ALSO BY MINDY THOMPSON FULLILOVE

Urban Alchemy: Restoring Joy in America's Sorted-Out Cities

Collective Consciousness and Its Discontents: Institutional Distributed Cognition, Racial Policy and Public Health in the United States (with Rodrick Wallace)

Homeboy Came to Orange: A Story of People's Power (with Ernest Thompson)

The House of Joshua: Meditations on Family and Place

ROOT SHOCK

ROOT SHOCK

How Tearing Up City Neighborhoods

Hurts America, and

What We Can Do About It

Mindy Thompson Fullilove, M.D.

newvillagePRESS

New Village Press Edition, November 2016

Published in the United States by New Village Press, New York
A division of Architects Designers Planners for Social Responsibility

bookorders@newvillagepress.net
www.newvillagepress.net

Originally published 2004 by Random House, Inc.

LIBRARY OF CONGRESS CATALOGING-IN-PUBLICATION DATA
Fullilove, Mindy Thompson.
Root shock: how tearing up city neighborhoods hurts America and what we can do about it/Mindy Thompson Fullilove
p. cm.
Includes bibliographical references and index.
ISBN 978-161-332019-8
1. Urban policy—United States—History—20th century.
2. Relocation (Housing)—United States—Psychological aspects.
3. Neighborhood—Psychological aspects. 4. Identity (Psychology)
5. African Americans—Social conditions. I. Title.
HT123.F85 2004
307.76'0973—dc22 2003063926

Front Cover design by Pam Shaw
Text design by Mary A. Wirth

Second Edition

This book is dedicated to
Della Wimbs and Charles Meadows,
who demonstrated through the way they lived their lives
how to love a neighborhood.

CONTENTS

FOREWORD

I tell everyone that it is worth listening to anything Mindy Fullilove has to say. For decades, she has pursued her ideas and intuitions with a singular intellect. *Root Shock: How Tearing Up City Neighborhoods Hurts American and What We Can Do About It* is an important and timely book that sprang from her work as a public health psychiatrist who thought deeply about her patients and followed their sources of suffering and resilience outward to locate them in communities, traditions, and history. This book marked Fullilove's emergence as one of the most important urban thinkers of our time, work that continues in her 2013 book *Urban Alchemy: Restoring Joy in America's Sorted-Out Cities*. Cities count, not just because they are large, they count because cities are the way humans now live, everywhere. How to make them settings where people not only live but thrive is a challenge that stretches across disciplines and belongs to us all.

In 1995, I was working in Harlem where Fullilove had just begun the work and thinking that would inform this book, first published in 2004 and now opportunely reprinted in a second edition. At the time, she was unravelling what had happened and what was happening in the Bradhurst section of Harlem. This was a devastated pocket of Harlem, itself a community that had lost fully one-third of its housing stock to abandonment and destruction in less than 30 years. We didn't know it yet, but Fullilove had begun her exploration of "root shock," a term she coined to capture what happens to a community and its people when its geography—its neighborhood—is destroyed. The telling begins with the end of the World War II and ends with current day 21st century, largely focusing on a retelling of "urban renewal," a federal project that targeted so-called "urban decay." Fullilove estimates that, as a consequence of what was billed as "upgrading," some 2500 city neighborhoods ceased to exist, mainly through large-scale clearances. Of these 2500 communities, fully two-thirds (about 1600 according to Fullilove) were home to African-Americans. "Urban renewal means Negro Removal" was a common catchphrase. The subsequent reconfiguration of cities was devastating to urban African-Americans. To this day, the loss of communities—told here from Roanoke, Pittsburgh, and Newark—still reverberates through families, neighborhoods, and entire cities, affecting all who live and lived there.

It was over 20 years ago that I listened at a Harlem community center as Fullilove wove together the strands from archival research, personal narratives she had collected, and experiences she had had through activities with the Harlem Congregations for Community Improvement. The result was a story that included architecture, history, activism, health, and the enduring power of place in our lives. I personally will never forget the way Fullilove described the importance of the entryway to a renovated apartment building and how it can signify respect for community, or not. Most people who listened knew that she had identified something important, really important, though admittedly there were some people who thought she had gone off the deep end. Today, all who care about health, dignity and wellbeing—and that should be everyone—owe Fullilove a great debt for carrying on this work (with others, I am sure she would hasten to add) and writing this book. If you have already read it, read it again. You will be inspired. If you are reading it for the first time, you will be both angered and enlightened. Most of all, Fullilove's *Root Shock* is a call to action to consider very carefully any effort that seeks to "protect and promote neighborhoods." Fullilove is clear that the legacy of urban renewal was that it literally tore up communities, squelching and squandering extraordinarily hard-won sources of community, culture, wisdom, and kindness. We may not know how to measure that elusive sense of what we call wellbeing, but each of us can easily summon the experiences that contribute to it. The neighbor who greets you, the yard you admire, the shop owner who goes to the back to find you something, the postal worker who stops to talk, the sense of safety and security in the known, the familiar. Lose all this and what's at stake is our health, our social fabric—our lives.

Root Shock emerged as a pioneering, synthesizing work that perches at the intersection of history, sociology, architecture, urban planning, and public health, all of which are embedded in where we conduct our everyday lives. Today, focusing on neighborhoods and place-based interventions is common in many fields. Across New York City government, city agencies seek to bring resources and programs to neighborhoods, treating them as settings that have the capacity to mold social outcomes independent of the particular individuals who live in them. In my field—public health—we talk a lot about how disease burden varies by community, with some neighborhoods—for example, Harlem or the South Bronx—experiencing enduring excess burdens of ill health and early death compared to wealthy enclaves such as the Upper East Side. These neighborhoods are the legacy of ghettoes segregated by both race and class, which in New York are virtually synonymous. What Fullilove conveys, often through the words of the residents whose narratives she has preserved and shared, is that all neighborhoods have assets, histories, and memory. Gone are the archetypal images of poor Black neighborhoods as sad, needy, and downtrodden—neighborhoods that need our benevolence, our help. Fullilove uncovers the complex histories of neighborhoods and debunks the enduring creation myth that troubled neighborhoods arise from troubled people. In some of the most moving passages of this book, residents of poor, largely working-class neighborhoods speak as powerful witnesses to and analysts of the destruction of the communities that nurtured them in a harsh world.

Deprivation is not a natural state, but one visited upon communities by bad policies, both past and present. When I first read this book, I was struck by its forthright exposition of the ongoing presence of structural and institutional racism. A decade ago, racism was a word that had practically vanished from both intellectual and everyday conversation. But racism is not gone, and, as groups like Black Lives Matter and other emerging movements articulate, racism will not disappear without attention to the structures that perpetuate it. Many such policies are embedded in our cities, in our housing policies and siting practices. And, while "slum clearance" I hope has ended, how to make cities places where people of all races and classes can survive and flourish is very much a challenge of today. Creating more affordable housing is critical, as the poor and middle class face escalating real estate prices, and gentrification continues to change and challenge neighborhoods. It is also critical to maintain the character of communities that makes cities—all cities, including my city—the vibrant places we love. Read this book as a cautionary tale and an extraordinary call to action.

—Mary T. Bassett, MD
New York City, July 2016

FOREWORD

Opening day for the Freedom Corner Monument, April 22, 2001, was a day of pride and healing celebration for the Hill District community, but it didn't feel that way to me.

City Councilman Sala Udin thanked everyone. He thanked God "for bringing us thus far along the way." He thanked the ordinary men and women who had performed extraordinary feats for the cause of freedom against all odds and whose names we may never know or inscribe onto granite. He thanked St. Benedict the Moor Church, whose various pastors acted as custodians of Freedom Corner for more than 40 years when it was just the broken-down sidewalk in front of their church. He thanked contributors, large and small, for their generosity and the members of the Freedom Corner Committee for illuminating the dream of Jake Milliones and countless Freedom Fighters. Finally, he thanked the architect Howard Graves and me, the artist, calling us two gifted men whose collaboration on the design and building of the monument was choreographed like a fine-tuned dance creation.

The community celebrated throughout the commemorative service on that special day, and rightfully so, for the monument does honor great people who marched and sacrificed for civil rights in America. However, within that rousing chorus, many celebrated the event not only as a commemoration but as a kind of resurrection of their beloved community. Many recognized what had truly manifested at Centre Avenue and Crawford Street had been born of emotions that stewed from 40-odd years ago when Pittsburgh Mayor David L. Lawrence and his wealthy renaissance men deemed the Lower Hill to have long outlived its usefulness. This declaration of the Hill to be a slum of no social value to anyone, soon thereafter, unleashed a sweeping urban renewal plan, that by March 1958 demolished every building in the area. Headlines called the mayor's ruthless plan 'Slum Clearing', but the urban renewal project, all for the sake of one civic auditorium, displaced 8,000 mostly black families and demolished the entirety of the Lower Hill District.

By springtime of 1957, we'd grown accustomed to hearing demolition sounding in the distance. Oftentimes, my brothers and I, taking pause from playtime, watched the buildings come down. I was delighted seeing the brick walls taking a hit, the way they'd stagger at first, seemingly poised for another mighty blow, but, when that 2-ton iron wrecking ball smacked again, walls faltered like shameless drunks, collapsing in dazzling clouds of dust. And to be there when they released that wrecking ball from way up sky-high—setting it free—letting it freefall from the tip of the towering jib—oh my!—did the sidewalks let out a bluster of dust and a thundering shuddering right up through our sneakers.

And then, there came the dusty black men from way up on the hill, strutting down our way looking for a day's work. Carrying tiny hammers for tending the fallen brick, they'd saunter about, some taking giant steps, their clodhoppers stomping, puffing up the dust. Some parked their Rocket 88s right next to a humped pile of brick and claimed it as their own. Others power-steered junkyard Buicks across vacant lots and still others backed their Fairlanes leaving the trunks gaping open wide, hungry to find whatever metals they could salvage from the dust.

Hunched over scattered bricks, they toiled, getting dustier than us, so heavily blessed under crowns of mortar dust, we could hardly tell the young men from the veterans. Most often, the old men sat straddled a crate. Gripping a brick with their calloused black hands, they'd flip the brick in one hand, tapping it with the hammer as if performing a magic trick; having struck off the mortar, they'd heave their bricks atop sorted heaps, each one landing with a clink among the chorus of many. By day's end, pennies earned accounted for the history that each man sweated to pile so high.

And then there was always that local man, the special man, the old one who'd lay his hammer down. Carefully brushing dust from his dirty overalls, he'd ascend woefully to the top of the highest mound. Gasping as if he'd climbed peaks of Mount Everest, sucking dust from his laden history, he'd scan the aftermath of his labor before looking toward the sky. And we'd be, right there, my brothers and I, stoning windows or playacting as pilfering pirates ransacking houses nearby. Oblivious to our sordid surroundings, we climbed atop those treacherous heaps—claiming ourselves kings of the hill.[1]

I was six years old then, the youngest in a poverty-stricken family of eight, twice displaced by the civic auditorium project. Nevertheless, my story is but one drawn from such a bad time experienced by many.

In time, the mayor's 1950's urban renewal project was proven to be nothing more than a giant steel chastity belt purposed to preserve white virtues, wow the wealthy, and, in the process, castrate the Hill District's cultural crotch. The brutal renewal plan nearly succeeded in destroying the Hill District in its entirety, but the Hill community, declaring the steps of St. Benedict the Moor Church and the run-down sidewalks at the intersection of Crawford Street and Centre Avenue as their recognizable line in the sand, fought heartily against the mighty political power of city hall.

Arm in arm, the community stood in solidarity, launching protest marches from the renowned intersection against the city's ongoing

---

1 Excerpt from *"Once Upon a Hill"*, a memoir by Carlos F. Peterson

aggression. Massive well-organized protest marches from that corner addressed loss of housing, employment, police brutality and social ills that coincided rightly with the nationwide Civil Rights Movement, and thereby thwarted Pittsburgh's 1950's renaissance plan and its potential expansion beyond Crawford Street. Understandably, and deservedly so, many people accepted the well-known intersection at Centre Avenue and Crawford Street as Freedom Corner.

In essence opening day for the Freedom Corner Monument was an unstated victory celebration for a community moving forward in its decades-long fight against displacement by the city's failed 1950's urban renewal project.

I was almost thirty-years old by the time I suspected any personal emotional damage done. Even as Councilman Udin praised the community and its achievements, I stood silent among them, for, even then, I had yet to recognize my place among the joyous people and truly appreciate my part in the daylong celebration.

Over a span of 16 years, I lived at 15 different addresses throughout the Hill, a love/hate relationship at best, never truly accepting the neighborhood as home. The Lower Hill was both playground and plaything for me, but coming of age there during its downfall made it seem that I was born into a bad time, conditioned by it, raised by it.

The familiar African proverb—It takes a whole village to raise a child—applied to my brothers and me. Although our home was a place of refuge and my mother cared for us, she didn't nurture by definition of the word, and, in that sense, a lesser-known African proverb—One knee does not bring up a child—extended beyond home and family to the pitiful neighborhood at large. More often than not, anonymous elders scolded, "you kids leave that alone, you kids stay out of there" or "stop throwing those rocks!" to quell our naughty ways. For the most part, time spent on the cobbled streets guided us. The weedy lots, ransacked houses, and stray cats game for chase were our calling. I recall more about the pathways, alleys, and byways I played in than I remember the workings of apartment spaces we lived in. Later, as I worked in white-collar America, I often denied ever having lived there.

Embattled for nearly a century, the district had welcomed generation after generation of immigrants into its swollen belly, and despite its broken condition, it had cradled my family too. Living there, on the brink of its demise, mine was a family without a legacy, so it seemed, for we did not have family traditions or practice ceremonial behavior in accordance with any ancestral wish, nor did we declare love for the decrepit places we lived in. I had not set any roots there, and I carried that shame with me to Freedom Corner's opening day.

Having designed the monument, I had reached the height of my art career, but, for reasons I had yet to understand, I felt unworthy.

I had left the Hill 1970 and moved to Pittsburgh's Manchester neighborhood, hoping never to return. But following a near-fatal head injury in a cycling accident, and haunted by my own mortality, I wanted to pursue my beginnings. Returning to the Hill, I wandered through the vacant buildings, just as I had done as a child on the Lower Hill many years before. For nearly a year, the few blocks between Crawford and Roberts Streets, where most all the dilapidated buildings waited for the wrecking ball, served as my place for introspection. Regarding the area as my sanctuary, I braved those unfamiliar places hoping to revive my dampened spirit. Sometimes sadness outweighed any desire to sketch or to make a photograph. I'd set up my tripod and camera, stand in the darkness and look through the viewfinder, hoping to sense that ineffable spirit of being. But no matter how angelic the view, my camera would have never captured what I was seeking, for there was no substitute for what I had been missing for so many years, the Lower Hill—my heritage so to speak.

Every trip to the Hill revealed a changing landscape, particularly between Arthur Street and Crawford Streets. Weeds outlined spaces where junked cars had rusted in place. Sagging telegraph cables no longer laced telegraph poles to the avenues and byways. Like odd-shaped tombstones, crumbled walls and twisted pipes marked block-long burial plots where homes had once stood. In a matter of weeks, dump trucks rumbled where the Hurricane Bar used to be, and bulldozers shadowed the façade of the Palace Hotel Bar. Within months, all of my sanctuaries were gone, every deserted space that

had provided stability and a sense of order. Nevertheless, the loss—
the demolition there—had somehow unearthed feelings for what I
had been missing from so many years before.

Addressing the matter through art and journaling, I never suspected that my reaction to conditions there had resulted from myr-
iad issues stemming from demolition of the Lower Hill years before,
nor did I realize how emotional my connection was. I didn't know
whether to address issues from my past or present. Attempting to
understand my dilemma more clearly, I created a diptych composed
of two photographs, in which one double-exposed image symbol-
ized past and future simultaneously, and a second image represented
the present.

Belonging to any single place and time seemed an impossible
task. Having one foot buried in the past and the other striving toward
an unknown future was a dilemma. While I searched incessantly for
my identity in both, I had neither. Nor did I feel a sense of place or
belonging to the Hill District.

No one was aware of my hidden, simmering feelings, not even
those closest to me. My artwork was the only mirror reflecting how I
felt. To the novice my art was "nice work," and always in demand for
Black History Month exhibitions. Oftentimes wondering, who am
I to exploit a downtrodden community for the sake of art, seemed a
pointed question through welling tears.

"In my Sanctuary" by Carlos F. Peterson, circa 1975

Unbeknownst to me, Dr. Mindy Fullilove had been working with inner-city communities around the country—including Pittsburgh's Hill District—over many years, guiding them through the aftermath of comparable development projects gone wrong and planting initial seeds toward healing and recovery. But, even if I had known that the gifted professor of clinical psychiatry from Columbia University was holding public workshops nearby, I would have never asked for help. Being the brooding artist, wallowing in misery, seemed to be more a part of my creative process than possible aftereffects of Pittsburgh's so-called urban redevelopment.

My emotional health wasn't perceptible to anyone—at least I didn't think it was. But then, Freedom Corner Committee Chairman Sala Udin introduced me to Dr. Fullilove. Dr. Fullilove sidestepped my artist façade and, getting straight to the point, defined root shock as a traumatic stress reaction to the destruction of all or part of one's emotional ecosystem. Hearing that, I didn't need to hear any more. I didn't need therapy—I didn't need diagnosis. She had answered provocative questions that the troubled artist within me had been tussling with for so long: what was I missing from my past, and how could a bad time from so long ago continue to touch my everyday life?

Having an advocate with such outstanding credentials addressing my realm of anxiety simply overwhelmed me. I felt validated. It seemed as if Dr. Fullilove had come to my rescue. What pleased me most was that she had given my questions a name. She had clearly articulated something that, up until then, had been a mystery to me. I wondered if she had known the extent of my mental health crisis. But then I thought, perhaps my artwork had reflected more of my state of mind than just the social commentary I had intended. Indeed, some of my artwork, along with anecdotes from my memoir, turned out to be important contributions to *Root Shock*.

I was especially moved by Dr. Fullilove's grassroots approach to the matter in *Root Shock*, particularly the sit-down-across-the-table, heartfelt interviews and workshops that struck at the core of the issue. Reading about others from different parts of the country who were grappling with similar issues to mine—knowing I wasn't alone—provided kinship and perspective toward healing. And how personable she was, advising us that it's OK to be sentimental about where we once lived—after all, those places were our homes!

Most of the interviewees, me included, responded to questions with nostalgia-flavored sentiment for neighborhoods that can never be experienced again. We had all been uprooted from close-knit places, thereby separated from enclaves supporting the traditional African-American ways of life. That similarity, at least in my view, revealed how far-flung the upheaval had been that weakened our shared traditions and moral values. In effect, urban renewal projects gone wrong made us party to our own cultural breakdown, resulting in bad times that are happening in black communities all over America today.

We must be free to attach to where we live without fear of being ripped away—sold down the Mississippi, in a manner of speaking. Bearing that in mind, as well as how threatened people of color in America are today, urban renewal projects displacing people of any color should be subject to public scrutiny.

Look in any direction from Freedom Corner today, and it is readily apparent that Dr. Fullilove's in-depth study and workshops helped galvanize the community. Good things are happening in the Hill. The contentious civic auditorium that spurred the urban redevelopment matter in the first place is gone—this, for some at least, settled the score a bit. In place of the civic auditorium a multi-use development, including affordable housing, is underway. More importantly, the new Crawford Square housing development and similar developments taking place throughout the Hill District attest to the community's ongoing recovery.

While recognizing that the demolition of the Lower Hill was a sad chapter in the community's long history, and should never be forgotten, the community works to reseed its roots. Residents have developed a beneficial master plan of their own—spurring revitalization and occupying a place at the table with the city and developers rebuilding the Lower Hill.

Through her book, *Root Shock*, Dr. Fullilove addresses an important societal problem that might have otherwise gone unnoticed, especially by politicians, developers, architects, and planners, and whoever else is making frontline decisions that affect many. She addresses matters of common civil rights owed to anybody, anywhere. Dr. Fullilove delivers her message to communities, the unknowing sufferers, comprised of individuals like me who dare not call ourselves the victims that we are.

I wanted to walk away from the Freedom Corner Monument on its opening day, but now, thanks to Dr. Fullilove's informative book, I not only recognize my contribution at Freedom Corner, I understand the traumas my family and many others suffered from the city's failed urban renewal project, as well as how that outlandish project hastened the civil rights movement in Pittsburgh. Moreover, thanks to Dr. Fulliove's undertaking, I accept that Freedom Corner stands in spirit of the many unscripted stories like mine . . . and as the place that welcomes me home.

—**Carlos F. Peterson**
Pittsburgh, July 2016

ROOT SHOCK

INTRODUCTION

When there is emotional pain, psychiatrists like me believe that we can help. But before we act, we need to find some handle for the problem, some name to guide action. Once in a while, we realize that these names are inadequate for the problems we are seeing. Then we search for new names, or new ways to group old names.

When I bumped into the emotional pain related to displacement, I had the option of using labels like "posttraumatic stress disorder," "depression," "anxiety," and "adjustment disorders." But I didn't think those labels—useful as they are—were enough to tell the whole story. Like Robert Coles, Oliver Sacks, and Arthur Kleinman, I wanted to understand displacement through the words of the people who had suffered from it. I wanted to walk the streets they were talking about, examine their photographs, visit their houses, and get a deep feeling for what they were sharing with me. I wanted to know the emotional truth of the experience through which they had lived. Between 1995 and 2003, I logged thousands of air miles, walked hundreds of city streets, examined archives, collected photographs, and talked to people who had stories to tell.

I had listened to many voices when, on December 2002, the truth hit me. At the time, I was sitting in the comfortable living room of Dr. Walter Claytor, listening to the story of his remarkable family, a family that in one generation went from slavery to professional education, a family that built significant buildings and provided a high level of health care for the surrounding community. I was so proud of Dr. Claytor and his father and his grandfather that I found it unbearable that this great American family had been dispossessed by urban renewal, a program of the U.S. government that had, between 1949 and 1973, bulldozed 2,500 neighborhoods in 993 American cities. A million people were dispossessed by the program, among them the Claytors.

I don't know if it was Dr. Claytor's charm or his insouciance that helped pull the pieces together for me. He was not seeking my pity. In fact, he strove to maintain his dignity while telling the story of his losses. But the pain was such that he couldn't quite keep it out of his voice. It was the breaking edge of his grief that linked it to the sound of pain that I'd so often heard, a sound that was obvious in some voices, and just beneath the cheerfulness in others. There was a remarkable emptiness in that pain. In that searing moment, I realized the loss he was describing was, in a crucial way, the collective loss. It was the loss of a massive web of connections—a way of being—that had been destroyed by urban renewal; it was as if thousands of people, who seemed to be with me in sunlight, were at some deeper level of their being wandering lost in a dense fog, unable to find one another for the rest of their lives. It was a chorus of voices that rose in my head, with the cry, "We have lost one another."

Being in touch with such sorrow was not easy. What popped into my mind were the famous words spoken by Jack Nicholson in the movie *A Few Good Men*: "You don't want the truth. You can't handle the truth."

Nope, I thought, I can't handle the truth. The phrase, though it seemed a bit irreverent, was rather comforting. This is one of those handy mental tricks that people use to manage intense emotions. I might have used denial ("That never happened") or repression ("What did you say, Dr. Claytor?") or intellectualization ("How many people feel the way you do?") but I used Jack. I must have told a hundred people, "I can't handle the truth," before I started to feel differently.

This process taught me a new respect for the story of upheaval. It is hard to hear, because it is a story filled with a large, multivoiced pain. It is not a pain that should be pigeonholed in a diagnostic category, but rather understood as a communication about human endurance in the face of bitter defeat.

There is a song written by an anonymous slave that has the line "I hear the archangels are rockin' Jerusalem, I hear the archangels are ringin' them bells." Imagine, for a moment, that songwriter: living in the oppression of slavery, torn from Africa, separated from family, driven by the lash, worked from sunup to sundown, yet able to imagine a rockin' Jerusalem. In the pain of upheaval, there is the unremitting effort of the oppressed to shake off the agony of unequal treatment. It is that effort that calls us, tells us not to be afraid of the truth, but to join the movement toward a more equitable future.

One hundred years ago, the distinguished African American scholar Dr. W.E.B. Du Bois wrote that the problem the twentieth century needed to solve was the problem of the color line. It took sixty more years for the United States to engage wholeheartedly in the battle for civil rights. Yet, as we have faced the truth of the color line, we have acted, reacted, thought, and felt differently. We are a better nation for it.

I venture to propose that displacement is the problem the twenty-first century must solve. Africans and aborigines, rural peasants and city dwellers have been shunted from one place to another, as progress has demanded, "Land here!" or "People there!" In cutting the roots of so many people, we have destroyed language, culture, dietary traditions, and social bonds. We have lined the oceans with bones, and filled the garbage dumps with bricks.

What are we to do?

I have seen people in many towns and cities working to reconnect after root shock. Whether it was building a labyrinth, or holding a flea market, they were gathering together as neighbors to re-form the web

Fig. 0.1. Carlos F. Peterson. "At Freedom Corner." This drawing represents the slow collapse of Carlos Peterson's community in the aftermath of urban renewal. It depicts the Church of St. Benedict the Moor, with the statue of the saint soaring above the sanctuary. Pittsburgh civil rights marches start at this corner, hence the name, Freedom Corner. COURTESY OF THE ARTIST.

of relationships. Within such a moment, people can recover and prosper. This highly respected type of healing, which is called "milieu therapy" by psychiatrists, works through the creation of healing places. For an environment to lift the spirit, attention must be focused on opportunities for relatedness. A psychiatric team might accomplish this by setting up a hospitable dayroom, or by having a meeting in which all the patients are encouraged to participate. The tools are many, and the intervention is powerful.

But milieu therapy is not an intervention that need be administered by licensed health care practitioners. In the psychiatric hospital, any member of the unit—staff or patient alike—can promote the common good. Similarly, each and every one of us has the power to improve the places we hold in common, whether we are concerned with the neighborhood, city, nation, or planet. A man in Berkeley, California, decided to stand by the road and wave at passersby. His death was mourned by the thousands of people who got a daily dose of friendliness from his white-gloved hand. We are each that man.

This book, then, tells a painful story, but it also offers hope. We have a century ahead of us: we have a treatment for root shock; we have the possibility of preventing further damage by nurturing the world's neighborhoods instead of destroying them; we who care about community are many.

I present here the words of the people who lived upheaval: the uprooted, the planners, the advocates, and the historians. Read their words with care for them and for yourself. Read their words not as single individuals living through a bad time, but as a multitude all sharing their morsel of the same bad time. Read in that manner and I believe that you will get the true nature of root shock. Read in that manner, and I believe you will be able to embrace the truth, not as a fearful thing, but as a call to join the struggle for a better tomorrow.

Chapter 1

THE BUTTERFLY IN BEIJING

Every once in a while, in a particular location and at a particular time, people spin the wheel of routine, and they make magic. One such location was Ebbets Field in the heart of Brooklyn, where, through World War I, the Roaring Twenties, the Great Depression, World War II, and the postwar struggles for equality in America, hard-working people enjoyed baseball. That small, unpredictable, and intimate ballpark was a gallery for characters to strut their stuff, and the characters in the stands took as much advantage of the opportunity as did the characters on the field. It was there that Jackie Robinson broke the color bar in Major League Baseball, and there that "Shorty's Sym-Phony Band" tortured the opposition. Words like "raucous" and "zany" are invoked to help those of us who were never present imagine the intensity and the uniqueness of what went on.[1]

In 1957, Walter O'Malley, the owner of the Dodgers, moved them to Los Angeles. The horror of that act is undiminished in the voices of fans. "I felt like a jilted lover," recalls a sixty-year-old physician of the catastrophe that darkened his young life. Forty-six years after the Dodgers played their last game there, it remains important to people to tell the story of Ebbets Field, and in particular, to try to take us into its magic. This is the real essence of "nostalgia," an emotion that is in one second bitter, and in another sweet, as the rememberer vacillates between the joy of what was and the grief of the loss. Enduring sorrow and untempered anger are hallmarks of the stories related by fans of the Brooklyn Dodgers. "I never rooted for them again," says my doctor friend, and he is not alone in the implacable anger that still seems the only reasonable response to that kind of pain.

Three years after the Dodgers left, Ebbets Field was destroyed, and apartment buildings were erected on the site. People have to get the address and specific directions to find the small plaque that is all that remains of the cathedral of baseball which once stood there. And so the team is gone, the fans dispersed, the stadium demolished. Of deeper importance for people who had lots of work and not much hope, a place of magic was ripped from their daily lives, leaving them dull and gray. The loss of Ebbets Field was a tragedy that could not be repaired: it changed Brooklyn forever.

But how could the loss of a baseball stadium undermine what would be the fourth-largest city of the United States (were Brooklyn independent of the rest of New York City)?

The answer to this conundrum lies in understanding that places—buildings, neighborhoods, cities, nations—are not simply bricks and mortar that provide us shelter. Because we dance in a ballroom, have a parade in a street, make love in a bedroom, and prepare a feast in a kitchen, each of these places becomes imbued with sounds, smells, noises, and feelings of those moments and how we lived them. When we enter an old classroom, the smell of chalk on the boards can bring back a swarm of memories of classmates and lessons, boredom and dreams. Walking toward a favorite bar awakens expectations of friends and drinks, good times, good food. The breeze on a certain hillside reminds us of a class trip, while the sun in the garden brings thoughts of Dad. Try to find the shortcut you used to take to your best friend's house and it is your feet that will carry you there. The cues from place dive under conscious thought and awaken our sinews and bones, where days of our lives have been recorded.

Buildings and neighborhoods and nations are insinuated into us by life; we are not, as we like to think, independent of them. We are more like Siamese twins, conjoined to the locations of our daily life, such that our emotions flow through places, just as blood flows through two interdependent people.[2] We can, indeed, separate from our places, but it is an operation that is best done with care. When a part is ripped away, as happened in Brooklyn when the Dodgers moved to Los Angeles, root shock ensues.

What Is Root Shock?

Root shock is the traumatic stress reaction to the destruction of all or part of one's emotional ecosystem. It has important parallels to the physiological shock experienced by a person who, as a result of injury, suddenly loses massive amounts of fluids.[3] Such a blow threatens the whole body's ability to function. The nervous system attempts to compensate for the imbalance by cutting off circulation to the arms and legs. Suddenly the hands and feet will seem cold and damp, the face pale, and the brow sweaty. This is an emergency state that can preserve the brain, the heart, and the other essential organs for only a brief period of time. If the fluids are not restored, the person will die. Shock is the fight for survival after a life-threatening blow to the body's internal balance.

Just as the body has a system to maintain its internal balance, so, too, the individual has a way to maintain the external balance between himself and the world. This way of moving in the environment maximizes the odds that he will survive predators, find food, maintain shelter from the harsh elements, and live in harmony with family and neighbors. This method for navigating the external environment is selected because, based on individual and collective trial-and-error experiences with the mazelike possibilities offered by the surrounding world, it seems to offer the greatest chances for survival. Using this analogy to mazes we can call the chosen pattern of movement "a way to run the maze of life," or, more simply, a "mazeway."[4]

When the mazeway, the external system of protection, is damaged, the person will go into root shock.[5] Just as a burn victim requires immediate replacement of fluids, so, too, the victim of root shock requires the support and direction of emergency workers who can erect shelter, provide food, and ensure safety until the victim has stabilized and can begin to take over these functions again.

Imagine the victim of an earthquake, a hurricane, a flood, or a terrorist attack. He suffers from root shock as he looks at the twisted remains of the known universe, searching for the road to the supermarket, which used to be there, but is now a pile of rubble. Imagining such a person—and knowing that these tragedies can happen to any of us—we open our hearts and wallets to the Red Cross and other relief organizations that show up immediately to be the temporary mazeway, the transfusion of an environment to those who are naked to the elements.

The experience of root shock—like the aftermath of a severe burn—does not end with emergency treatment, but will stay with the individual for a lifetime. In fact, the injury from root shock may be even more enduring than a burn, as it can affect generations and generations of people. Noah's ark—and his effort to rebuild the world after the flood—is the true story of a lost world. We keep telling that story because we keep living it, not simply when the floods come, but after they have receded and we try to rebuild.

Carlos Peterson, a resident of the Lower Hill, was deeply affected by the bulldozing of his neighborhood. He related, "I remember being able to look from the third floor and actually see the bulldozers and the destruction of where we once lived. This urban renewal process was preparation for Pittsburgh's Civic Arena. I was young and did not fully understand what was happening. I only knew this process was coming towards us. Coupled with the sense of personal loss of friends and neighborhood, this event had quite an influence on my life." As an adult, he gained a deeper understanding of the process that continued to destroy the neighborhood. It was with a sense of increasing urgency that he sought to document what was happening around him. The photograph shown here depicts the bulldozing in the area of Crawford Street, with the dome of the Civic Arena in the background, and exposed tree roots in the foreground. The disrupted context, exterior to the individual and the group, is the fundamental process that engenders root shock.

Fig. 1.1. Carlos F. Peterson. "Hill-o-Phobia." Carlos Peterson took this photograph after the bulldozing of a section of the Lower Hill. It shows the Civic Arena just behind the tree root. It is an image of the world torn apart that we will revisit in the work of other artists. COURTESY OF THE ARTIST.

Carlos Peterson worked, as well, to depict the emotional impact the environmental devastation had on him. "I decided to express my feeling using drawings and photography. . . . I decided to look at my surroundings from a grassroots level, with the perspective of knowing how such conditions made me feel. My impression was that we were like a bunch of nomads always fleeing, that was the feeling I had.

"When creating my drawings I attempted to look at a building from within, and the structure's exterior. I would go into a vacant structure and photograph how it was, allowing memories of my experience to influence art. I would seek to tie in my impressions of what it would feel like had I been the last resident. Therefore, I would end up with a lot of stretched and distorted images that I thought reflected the economics in a downtrodden neighborhood."

In "Stream of Consciousness," the drawing shown here, the isolated buildings, open grave, and looming cross create a landscape of loss. The artist has placed his profile among the doomed buildings on the horizon. A dressmaker's model and a fallen stop sign are poignant reminders that this world once worked and moved and meant something to the people who lived in it. Thus, Carlos Peterson attempts to reveal the texture and content of the painful emotions that accompany root shock.

"This drawing contains symbolism that characterized my state of mind during the time when the Hill District was at its lowest ebb. My drawings were my therapy through the smothering depression that came with the area's carcass-like landscape. During that time I saw contradiction between religion and nature. Man-made structures and man always succumb to nature no matter how strong man's faith, prayer, or objects. . . . Nature renews itself through death and dying. With this realization, I included my profile near the horizon just beyond the fence, upper right."

Root shock, at the level of the individual, is a profound emotional upheaval that destroys the working model of the world that had existed in the individual's head.[6] Root shock undermines trust, increases anxiety about letting loved ones out of one's sight, destabilizes relationships, destroys social, emotional, and financial resources, and increases the risk for every kind of stress-related disease, from depression to heart attack. Root shock leaves people chronically cranky, barking a distinctive croaky complaint that their world was abruptly taken away.

Root shock, at the level of the local community, be it neighborhood or something else, ruptures bonds, dispersing people to all the directions of the compass.[7] Even if they manage to regroup, they are not sure what to do with one another. People who were near are too far, and people who were far are too near. The elegance of the neighborhood—each person in his social and geographic slot—is destroyed, and even if the neighborhood is rebuilt exactly as it was, it won't work. The restored geography is not enough to repair the many injuries to the mazeway.[8]

Fig. 1.2. Carlos F. Peterson. "Stream of Consciousness." In this drawing, Carlos Peterson included a series of images of loss and confusion, as he tried to make sense of the disintegration of the world around him. COURTESY OF THE ARTIST.

Root shock, it is important to recognize, ripples out beyond those who are affected—in the way we like to measure these things. September 11 demonstrated our society's great love for distinguishing an "affected" group that needs help from an "unaffected" group that doesn't. While the "affected" people did need help, many more people were affected than was generally conceded. I was part of a call-in television show that aired just before the first anniversary of the attack. People from Queens or Staten Island called to say, "I feel bad, but nothing happened to me. It's making me feel guilty." I insisted, over and over again, that September 11 had happened to all of us and that the bad feeling was a natural reaction to having one's city attacked by terrorists.

But root shock goes even further than one city, linking a local tragedy to events around the globe. During the 1950s and '60s, a federal program called "urban renewal" destroyed hundreds of African American neighborhoods, many of which were home to jazz, a music that flowed through the communities from home to street to club. The young kids learning to play would linger outside the clubs to hear the music, dreaming of the day they might participate. Major chunks of the jazz world—the Fillmore in San Francisco, the Hill District in Pittsburgh, and the South Side of Chicago, among them— were torn up by urban renewal, and the structure of home-street-club was destroyed. Jazz nearly disappeared in the United States, surviving by dint of becoming an academic subject in high schools and colleges, played in a few austere clubs in New York and other big cities. The fact that the music endured had much to do with Europe and Japan, which offered performance sites where musicians might hone their craft and earn a living. Japan is now the top consumer of jazz CDs and Tokyo a "must stop" on a jazz ensemble's touring schedule.

Tobias von Shöenebeck, a tour guide in Berlin, applied this principle of ripple effects on August 3, 2003, while watching fellow citizens participate in a new fad called "flash mob," which had apparently originated in New York two months earlier. At the Berlin event, the flash mob, called together by email and cell phone, gathered in front of the American embassy to pop bottles of champagne, toast Natasha, and disperse. Von Shöenebeck shook his head, and muttered, "This is just the sort of thing that happens when you forbid New York to smoke."[9] He was referring to the implementation in April 2003 of tough new laws outlawing smoking in New York City bars and restaurants. While few might have made the connection between New York's smoking laws and the fads that catch on in Berlin, it is exactly the kind of idea to which I am referring.

This lesson of interconnectedness is as hard to learn as differential calculus or quantum mechanics. The principle is simple: we—that is to say, all people—live in an emotional ecosystem that attaches us to the environment, not just as our individual selves, but as beings caught in a single, universal net of consciousness anchored in small niches we call neighborhoods or hamlets or villages. Because of the interconnectedness of the net, if your place is destroyed today, I will feel it hereafter.

Though a simple principle, it is hard to learn because the effects of root shock immediately get caught up in everything else that's going on in the world. As the message moves around the world, it is possible to think of many other explanations for an initial cause. Imagine how many factors, other than New York City's smoking laws, helped create the Berlin flash mob. The idea that your hurt has an effect on my life requires us to believe in "action at a distance," which makes the average scientist go rigid with skepticism.

The emergence of theories of complex systems, chaos theory among others, has helped us. We now understand the seemingly impossible proposition that the flapping wings of a butterfly in Beijing could affect the weather in New York.[10] It is from that perspective that we must view the ecosystem of emotions. Root shock rips emotional connections in one part of the globe, and sets in motion small changes—jazz musicians in search of a venue, smokers acting out their annoyance—that spread out across the world, shifting the direction of all interpersonal connections. Imagine it as a version of six degrees of separation, the idea that each American is only six handshakes away from the president of the United States. We are each of us only thirteen handshakes away from anyone's root shock—not much distance in a global world.

Where Are People Rooted?

Though I have already argued that people go into shock if uprooted, it is useful to consider: Where are people rooted? Before people moved to cities, this was a fairly straightforward question. They were rooted where they lived, and they lived where their fathers, and their fathers' fathers, had lived. Of course, this is more complicated than it seems, as armies swept back and forth across the continents, trade routes linked distant lands, tribes exhausted their lands and had to move to new pastures, and adventurers wandered the world. Yet for a long time in human history, people lived for generations in small places—a few miles in diameter—and that is where they were rooted.

Things got complicated when people started to move to cities. After all, cities are much more unstable—people will leave a neighborhood within months or years, rather than decades or centuries, and they live with a fairly high level of anonymity. A few will live in stable neighborhoods, like the urban villagers who inhabited Boston's West End before it was destroyed by urban renewal.[11] But most live in a city neighborhood much looser and less secure. So where are they rooted?

The renowned urbanist Jane Jacobs had a profound insight into this puzzle. She identified the way in which people made the mazeway in the urban setting, what she called the "sidewalk ballet." In one of the passages fundamental to our current understanding of rootedness, she wrote:

> The stretch of Hudson Street where I live is each day the scene of an intricate sidewalk ballet. I make my own entrance into it a little after eight when I put out the garbage can, surely a prosaic occupation, but I enjoy my part, my little clang, as the droves of junior high school students walk by the center of the stage dropping candy wrappers. (How do they eat so much candy so early in the morning?)
>
> While I sweep up the wrappers I watch the other rituals of morning: Mr. Halpert unlocking the laundry's handcart from its mooring to a cellar door, Joe Cornacchia's son-in-law stacking out the empty crates from the delicatessen, the barber bringing out his sidewalk folding chair, Mr. Goldstein arranging the coils of wire which proclaim the hardware store is open, the wife of the tenement's superintendent depositing her chunky three-year-old with a toy mandolin on the stoop, the vantage point from which he is learning the English his mother cannot speak . . . It is time for me to hurry to work too, and I exchange my ritual farewell with Mr. Lofaro, the short, thick-bodied, white-aproned fruit man who stands outside his doorway a little up the street, his arms folded, his

feet planted, looking solid as earth itself. We nod; we each glance quickly up and down the street, then look back to each other and smile. We have done this many a morning for more than ten years, and we both know what it means: All is well.[12]

The street, bordered by buildings, is the stage of the local world, Jacobs proposes to us, as she describes her entry onto the "scene." She recounts the interactions she experiences daily, informing us through her interchange with Mr. Lofaro that she is part of this little spot and she knows its rules. "All is well," she writes, letting us know how content she is to be a part of this small theater piece. This construction of theater and actors, all knowing their parts and performing them well, is what makes up the street ballet. It is another way of describing our ability to master and run the maze of life, the mazeway, the near environment within which we find food, shelter, safety, and companionship. We love the mazeway in which we are rooted, for it is not simply the buildings that make us safe and secure, but, more complexly, our knowledge of the "scene" that makes us so. We all have our little part to play, carefully synchronized with that of all the other players: we are rooted in that, our piece of the world-as-stage.

Try the following thought experiments.

First, imagine Jane Jacobs's street altered in any way you like—change the size of the buildings and their use; reorganize the street—move the subway entrance, relocate the school—and then imagine people making use of it. If you look closely, a sidewalk ballet, albeit different from Jacobs's version, will emerge before your eyes. In this thought experiment, you are observing the degree to which people can adapt to different settings, and not just adapt, but attach, connect. They are connecting not to the negatives or even the positives of the setting, but to their own mastery of the local players and their play.

Second, take any setting, and reduce it to shreds. The fundamental geographic points cuing the ballet are now gone. Center stage has disappeared. Jacobs's entry is gone, and so are the stores and the stoop that made possible the three-year-old's English lessons. For a long moment, the actors will be frozen in horror. As the horror recedes, confusion will set in. Where is food? Where is shelter? Should I still go to school? What you have just imagined is root shock, the traumatic stress from the loss of a person's stage set, lifeworld, mazeway, home.

Just as Walter O'Malley, owner of the Brooklyn Dodgers, uprooted his team without regard for Brooklyn, so too other entrepreneurs of that era reorganized the landscape so that they could make more money. The tool that they used was urban renewal, a program of the federal government that provided money for cities to clear "blight."[13] Blight, like beauty, is in the eye of the beholder, and it happened, more often than not, that the part of the city the businessmen thought was blighted was the part where black people lived.

By my estimate, 1,600 black neighborhoods were demolished by urban renewal.[14] This massive destruction caused root shock on two levels. First, residents of each neighborhood experienced the traumatic stress of the loss of their life world. Second, because of the interconnections among all black people in the United States, the whole of Black America experienced root shock as well. Root shock, post urban renewal, disabled powerful mechanisms of community functioning, leaving the black world at an enormous disadvantage for meeting the challenges of globalization.

Urban renewal is the butterfly in Beijing, the unseen actor who caused the tempest. The vigor of the civil rights movement led to the expectation that black Americans would be better off when segregation was defeated. In fact, by 1970, some were but many were not. Instead, the have-nots had tumbled deeper into poverty and dysfunction. The great epidemics of drug addiction, the collapse of the black family, and the rise in incarceration of black men—all of these catastrophes followed the civil rights movements, they did not precede it. Though there are a number of causes of this dysfunction that cannot be disputed—the loss of manufacturing jobs, in particular—the current situation of Black America cannot be understood without a full and complete accounting of the social, economic, cultural, political, and emotional losses that followed the bulldozing of 1,600 neighborhoods.

But we cannot understand the losses unless we first appreciate what was there.

Chapter 2

IMAGINING NEON

In 1995, Richard Chubb took me for a drive through territory that, before urban renewal, housed Roanoke, Virginia's black neighborhoods. We passed a series of businesses sitting in such wide swaths of grass, they seemed dwarfed by nature. Pointing in succession at Magic City Ford, the post office, and the civic center, he said with bitter insistence, "There used to be houses here. Those are just buildings."

As we crossed out of that business area over a bridge, his bitterness dropped away. With pride he told me, "This is Henry Street. This used to be jumping. We had neon."

I saw a mass of vacant land and a bunch of leftover scraggly buildings typical of a burned-out ghetto. We stopped in front of one of the buildings. "Come in. I want to show you," he said.

We went up to his second-floor office. "When I was a kid I dreamed of having a business on Henry Street, but my life didn't turn out that way. I became a school principal instead. But I felt that there was something missing, so in 1986, I left that job and opened my counseling business here on Henry Street.

"Come over to the window," he beckoned.

We stood shoulder to shoulder and he pointed up the empty street. "Sometimes I just stand here and the tears come down, thinking about what used to be."

What used to be: houses not buildings, neon not vacant lots, neighborhood not emptiness. I wanted to see what he saw, and to understand how it came into being. In every city, where I was studying the effects of urban renewal, I asked people, "What was it like before urban renewal?"

Before the City Lights . . .

Though black people have been a part of American cities since their importation from Africa began in 1619—the Haitian fur trader Jean Baptiste Point DuSable was the first permanent resident of Chicago, for example—for the vast majority, urbanization was a twentieth-century phenomenon. It followed a long detour from auction blocks in ports serving the slave plantations, where blacks sojourned under the slave regime's reign of terror. The languages and cultures of many different groups slowly yielded to a common present of oppression and a shared dream of a better future in a faceless place of opportunity they sang of as "New Jerusalem." It was in New Jerusalem that people torn from their homes and forced into servitude would be able to make a home again.

During Reconstruction—in the immediate aftermath of the emancipation of the slaves and the Civil War—it seemed that the freed people might be able to make this New Jerusalem throughout the South. Between 1865 and 1876, black people were able to own land, establish schools, and elect representatives to every level of government. The violence that followed the federal abandonment of Reconstruction in 1876 inaugurated a frightful new epoch of oppression that greatly resembled slavery in its methods and its intent. As the white power structure solidified its dominance, it was able to introduce a system of segregation popularly known as Jim Crow.[1] Between 1890 and 1910, Jim Crow laws created an elaborately divided world, such that the domain of resources and power was inhabited by whites, and the domain of deprivation and powerlessness was inhabited by blacks. The weight of this system fell with greatest force on those in the rural areas, who were tied to the land by debt slavery and peonage.

So much power was concentrated among the white landowners that it must have seemed that the divided world would last forever. But the confluence of worldwide instability and worsening of conditions in the South acted—as did the Black Death in the Middle Ages[2]—to create an opportunity for those living in feudal conditions to flee to the city for their freedom.

In 1916 the black mass movement to the city began. By 1930, 1.5 million black people had left the privation and oppression of the rural South to make a new life there. In 1941, Jacob Lawrence, then a young painter in Harlem, created sixty panels describing the Great Migration. The stark pictures painted in poster colors on butcher paper cut to the core of the transition between rural oppression and urban opportunity. To help us understand the tension, he adds a refrain about the importance of the train:

- "Families arrived at the station very early in order not to miss their train North . . ."[3]
- "[White people] made it difficult for migrants leaving the South. They often went to railroad stations and arrested the Negroes wholesale, which in turn made them miss their train."[4]

To make the move, you had to get on the train. When you arrived at your destination, the work of building New Jerusalem began. Geographer David Seamon has called this kind of voyage the "Dwelling-Journey Spiral."[5]

Seamon traced seven steps in a novel about Swedish immigrants. Forced to leave home because of famine, the Oskar family set out in the 1850s to make a new home in America. They found land, built a home, and created a farm, thus establishing a place. But they were terribly lonely. In time, a group of other Swedish families gathered near, and together with their new neighbors, the Oskars began to create community. It was in the presence of this new community that all of the families found, once again, the opportunity to be at home in the most profound sense of the word, to be *dwelling*.

A story about Swedish immigrants helps us to see the journey to a new home in its ideal form. African Americans, by contrast, struggled toward their goal against great obstacles. The African American story teaches us that being "at home" requires freedom. Because of racist oppression, the African American journey involved finding a place, building homes, making community, winning the battle for civil rights, and then hoping to dwell.

To Dwell in the City: Build Community

To move from the fictional version of white settlement to the reality, we can turn to the sociologists at the University of Chicago, who were watching the arrival of waves of immigrants from other countries, as well as from rural America. They observed that people arrayed themselves on an urban grid in a particular pattern. Poorer, industrial neighborhoods occupied the center, while wealthier, more residential neighborhoods were located at the edges. As the years passed, the sociologists decoded movements among the neighborhoods, such that white people, when they first arrived, would live in the poor neighborhoods in the center of the city, which we may call "newcomer neighborhoods." When they got a little money, they moved on to more peripheral neighborhoods.

The newcomer neighborhoods were centrally located, close to mills and factories. They were eccentric places, built at hazard, bisected by alleys and overhung by industrial pollution. Although they were areas of filth, crime, and poverty, those funky neighborhoods provided the doorway into the American dream.

For blacks, the newcomer neighborhoods were the beginning and the end of their options for housing. As the neighborhoods became "black," segregation created a boundary that was rigidly, and even violently, enforced. The newcomer neighborhoods were transformed into Negro ghettos. A 1946 map, created by the Chicago Council Against Racial and Religious Discrimination, showed vigilante attacks that had occurred on the periphery of the South Side

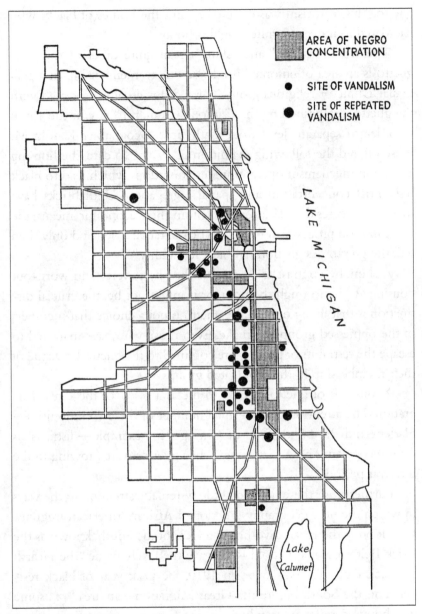

Fig. 2.1. Terrorist Attacks Against Negro Homes in Chicago, May 1944–August 1946. Adapted from chart of the same title issued by the Chicago Council Against Racial and Religious Discrimination. ROBERT WEAVER, *THE GHETTO*, 1948.

ghetto. This terrorism was directed against the homes of blacks who had dared to move to white neighborhoods.[6]

The words "ghetto" and "slum" mean quite different things. A ghetto is an area of enforced residence due to membership in a particular ethnic or religious group. The word is usually associated with the ghettos established by the Catholic Church in Italy in the 1500s in order to separate Jews from Catholics.[7] Geographer Harold M. Rose offered the following definition in 1971: "To date, the housing allocation mechanism operates under conditions which lead to black residential concentration and spatial segregation. Until blacks have free access to residential locations within their economic means, the ghettoization process can be said to be operative. Then and only then will the ghetto designation have lost its validity."[8]

A slum, by contrast, is an area marked by poverty and worn-out housing. A ghetto might be poor, or it might not be: the crucial distinction is that living outside the ghetto is not a choice that members of the oppressed group can make. Even those who have managed to escape the restraints of poverty are confined to the ghetto by virtue of their membership in the subjugated group.

Thousands of ghettos sprang to life as a result of the Great Migration. The attention given a small number of these communities—Harlem and the South Side of Chicago, for example—distracts us from recognizing how very many urban ghettos were growing in the interwar period.

Furthermore, there has been little systematic attention to the ways in which the new geography functioned. African American migrants were leaving the rural, slave-holding areas of the South, known as the Black Belt, to which Harold Rose gave the lovely name "the Hearth of Black Culture." This was—in 1910, the peak year of black residence in the South before the Great Migration—an area ". . . some two hundred miles wide which spanned the plainsland South from the Black Prairies of Texas to Virginia, and then tapered to a narrow tip in Megalopolis. This belt widened perceptibly where it crossed the Mississippi River bottomlands, sent a finger curling into northern Florida, and had outliers in the middle Tennessee River Valley—

Nashville Basin–Pennyroyal Plain area and in the Kentucky Blue-grass."[9]

One and a half million black people left the South between 1910 and 1930, settling in major cities in the Northeast and Midwest, while others moved from rural areas in the South to the southern cities. The years 1940–70 marked another great wave of migration, during which millions more moved to the nation's cities. Though African Americans were 90 percent rural at the beginning of the twentieth century, they were 90 percent urban one hundred years later.

In the usual manner of migration, such a diaspora would have been the beginning of the decline of the culture of the old country, in this case, the culture of the Black Belt. Immigrants themselves hold on to their culture, but their children and especially their children's children stop speaking the old language and switch to the customs of the American mainstream. However, the virulent racial segregation that was instituted all over America—and which remains at the time of this writing a potent force influencing residential life—has impeded the African American people's transition from the culture of the Black Belt to the dominant American culture.

Instead, the geography created by dispersal-in-segregation created a group of islands of black life. "Archipelago" is the official geographic term for a group of islands. Black America is an archipelago state, a many-island nation within the American nation. The creation of the archipelago nation had two consequences for African Americans. The first is that the ghettos became centers of black life; the second is that the walls of the ghetto, like other symbols of segregation, became objects of hatred. In this ambivalent, love/hate relationship, it was impossible to choose to dwell. Yet people did choose to make life as vibrant and happy as they possibly could.

Black people worked hard to help one another. They worked especially hard to help the gifted child realize his potential. Paul Robeson, who spent his early childhood in the ghetto in Princeton, New Jersey, described the nurturing that accompanied the community's conviction that he was a gifted child who would express their culture. "Hard-working people, and poor, most of them, in worldly goods—

but how rich in compassion! How filled with the goodness of humanity and the spiritual steel forged by centuries of oppression! . . . Here in this little hemmed-in world where home must be theatre and concert hall and social center, there was a warmth of song. Songs of love and longing, songs of trials and triumphs, deep-flowing rivers and rollicking brooks, hymn-song and ragtime ballad, gospels and blues, and the healing comfort to be found in the illimitable sorrow of the spirituals . . .

"There was something else, too, that I remember from Princeton. Something strange, perhaps, and not easy to describe. I early became conscious—I don't quite know how—of a special feeling of the Negro community for me. I was no different from the other kids of the neighborhood—playing our games of Follow the Leader and Run Sheep Run, saying 'yes ma'am' and never sassing our elders, fearing to cross the nearby cemetery because of the 'ghosts,' coming reluctant and new-scrubbed to Sunday School. And yet, like my father, the people claimed to see something special about me. Whatever it was, and no one really said, they felt I was fated for great things to come. Somehow they were sure of it, and because of that belief they added an extra measure to the affection they lavished on their preacher's motherless child."[10]

Ralph Ellison experienced the same investment in the "special" child while growing up in Oklahoma City. "During summer vacation I blew sustained tones out of the window for hours, usually starting—especially on Sunday mornings—before breakfast. I sputtered whole days through M. Arban's (he's the great authority on the instrument) double- and triple-tonguing exercises, with an effect like that of a jackass hiccupping off a big meal of briars . . . Despite those who complained and cried to heaven for Gabriel to blow a chorus so heavenly sweet and so hellishly hot that I'd forever put down my horn, there were more tolerant ones who were willing to pay in present pain for future pleasure. For who knew what skinny kid with his chops wrapped around a trumpet mouthpiece and a faraway look in his eyes might become the next Armstrong? Yes, and send you, at some big dance a few years hence, into an ecstasy of rhythm and memory and brassy affirmation of the goodness of being alive and part of the community? Someone had to, for it was part of the group tradition, though that was not how they said it."[11]

And when the special child appeared, was nurtured, and took the stage of some city club, the ecstasy happened, as the people knew it would. In 1944, Billy Eckstine's legendary big band went to St. Louis to play at a white nightclub called the Plantation Club. The owners insisted that Billy enter through the back door. He walked in the front door and they fired him on the spot. He took his band to the Riviera Club, an all-black club on Delmar and Taylor. The band included Dizzy Gillespie and Charlie Parker. Standing in for an absent trumpet player was eighteen-year-old Miles Davis.[12]

"Listen," Miles wrote in his autobiography. "The greatest feeling I ever had in my life—with my clothes on—was when I first heard Diz and Bird together . . . when I heard Diz and Bird in B's band, I said, 'What? What is this!?' Man, that shit was so terrible it was scary. I mean, Dizzy Gillespie, Charlie 'Yardbird' Parker, Buddy Anderson, Gene Ammons, Lucky Thompson, and Art Blakey all together in one band and not to mention B: Billy Eckstine himself. It was a mother-fucker. Man, that shit was all up in my body. Music all up in my body, and that's what I wanted to hear. The way that band was playing music—that was all I wanted to hear. It was something. And me up there playing with them."[13]

The triumph of the legendary band of Billy Eckstine was in part a result of the nurturing those amazing musicians had received throughout their lives.

There is another piece to the puzzle of "neon" and that is understanding that places can have a special quality that is greater than the sum of their parts. Neighborhoods can have magic.

Among the truly magic places on earth is the Hill District in Pittsburgh. I believe that, pound for pound, the Hill District was the most generative black community in the United States. When I say "pound for pound," it is like arguing whether the lightweight Sugar Ray Leonard was a greater boxer than the heavyweight Muhammad Ali. The size difference is so great, the two would never have met head-to-head. So the discussion is always framed "pound for pound." Take, for example, photographs. The Hill was so photogenic that

Charles "Teenie" Harris took eighty thousand photographs. Richard Saunders was only in Pittsburgh a few months, but took three thousand pictures, mostly of the Hill. W. Eugene Smith almost succumbed to the photographic equivalent of narcosis of the deep, he struggled so hard to capture the images of the city, and the Hill District. The key is this: it was so lively, so absorbing, so hilly, that every picture was interesting. And that's just for openers.

Eighty-six-year-old tap dancer Henry Belcher told me, "[The Hill District] was amazing. There was people all up and down the street all the time. It was like, well, I never did go to New Orleans, but I would say it was like in New Orleans or something, where if something was going on, people would be out mingling. The only place that I see now, that reminds me of what it used to be here, is on Carson Street on the South Side. See, on Carson Street after dark, people are mingling all up and down the street and in the joints. Well, that's the way it used to be here. All up and down Centre Avenue."

Everyone was in the streets, the fundamental place where the magic was created. The young boys were in the streets a lot, trying to make money to help their families and to take care of their own needs. Lots of men told me stories about their adventures doing little jobs. Ken Nesbitt, who was part of a focus group I led, talked of delivering dinners to the brothels and deciding that a pimp's life was definitely better than the iceman's. "The iceman, he had a horse and buggy. And I used to watch those guys, and say, 'I'm never going to be like that, carrying ice, and shoving that coal down that cellar.' You know, you getting two tons of coal, you got to shovel it down there in the cellar, you get up every morning, you are going to make their fire, and you are going to fix their stove because the stove is run by coal. And I didn't want to be none of them guys there. Them guys worked too hard."

Ken shared his discovery, made at an early age, of how to get change. "I'm talking five or six years old. My dad used to frequent Centre Avenue, the bars, and with us being on Clarke Street, it wasn't that far. And I remember some of the bars had brass rails and sawdust on the floor, and I would go up there looking for my dad, and I knew I wasn't supposed to be up there, but everyone knew my dad and knew I was his son, so they'd give me quarters. And I said, 'Hey, I can get some money!' And even if I knew my dad wasn't up there, I would be up there."

George Moses, in the same group, remembered, "Every Saturday, it was just an unwritten law; every Saturday [the numbers runners] would come down there, and all the boys, there might be thirty of us, they'd take us out to Forbes Field, they'd buy us baseball tickets, and they got kind of like into that, they would support our little sandlot baseball team in the Lower Hill."

Henry Belcher said, "Yeah, we was on the streets, selling papers. And we used to have little jam sessions on the corners. And someone would come around and he done got a new step or something. 'Hey, look, man, here's a step I got!' And we would show each other steps, and we were actually teaching each other that way."

When I asked him who invented that art form, he stressed, "The kids on the street accomplished these things themselves, like." The exchange of dance steps was nourished by the existence of a performance circuit. Henry Belcher explained, "There were certain steps that every new dancer you'd meet knew. 'Cause, times we'd leave Pittsburgh, maybe we'd go up to Harrisburg and work in the clubs. Well, maybe some of them come from Philly or Washington, New York or something, can come up over there to work too. We'd be working on the same deal together. Well, there were certain things that we all knew, these routines. One was called a 'sham' and one was called the 'be-scorts' and we used to use them as an opening or a closing, because everybody already knew them. You didn't have to make up no ending on the show."

The interconnections—in this case, the young boys developing their individual virtuosity, the group establishing a common core of ideas, nurtured both by the local street scene and the national circuit—were essential to the survival and prosperity of the community. Because of the generative nature of the interconnections, those that showed true talent had many venues in which to nurture their talents—Henry Belcher said there were ten or twenty clubs in the Lower Hill, including the Sonia Club, the Crawford Grill, the Ritz Club, Stanley's, Lopez, Javel Jungles, and the Washington Club, as well as the big theaters, such as the New Granada and the Roosevelt Theater.

"You had clubs, like, maybe two or three on every block . . . And then they had the after-hour clubs, they used to run all night long. People would be coming out of there and it would be daylight. People would be running to catch the streetcar. They had streetcars then; they didn't have buses. And the people would be running to catch the streetcars and things. But it was amazing, you know? And you didn't realize, you were just living with what was going on. But that's just like the Hill House here.[14] This was a Jewish place called the Irene Kaufman Settlement. But the Jews never realized that they would have to give that up to the blacks."

The clubs were supported by the men and women who were working in the factories and mines of the Pittsburgh area. Henry Belcher said that, though they were uneducated people from the South, they had more money than they'd ever had in their lives. "And when they got their pay at the end of the week, they just had a ball."

Interactions of all kinds kept the Hill afloat and made sure that everybody ate, had clothes to wear, and behaved properly. The boys on the streets got advice from older men: the dancers and musicians taught them how to refine their arts; the pimps showed them an easy way to make money; the regular guys urged them to go straight— "Even if you see me do it, don't you do it."

Thelma Lovette, who is a matriarch of the Hill, spoke with me about what the community was like when she was growing up in the 1920s and '30s.[15] She was the fifth of eleven children. Her mother had been born in the Hill, and her father had migrated there. She recalled how white shopkeepers helped her father get started in business. "In May 1919, [Papa] decided that he would work for himself. I know the date because my mother delivered a set of twins. The Gross brothers, a set of Jewish brothers who owned a confectionery store at the corner of Wiley and Crawford, were the ones who suggested that Papa use the converted stable behind Burke's [Theater] and set up a shop. Father was a self-taught plumber. His skills and talents were often sought after by many who needed various plumbing jobs done. Outhouses had been outlawed and indoor plumbing was required. They were putting the bathrooms in the homes, so Papa had lots of work to do."

In another story she related, she put across the same message of mutual aid and comfort. "I remember Papa telling us, 'Always remember the neighborhood grocer. Because when you need, he will help you.' The government was rationing sugar and butter. We had a neighborhood grocer—Rosenfield was the name of the family. He would always find a square of butter for Papa. We always had butter."

Such reciprocity depended on connection, both within the Hill and among the Hill and other Pittsburgh communities. Though everyone assured me that it was not necessary to leave the Hill, as everything you needed was there, people did leave for work and shopping. One of the ways to travel was the incline, Pittsburghese for a railroad that runs up the side of a mountain. Agnes Franklin filled me in on the role the incline, which ran from the top of the Hill to the Strip Market, played in the community. "[The incline] is a big thing. And because [my family] didn't live far from there, we were the first ones that those hucksters were in contact with. I remember my grandmother who would want something from down the Strip, she would watch me out the window: go down the incline, get off the incline, go buy her what she wants, and get back on the incline. And she would watch me the whole time.

"And they started to tear down inclines, right? But they only tore *our* incline down," she remembered with bitterness. "The other inclines today are in storage, or monuments, but they tore this incline down. But that incline, you know the sign is still there. But whenever I think about the incline they have over on Mount Washington? *We* had an incline! It cost five cents, didn't it? Something like that."

The comings and goings included treats, as well as chores. Barbara Suber told me, "I feel sorry for the kids today. We didn't have money, but we didn't miss a parade, and the circus used to come down on Gray Street, and the trains. And we was always there. The kids haven't had that experience."

The active, creative life of the archipelago ghetto nation was the result of its interior processes: artists nurtured by the collective and, in turn, giving expression to the people's moods, issues, and tribula-

Fig. 2.2. Charles "Teenie" Harris. "Mother and Daughter in Front of the YMCA in the Hill District." 1942. COURTESY OF THE CARNEGIE MUSEUM OF ART, PITTSBURGH.

Fig. 2.3. Charles "Teenie" Harris. "Iron City Marching Band in front of the Carnegie Library on Wylie Avenue." 1940s. COURTESY OF THE CARNEGIE MUSEUM OF ART, PITTSBURGH.

Fig. 2.4. Esther Bubley. "Art Class at Irene Kaufman Settlement House." June 1950. From the Pittsburgh Photographic Project. COURTESY OF THE PENNSYLVANIA ROOM, CARNEGIE LIBRARY OF PITTSBURGH.

tions. In addition, different neighborhoods developed along particular pathways, each making unique contributions to the strength of the whole. But the wall of oppression that ringed the ghetto remained an obstacle to dwelling that had to be removed. Just as with the creation of art, the fight against oppression was the result of both the contributions of special individuals—in this case, especially brave individuals—and the will of neighborhoods.

The Extra Step: Fight for Freedom

Lorraine Hansberry wrote of black Chicago, "All travelers to my city should ride the elevated trains that race along the back ways of Chicago. The lives you can look into!

"I think you could find the tempo of my people on their back porches. The honesty of their living is there in the shabbiness. Scrubbed porches that sag and look their danger. Dirty gray wood steps. And always a line of white and pink clothes scrubbed so well, waving in the dirty wind of the city.

"My people are poor. And they are tired. And they are determined to live.

"Our Southside is a place apart: each piece of our living is a protest."[16]

Because segregation was the major enemy of the community, the defeat of segregation was a major goal. Just as the music evolved with the changing times, so did the style of activism shift with urbanization.

Angelo Herndon, a young black Communist labor organizer in the South, told of many clashes with the old "accommodationist" leadership. The following story, from his experiences in Birmingham in 1930, reflects both the urgency of his wish to be free, and his rage at the old styles of fighting.

"On my way home one day I got on a trolley. I sat among the Negroes in the Jim Crow section in the rear. Iron bars separated us from the whites. As many of the latter kept coming on we were shoved back into the rear behind the bars, which were movable. I felt like a monkey in the zoo. I knew I was going to lose my temper upon the slightest provocation. I had been sitting on a bench right behind these bars when some white boys in front of me asked me to move back. This made me angry. I said:

" 'What do you mean? I paid my cold cash to ride on this car just as you did and you can bet your sweet life I won't budge.'

"Meekly other Negroes on the car began moving back, urging me to do the same. I felt so ashamed of them! A Negro preacher sitting across from me came over to me and whispered in my ear:

" 'Please, son, for the Lord's sake, don't do that. You'll only cause trouble for yourself and for all of us. What need is there for it? You know you don't own this car. White people run things like they want to, and it's not up to us to tell them what to do.'

"Revulsion seized me, and I said to him:

" 'Dear Reverend, will you please go and take ten steps to hell!'

"The conductor finally came back and rudely asked me to move over. I rose from my seat and said to him:

" 'You white people are so civilized that you seem to think that you can afford to behave worse than savages toward us defenseless Negroes. I know you hate us, but it strikes me awfully funny that you are ready to accept money from a black hand as well as from a white. Now understand me clearly, I've paid my fare to ride this car and I won't give up my seat to any white man until hell freezes over!'

"The conductor said to the white boys:

" 'Leave him alone—he's crazy.' "[17]

Angelo Herndon, who was crazy for freedom, was jailed shortly thereafter for "attempting to incite insurrection," a charge that carried the death penalty. A young black Harvard-educated lawyer, Benjamin J. Davis, stepped forward to represent him. It is possible that Ben Davis recognized in Angelo Herndon the "crazy-for-freedom" characteristics of his Grandfather Davis, who was beaten half to death by his owner, yet refused to give up his defiance. Finally, after protecting his wife from a beating, Grandfather Davis was sold away from the plantation and never seen again.

That ferocious appetite for freedom was passed along to Ben Davis's father, who published a small black newspaper, the *Atlanta Independent*. On one occasion a bundle of papers was returned from a small town called Covington, and someone had scribbled the words "Nigger Ben, we don't allow this paper in this town stirring up trouble among our niggers. Keep it out of here and stay out of here yourself."

The elder Davis refused to be intimidated by the Ku Klux Klan; a few weeks later he set off for Covington, where he had arranged to give a talk on the Constitution. That subject entitled the black people of the area to secure a room in the Covington courthouse. Young Davis accompanied his father. A group of two hundred black people and fifty whites awaited their arrival. On entering the courthouse, all the black men removed their hats, but the whites did not. Ben Davis remembered the tense atmosphere, and the pockets of men, black and white, bulging with firearms.

"My father rose to speak, and my heart was in my mouth. 'Fellow citizens,' he began, 'white and black. I am glad to see that my people respect this courthouse by removing their hats.'

"That was the challenge and my father had boldly chosen the issue—it was an audacious one. We looked around at the audience. Naturally, our eyes fell on the white men standing around the wall with their hats on. What would they do?

"My father paused a full minute, awaiting the reaction to the blow he had struck. As he later explained, he wanted to see whether the whites hated the Negroes so much that they would not respect their own courthouse.

"The next move was up to the badly outnumbered whites slumped along the walls. After about two minutes, one removed his hat. Then another followed suit. One of them walked out. Slowly and sullenly, as if they realized they were beaten, all who remained removed their hats.

"The tension relaxed."[18]

Not only did he win the moment, but the senior Davis won subscriptions as well. His son went on to become a councilman from Harlem, the first member of the Communist Party to hold such a position. He was jailed for his beliefs during the McCarthy period. His activism took a different political course from his father's Republicanism, but like his forebears—and like his client Angelo Herndon—he remained crazy for freedom.

At about the time Ben Davis was getting out of federal prison, Rosa Parks started the modern civil rights movement by refusing to give up her seat on a Montgomery, Alabama, bus. In Montgomery, black bus riders were exposed to a degree of humiliation and danger that is nearly unimaginable, considering—from the perspective of our times—that blacks were consumers paying for a public service. Astounding as it may seem, bus drivers, as enforcers of segregation, were given free reign in abusing the black passengers:

- Blacks couldn't sit in the first rows of seats reserved for whites, even if there were no whites on the bus—even if there were no whites on the bus route!
- If the white section of the bus became full, black people were expected to give up their seats to the white people—and not simply the seat needed for the person, but to vacate the row of seats so that the white person might sit in a "white row."
- Blacks were forced to pay at the front of the bus, then dismount and enter via the rear entrance. It was not uncommon for black people to be left behind, even though they had paid their fares.
- Angry bus drivers could—and frequently did—throw blacks off the bus, have them arrested, yell at them in a humiliating manner, and hit them. In some cases this led to the permanent injury and even death of the black bus rider.

The black community of Montgomery, dependent on the buses for transportation, was thoroughly and repeatedly traumatized by these racist practices. They had tried to meet with the city and the bus company to win courteous treatment. One brief interlude of peace was won, but matters quickly reverted to the high levels of abuse and traumatization.

Jo Ann Robinson and other members of the local Women's Political Council, frustrated by the failure of their efforts to negotiate with the bus company, had agreed years before to boycott the buses when the time was right. They had even worked out some fundamental logistics, such as how to spread the word throughout the black community.

On December 1, 1955, Rosa Parks, who was known to all as a "respectable seamstress," was arrested for refusing to give up her seat in the "colored" section to a white man. Jo Ann Robinson and her colleagues agreed the time had come. Rosa Parks was a beloved woman and dedicated community leader. She was one of the "best people" in the community. This led people to ask themselves, "If they can do that to *Rosa Parks,* what will they do to *me*?"

Telephones rang all over the city and children raced from house to house, spreading the word. By the next morning, Jo Ann Robinson and coworkers had run off enough leaflets to reach the fifty thousand people in the community, and the Women's Political Council's network was passing them out door-to-door and in stores, beauty parlors, beer halls, factories, and barbershops—as well as at Hilliard Chapel AME Church, where a group of Montgomery's black ministers were meeting. They, like everyone else, embraced the idea of the one-day boycott, called for December 5, 1955.

Everyone who was in Montgomery on that day has testified that it was nerve-racking waiting for the first buses to pass by. Would the black community stand together? Would this effort fizzle out as others had before it? Could people make the sacrifice?

The answer—and we cannot cease to marvel at this—was that not only could and would people make the sacrifice, but they would do it for thirteen months, against great brutality, enjoying every minute of the assertion of their right to respect. The true, mass nature of the boycott was revealed in many ways, among them, the testimony of Gladys Moore, given during the March 1956 conspiracy trial of Dr. Martin Luther King, Jr. Asked to explain why she had stopped riding the buses on December 5, Gladys Moore replied:

> MOORE: I stopped because we had been treated so bad down through the years that we decided we wouldn't ride the buses no more.
>
> JUDGE: What do you mean "we"?
>
> MOORE: All the fifty thousand Negroes in Montgomery.
>
> JUDGE: When did you all decide?
>
> MOORE: Well, after so many things happened. Wasn't no man started it. *We all started it overnight.*[19] (emphasis added)

Jo Ann Robinson wrote in her memoir, "Our first day did everybody good, for the angry ones had released pent-up emotions. The maladjusted, frustrated ones 'walked off' the feeling during the day's routine and felt better. Those who suffered from inferiority complexes felt important. So there was definitely no stopping it now . . . The one day of protest against the white man's traditional policy of white supremacy had created a new person in the Negro. The new spirit, the new feeling did something to the blacks individually and collectively, and each liked the feeling. There was no turning back! There was only one way out—the buses must be changed!"[20]

The stresses and strains of those thirteen months were managed collectively by the Montgomery Improvement Association, but it was Martin Luther King, Jr., who gave the boycott the character of redemptive love, and planted the first seeds of the idea of the Beloved Community.

That fifty thousand people shared a common torture, that they shared networks via which messages might spread at lightning speed, that they had a vast concern for preserving one another, that they had a common religious history and moral tradition: these are the ingredients of what we might call the "Beloved Neighborhood," the urban ghetto that was built by migrants from the rural South, hoping to find a better life in the cities. The "better" that they found was not good enough, so they began to work, to organize, to struggle, to make the "better" better, the real New Jerusalem.

What did they want? Dr. King offered, in answer to that question, a vision of total relatedness. Religious scholars Kenneth L. Smith and Ira Zepp have pointed out, "Behind King's conception of the Beloved Community lay his assertion that human existence is social in nature. 'The solidarity of the human family' is a phrase he frequently used to express this idea. 'We are tied together in the single garment of destiny, caught in an inescapable network of mutuality,' he said in one of his addresses. This was a way of affirming that reality is made up of structures that form an interrelated whole; in other words, that human beings are dependent upon each other. Whatever a person is or possesses he owed to others who have preceded him. As King wrote,

'Whether we realize it or not, each of us lives eternally "in the red." ' Recognition of one's indebtedness to past generations should inhibit the sense of self-sufficiency and promote awareness that personal growth cannot take place apart from meaningful relationships with other persons, that the 'I' cannot attain fulfillment with the 'Thou.' "[21]

During the Montgomery bus boycott, the people of that place used the linkages they had forged to create a better place. They gained, and passed on, a vision of an even better place: one in which the color of one's skin did not matter, in which all people were invested in the well-being of other people, and, one might hope, all living beings on the planet.

Jo Ann Robinson explained, "At the beginning, black bus boycotters had learned to hate, and they had hated 'with a vengeance.' But they learned one thing: hate does more harm to the hater than to the hated. The body, the state of mind of the one hating responds to the hate, and, like an illness, the hate begins a deterioration of that body, that mind. Illness, even death, can result.

"All boycotters learned this lesson. Dr. King had taught them that love is *redemptive*. That is why, though they had continued to boycott, they had dismissed the bus drivers from their thinking. They learned to guide their thoughts to pleasant things. This was why they stopped 'hating whitey,' why they laughed so much as they walked, why they could boycott for thirteen months while still working at their jobs and keeping their children in school, their bills paid, and their bodies well. Hate destroys, but love revitalizes!"[22]

Jo Ann Robinson pointed out that, prior to the boycott, the stress of riding the buses had contributed to violence in Montgomery families. The boycott was so effective in changing people's state of being that hospitals reported many fewer injuries related to family anger. King's fundamental thesis was that racism hurt whites as much as it hurt blacks. Though blacks were the ones fighting to make Montgomery a better place, the victory was not for themselves alone, but for all of the city.

This is the nature of neighborhood: the way of life evolves over time, as each effort at problem resolution becomes part of the collective memory and the collective foundation for problem solving. In such a way, living for millennia in a place, the aboriginal people of Australia mastered the subtle signs of the bush country, and the Inuit invented names for many kinds of snow. "Generational knowledge," Roanoke reporter Mary Bishop called it, and I think that is an excellent name for the information which belongs to a community that has lived together for a long time. This is the essence of the ghetto neighborhoods that evolved over several generations. It is, we learn from the story of the Montgomery bus boycott, the ghetto, rooted in place, that is the material basis for Martin Luther King's Beloved Community—the slaves' dream of New Jerusalem, the highest expression of people living together in justice and compassion.

To Dwell or Not: The Uncertain Future of the Ghetto

A dilemma was embedded in the effort to defeat segregation. It was segregation that had made the ghetto. The ghetto, in turn, had made the archipelago state and its local representative, the neighborhood. The alteration—if not the death—of the neighborhood-based community was planted in the death of segregation. Segregation—and the accompanying violence and maltreatment—was intolerable. But what was to become of the ghetto once segregation was defeated?

Among the leaders who faced this issue was my father, Ernest Thompson, who, in the mid-1950s, was a nationally recognized trade union leader. He had been part of the Great Migration, leaving the oppression of rural Maryland in 1922 to make a better life in New Jersey. He immediately took up the struggle for better working conditions. Against great odds he worked to form unions and threw himself wholeheartedly into the union drives that took off after the 1932 election of Franklin Delano Roosevelt.

The union movement, he often pointed out, was a coalition among the workers of different nationalities who worked together in the same plants. The union movement was neither of the ghetto nor in the ghetto. Under the onslaught of McCarthyism, many unions retreated from progressive positions on rights for black people. My father realized that the leadership for the struggle for Negro freedom would come from the ghetto itself. "The Negro must embrace the ghetto like a mother her child," my father said, as he turned his efforts toward organizing the political power of the ghetto.[23] His was not a position of separatism, for he understood clearly that decisions about the ghetto were made outside its boundaries, in city hall or in Congress. Rather, he hoped to use the ghetto as a base of power from which to work in coalition with other groups in the fight for basic necessities, education and housing chief among them. Desegregation, in his view, was the beginning of a new life for the ghetto, not its end. But how was this to be?

It was the urbanist Jane Jacobs who provided a vision of the possible future of the ghetto postsegregation.[24] She argued that, though we call all poor neighborhoods "slums," we should distinguish between two kinds of poor neighborhoods: perpetual slums and unslumming neighborhoods. They might look the same initially, she noted, but they were on distinctly different trajectories due to the actions of area residents. A slum would endure if residents left as quickly as they could. A neighborhood could transform itself, if people wanted to stay. It was the investment of time, money, and love that would make the difference. Following this line of reasoning, one might imagine some ghettos that would flourish and others that would flounder, depending on whether or not the area received investment from residents and attention from the larger body politic.[25]

It is significant that much of the Jewish ghetto in Rome is still standing, nearly 450 years later. Laura Supino told Carol Shapiro, "Jews have been living in this neighborhood for 22 centuries, two hundred years before the common era, with no break in their presence. So we are the only Jewish community to be present always in the same place before the Diaspora. Jewish people still live here, but of course all Italian citizens can live here and Jews can live in every other part of the town. But this quarter has always been a meeting place and a place for Jewish memories."[26]

Sentiment aside, make no mistake about it, the ghetto of Rome was not just a ghetto: it was also a slum. According to Anya Shetterly, "There was just tiny narrow streets, all the garbage went out on the street. You can just imagine the smell." But, in 2002, *Let's Go Rome* tells tourists, "Although Dickens declared the area 'a miserable place, densely populated and reeking with bad odours,' today's Jewish ghetto is one of Rome's most charming and eclectic neighborhoods, with family businesses dating back centuries and restaurants serving up some of the tastiest food in the city."[27]

Segregation in a city inhibits the free interaction among citizens and invariably leads to brutality and inequality, which themselves are antithetical to urbanity. When segregation disappears, freedom of movement becomes possible. That does not necessarily mean that people will want to leave the place where they have lived. The ghetto ceases to be a ghetto, it is true, but it does not stop being a neighborhood of history. Postsegregation, the African American ghetto would have been a site for imaginative re-creation, much like the ghetto in Rome.

The Second Great Migration, which began in 1940 and ended in 1970, posed another extraordinary set of challenges to the ghetto and to the city. The ghettos, largely built by the hopeful and resourceful migrants who arrived during the course of the Great Migration, were now the destination of millions of refugees, forced off the land by the mechanization of the cotton harvest. The new arrivals swelled the populations of the ghettos, bringing with them a welter of needs that far exceeded the kind most neighbors might have to offer. Whereas the earlier generation was urbanized by the factories that stood on every corner, the era of unskilled labor was drawing to a close as this second group of country people showed up looking for work. Who was to meet their needs? Where were they to be housed? Who would help them make the transition from the rural to urban life?

For if the city had been unhappy with the ghetto before 1940, the numbers and the rawness of the new arrivals were an even more severe aggravation to white sensibilities. The city would have to help meet the needs of its new citizens, and somebody had to find some room for them.

The third challenge facing the urban ghettos was the loss of unskilled jobs, some due to "runaway" plants that had left the older industrial areas for the South and other places with nonunion labor, and some due to automation of factory work and the transition to an information economy. The handwriting was on the wall: if people were not ready to compete for jobs requiring mastery of a high level of reading and writing skills, they were going to be shut out of the re-configured urban job market.

Given the vitality of the civil rights movement, and the strength of the ghetto communities, it is possible they could have solved all these problems and more. But what happened next was an enormous setback, one that threw the homeward journey completely off course. What happened next was urban renewal.

ZENOBIA FERGUSON

The following excerpts are from an interview with Zenobia Ferguson, a resident of Roanoke, Virginia, who was displaced by the urban renewal of the Northwest section. This is the story of how she moved to the city and made a home for herself.

I had never lived in an all-black neighborhood until I came to Roanoke. Because where I lived was out on a farm, and all around it, people were white, and I didn't see black people until I went to church, or Sunday School, or in the winter when I went to school. All of my schoolmates were black. That's just the way it was. We played together. Fought and played. Country life, you were very isolated from people because most people were on a farm, and unless there was some kind of activity at the church or at school, you just didn't see people. But you know, black people, that is. The Pullens, they lived across the road, we all played together, and they were all white.

And the neighbors we had that were black were just an old couple, Mr. and Mrs. Wax. We'd go down to see them, but they didn't have any children. And see, I left Fincastle when I was twelve and went to Christiansburg Institute for high school, because there was no high school in my area for black people.

It was nice. They were strict. They were really strict, and I was the youngest student there. We had dormitories. We had matrons, and founders of that school were people from Pennsylvania, they call them the Quakers. But the atmosphere of that school was sort of like Tuskegee Institute in Tuskegee, Alabama, because I understand that Booker T. Washington was instrumental in getting that school started.

Mostly the boys learned the trades. We had students from all over Virginia. Some from New York and some from Pennsylvania. It was a boarding school and a day school also.

[Commenting on the strictness] I had been over in the Edgar Long Building and I had to come back and get something I left in the dormitory, and I would run up the steps, and the matron would say, "Go right back down where you started running, and start walking like a lady." And on Saturday night we had what was called the Douglass Literary Society, named after Frederick Douglass. And that was where you learned poetry and society, and then they would talk to us about the social graces and this kind of things.

We had to line up on Sunday morning, and we would walk over to the Christiansburg Church. And the matron would walk down the line and inspect you.

And on Monday nights, we would have a Monday night meeting, and everything that you did wrong was written in her black book. And she would go down the line, and point you out, and she would say to me, "I don't have your name here, but I know you did something. And I'm going to find out!" And she was always on my case. Always on my case! And I saw her in Washington later, and she was with her daughter, and she said, "I just loved this girl!" And I thought to myself, "God!"

And at boarding school, you had calling hours on Sunday. And boys would put your name down, and then if you had been good, you could come down and sit in the living room and talk, but he couldn't touch you. No handling, no, no no! You used to have to cross your ankles. I think about that and think, "God, look at kids today." But other things that the kids do, I think, you know, it all comes in time. Because I remember when I was up there in Christiansburg, my mother sent me a new pea coat, that's what we were wearing then. And I had everybody autograph my coat with a pen. That was what you did with it. When I went home, my mother was furious. She said, "What's this?"

And I said to her, "Mom, if I knew I couldn't have it autographed, I wouldn't have worn it."

And she smacked me. She thought I was being smart. But that was just what kids were doing. And I was so proud of my autographs.

Of course, I have never let anything stop me. I just keep on going. When I finished Christiansburg Institute, I marched with my graduating class, but two days before graduation, I was called into the principal's office. Botetourt County was supposed to have paid my fee, and they didn't. And they didn't give me a diploma. I had to march with a blank diploma. And I had to fight back the tears, because I had worked, waiting tables, and washing dishes, and doing everything I was supposed to do, but they messed up.

[Mrs. Ferguson moved to Roanoke at that point.]

I had so many people who were good to me here. Mrs. Pullen and her daughter Ethel. We had a drama club in Christiansburg and Edison had one too, and we used to exchange plays, so I knew Ethel, when I was going to school, and when I would come here I would go down and see her, and everything. And I would ask Mrs. Pullen, her mother, "Can Ethel go with me this place or that place?"

She'd say, "No. Ethel can't go and you're not going either!"

I had a lot of people like that, Mrs. Pullen [another Mrs. Pullen; this one was black], Mrs. Martin, and all those people would just tell me what I could and couldn't do. That, I used to appreciate. I really did.

I remember hearing about Henry Street; there was a club called the Morocco that you could go in, and it had bands and those kind of things, and that's where I met my husband, you know? And he had just come back from World War II, and that is where I saw him. And Henry Street is where if you wanted to dance or anything, this is where you went. If you wanted to go to the movies or the theater, that's where you went. You could go downtown to the theater but you had to go up to the mezzanine, or the balcony. You had to go up all those steps. So we felt like the Virginia Theater was ours, we could just go there. And then there were restaurants and things like that. And most of the people we knew, like, I'm trying to think of the name of the restaurant, but his daughter and I, we were buddies. We used to go over there and get these big old steaks and all that kind of things at his restaurant at Henry Street.

And we didn't *hang* on Henry Street. Because I've always been this kind of person: if I'm going somewhere, I'm going. But I don't go out on the street when I don't know where I am going. I wasn't that way.

So, we had four social clubs that had formal dances, and there used to be the Roanoke Auditorium. We used to go dancing there, and hear Ella Fitzgerald, Erskine Hawkins, and Cab Calloway, all those fellows. They used to come to Roanoke and we used to go to those dances and have a ball. The Hotel Dumas had a private band, that is where the music center is now. And they had a private band and you could go and dine more elegantly. And we used to go there. And of course there was the Royalton, where they used to have the Red and White Ball. We would go there.

[I settled at] 402 Chestnut Avenue, Northwest. It was just a close-knit neighborhood. The neighbors were, okay, I'll give you an example. My daughter, and she is really my stepdaughter, my husband had her before we got married. I have a son and he has a daughter. But when she went to college she said that somebody took her bag with all of the clothing that she could wear at that time, because it was September, and it was hot. And she called back home crying. My neighbors across the way started buying clothes for this girl, and gave them to me so I could take them down there to her. That is the kind of neighborhood I lived in. It was just, "What can we do?" You know? And she wanted to come home, you know. She didn't want to stay at college, but I was determined that she was going to stay there.

Now people weren't always in each other's homes, I don't mean that. But it was just a lot of love and caring. But I'm going to tell you something, it's the same thing in this community. I have been lucky and thankful that people have a sense of belonging. And in Northwest, there was a lot of pride of ownership, pride of belonging. Our families and our schools and our churches, all were sources of pride. I shall never forget when Four Sounds sang down at Roanoke Auditorium. And everybody applauded them. They were just magnificent.

You have never seen anything like it. We were so proud we didn't know what to do.

One day I was on Chestnut Avenue, looking out the window of my beauty shop, and I said, "I am going to get my degree." I called Lawyer Muse and told him my situation, and he said, "Mrs. Ferguson, you stay on the line, and I will put my secretary on, and I am going to dictate a letter to Mr. Wilkerson," I think his name was, the superintendent of the state. And, he did that. He said he would get my diploma papers for me, and he did it. And when I got them, I decided, I will never argue with anybody about a high school diploma. I went to Virginia Western Community College, and I enrolled and I graduated from there. And then for my last two years I went to Hollins. And I graduated from there in May 1972.

Nothing could stop me. I just made up my mind I was going. I said I would do whatever I can, and I did that. I just made up my mind; when things are going bad, I just get going.

Chapter 3

URBAN RENEWAL . . .

Cities are always growing or shrinking, hence remaking themselves. Sometimes this reordering is haphazard, and sometimes it is planned, carried out according to the agendas of those paying for the improvements. The messy, medieval city of Paris came in for such planned improvement, and it was the first capital city to be rebuilt without a massive fire first clearing the land. The coup d'état that made Louis Napoleon Bonaparte emperor of France in 1852 gave him the absolute power needed to undertake the massive renovation of Paris. He had three major goals: to bring water into the city and to improve the circulation of air among the buildings; to unify its parts; and to make it more beautiful. A powerful administrator was needed, given that this massive project was to be carried out while the busy life of the capital went on around it. In 1853, the emperor selected Georges-Eugène Haussmann, whom he made a baron, to be that man.[1]

Though Haussmann's name is the one attached to the changes in Paris and many other French cities, he was not the person who created the ideas. Rather, the plans drew on wisdom acquired during several hundred years of city making. Years earlier, kings of France, eager to make their capital as beautiful as Rome, had begun deciphering the strategies needed to achieve that end. The leaders that followed them added to those aesthetic concerns the need to control frequent epidemics, such as those caused by raw sewage running in the narrow alleyways of the city. As the years passed and modes of transportation changed, the people of Paris found that they couldn't move through the narrow medieval streets squeezed between the tightly packed buildings; street widening became a pressing goal of city beautification.

Over the years, a concept evolved. At its heart was the creation of wide avenues called *percées* ("pierced"), because they were to cut diagonally through the old city's massive blocks of housing. By the mid-nineteenth century, a few of these avenues had been created with great success. Their width permitted light and air to enter the city and their style added to its beauty.

Haussmann's job was to apply these proven techniques on a scale large enough to transform the city. At the same time, while the streets were being carved out of the old city, sewers could be installed. A new street face was installed, incorporating buildings, street lamps, *pissoirs,* and other "street furniture" carefully designed to create unity in the "look" of Paris as one traveled from arrondissement to arrondissement, ward to ward.

In the series of figures shown here, we see the section of Paris that was "pierced" to create Avenue de l'Opéra, one of the greatest of the Haussmann boulevards. In the first map, we see the outlines of the tight and somewhat random streets of the old Paris. In the second map, we see the proposal for a boulevard to cut diagonally through the urban tissue. In the final map, we see the Paris of today, with Avenue de l'Opéra successfully built.

Lithographs drawn while the piercing was in progress show the deep trenches that were dug to permit the placement of the sewers. We also see the sorrow of those who were moved away. Although most of the housing destroyed in the center was eventually replaced, its costs were prohibitive for the poor, who were forced to move to outlying areas that were added to the city during the Haussmann period.

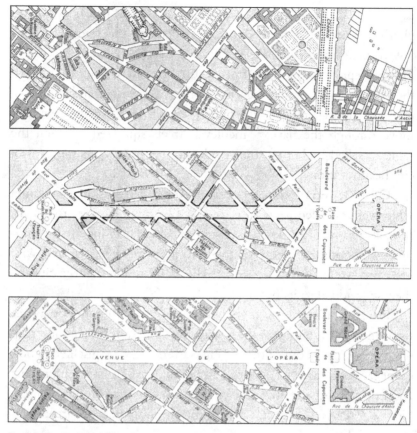

Fig. 3.1. The strategic design of renovations in Paris in the area of the Avenue de l'Opéra. Upper plan: the area as it appeared under Louis XV, 1773. Middle plan: the plan for the new avenue overlaid on the existing street grid, in 1876. Lower plan: actual construction (in 1929). REPRODUCED FROM *L'ILLUSTRATION*, 1929.

It is not, I think, an accident that social critic Victor Hugo—one of thousands of republicans exiled under the Empire—used the images of sewers to animate the persecution of Jean Valjean in his 1861 masterpiece, *Les Misérables*. Nor was it an accident that the new boulevards became a central character in the paintings of the Impressionist school and on the picture postcards of the era. The city's transformation aroused the pain and the wonder of the population.

In 2000, I spent two months living in a neighborhood bounded by two great Haussmann boulevards—Boulevard Saint Michel and Boulevard Saint Germain des Prés. Every day I walked through the old city into the new, examining the manner in which Haussmann

Fig. 3.2. Root shock in Paris. Compare with root shock in Pittsburgh, fig. 7.3, and root shock in New York after 9/11, fig. 8.5. Upper lithograph: Honoré Daumier. From the series "Locataires et Propriétaires": Scene from a neighborhood in process of demolition. REPRODUCED COURTESY OF THE PHOTOTHÈQUE DES MUSÉES DE LA VILLE DE PARIS. Lower lithograph: Demolition for the Avenue de l'Opéra. REPRODUCED FROM *L'ILLUSTRATION*, 1929.

had cut the great boulevards at an angle through the urban fabric and had pasted the new Paris over the old.

French urbanist Michel Cantal-Dupart wrote of that neighborhood, "At the base of Boulevard Saint Michel, Haussmann had demolished the Church of Saint André des Arts, which was the parish church for the riverside neighborhood that stretched from the Pont Neuf to the Pont Saint Michel. According to their residence east or west of the new boulevard, the parishioners were reassigned to Saint Germain or Saint Séverin. One was in the 6th *arrondissement,* and the other in the fifth. Boulevard Saint Michel, although it united traffic towards Paris, proved to be an almost unassailable obstacle to the urbanism of the neighborhood. Though it has been more than a century since the demolition of the church, the neighborhood has remained disorganized. The village never regained its authenticity. It had lost an essential organ."[2]

The sense I was getting—that the renovation entailed a massive, irreparable upheaval—was heightened by the realization that Haussmann was thrown out of office in 1870. At about the same time as the fall of Haussmann, Emperor Napoleon III entered into a disastrous war with Germany. France was quickly beaten back, and a siege laid around Paris. Over the months of the siege, and during the peace negotiations that followed, residents of the city lost whatever faith they had had in the emperor's government. In fact, that government collapsed and was replaced by a provisional government, which appeared to be just as unreliable in its negotiations with Germany and in its treatment of the capital. Obviously, much had happened by the point at which, in an effort to save the country and themselves, the working people of Paris rose up in revolt and declared a new democratic government, the Paris Commune.

War, siege, and abandonment by the national government might seem to have been enough to provoke the Commune. Research has demonstrated that upheaval played a part as well. The Commune was organized by people who had been displaced from the center of the city by the Haussmannian renovations. Living and struggling together in the newly annexed peripheral arrondissements, the displaced people had gathered strength and solidarity from one another.[3] Displacement both added to the other layers of frustration and reorganized neighboring, creating new spaces within which relationships and ideas were developed.

The Commune, with its generous reforms and democratic concerns, was quickly overthrown. A bloodbath ensued, during which as many as thirty thousand Communards were murdered. Reading this part of the story of Paris provided me with new ways to think about urban renewal and its consequences. I thought it was probably a good idea that the United States hadn't gone to war just after urban renewal. Then I remembered Vietnam.

The Housing Act of 1949

The term "urban renewal" is used generically to refer to improvements in cities. In the United States the phrase is also used to refer to a program of the federal government, begun under the Housing Act of 1949, and modified under a number of later acts, the most important of which, the Housing Act of 1954, actually introduced the term into the law. Those acts were designed to provide the money for retooling the city, preparing for the postwar era, and switching from the war machine to new means of productivity. In 1950s America, urban renewal was a synonym for "progress."[4]

Progress meant new technologies, new jobs, and—here is where urban renewal comes in—new uses for the land. Those who sought to maintain the old city stood in the way of progress, and *progress* was a magic word back then: normally honest people would hide their true feelings on any issue in order to be able to say, "I'm for progress."[5] General Electric went a step forward, reminding us through its advertisements, "Progress is our most important product."

Reclaiming land for new uses has an important precedent in American history in the abrogation of treaties with Native Americans. In the beginning of the westward push, Native Americans were asked to move west of the Appalachians. Then they were asked to move west of the Mississippi. Then they were settled on reservations, which were relocated repeatedly. In the 1950s, children like me grew up with the story of Native Americans being settled on wasteland dotted with black puddles, but being moved when it was discovered that those black puddles were oil.

There is a joke that circulated on email a few years ago. It went like this. Two Navajos, an old man and his grandson, were walking on the reservation one day and ran into a group of white scientists from NASA, standing around a spacecraft. The grandson asked what they were doing and the scientists explained they were preparing a trip to the moon. The grandson translated this to the old man, who spoke only Navajo. The old man pondered this information for a moment, then asked if he could send a message to the Man in the Moon. The NASA scientists, amused by this request, got out their tape recorder. The old man spoke briefly in Navajo and nodded with satisfaction when he was done. The scientists asked the grandson what he had said. He told the Man in the Moon, "Watch out, they've come to take your land."[6]

The land-claiming strategy embodied in the Housing Act of 1949 was straightforward. An interested city had first to identify the "blighted" areas that it wished to redo. Having defined "slum" and "ghetto," we must add this concept of blight, which was invented specifically for purposes of redoing aging downtown areas, and meant, quite simply, that buildings had lost their sparkle and their profit margin.[7] Quite a remarkable array of buildings could fit under the definitions of blight that were enacted into law.[8]

Once those areas had been defined, the city had the task of developing a "workable plan." This had largely to do with figuring out a new use for the area once it was cleared of blight. The workable plan was forwarded to regional urban renewal offices for approval by the federal government. Once the plan was approved, the designated areas could be seized using the government's power of eminent domain. The people and businesses that occupied the site were given a minimal amount of compensation and were sent away. The seized land was then cleared of all buildings and, thanks to federal subsidies, sold to developers at a fraction of the city's costs. The developers then built businesses, educational and cultural institutions, and residences for middle- and upper-income people. In some instances, high-rise public housing projects were built on the cleared land.[9]

Marc Weiss summed up the overall impact of the twenty-four-year program by saying, "Urban renewal agencies in many cities demolished whole communities inhabited by low income people in order to provide land for private development of office buildings, sports arenas, hotels, trade centers, and high income luxury buildings."[10] Rather than providing decent homes and suitable living environments, urban renewal created a massive housing crisis. Weiss noted, "As of June 30, 1967, 400,000 residential units had been demolished in urban renewal areas, while only 10,760 low-rent public housing units had been built on these sites."[11] You might well ask: How did a plan that subsidized developers, and dramatically worsened the conditions of the poor, come to be the law of the land?

Saving Downtown

American business leaders and mayors of large cities believed that the civic organization that had evolved over the first part of the twentieth century, that is, a central downtown surrounded by an array of manufacturing, trading, and residential areas, was becoming obsolete as the population began to overrun the borders and fill the nearby suburbs. In their view, a postwar retooling of the American city was needed, one designed to respond to the changing spatial dynamics and to prepare for competition with other nations. The changing needs of American capitalism were the impetus for the reorganization of the cities, and it was powerful men who sought solutions and pushed for their enactment into law. Weiss noted: "Urban renewal owes its origins to downtown merchants, banks, large corporations, newspaper publishers, realtors, and other institutions with substantial business and property interests in the central part of the city."[12]

In Pittsburgh, for example, the leadership for urban renewal came from the Allegheny Conference on Post-War Community Planning, a group of civic and business leaders that was started in 1943 to chart the course for ensuring the city's prosperity. A photograph of the executive committee of the conference depicts a large group of white men, dressed to suggest wealth and authority, and seated under portraits of two members of the Mellon banking family.[13] Just to list those seated in the first row:

- Edward J. Hanley, vice president of the conference and president, Allegheny Ludlum Steel Corporation;
- Edward J. Magee, executive director of the conference;
- Leon Falk, Jr., industrialist;[14]
- John T. Ryan, Jr., chairman of the conference and president, Mine Safety Appliances Company;
- Carl B. Jansen, president of the conference and chairman of the board, Dravo Corporation;
- Gwilym R. Price, vice president of the conference and chairman of the board, Westinghouse Electric Corporation;
- Leslie B. Worthington, president, United States Steel Corporation;
- John A. Mayer, vice president of the conference and president, Mellon National Bank and Trust Company.

Conspicuously absent from the picture, and from the decision-making processes, were poor people, black people, and women. One way of understanding urban renewal is to contrast the discourse that was taking place in different settings. Clearly, when the industrialists themselves were at the table, the looming and fundamental changes in methods and places of production were part of the conversation.

Outside of those rooms, however, the public concern of white officials was largely cast as physical improvements that entailed "no social loss." George Evans, a member of the Pittsburgh City Council, wrote a 1943 article that put forward the public face of urban renewal. In "Here Is a Postwar Job for Pittsburgh . . . Transforming the Hill District," Evans argued, "The Hill District of Pittsburgh is probably one of the most outstanding examples in Pittsburgh of neighborhood deterioration . . . There are 7,000 separate property owners; more than 10,000 dwelling units and in all more than 10,000 buildings. Approximately 90 per cent of the buildings in the area are sub-standard and have long outlived their usefulness, and so there would be *no social loss* if they were all destroyed. The area is criss-crossed with streets running every which way, which absorb at least one-third of the area. These streets should all be vacated and a new street pattern overlaid. This would effect a saving of probably 100 acres now used for unnecessary streets."[15] (emphasis added)

The Hill District, which served as a newcomer neighborhood of Pittsburgh, had welcomed tens of thousands of African Americans to the city in the first half of the twentieth century. For those migrants, the tight streets of the Hill were not a waste of territory, but the nidus for making essential relationships.

As Sala Udin, who grew up in the Hill District and later served as its councilman, put it, "The sense of community and the buildings are related in an old area. The buildings were old, the streets were cobble-stone and old, there were many small alleyways and people lived in those alleyways. The houses were very close together. There were small walkways that ran in between the alleyways that was really a playground. So, the physical condition of the buildings helped to cre-ate a sense of community. We all lived in similar conditions and had similar complaints about the wind whipping through the gaps be-tween the frame and the window, and the holes in the walls and the leaking and the toilet fixtures that work sometimes and don't work sometimes. But that kind of common condition bound us together more as a community. I knew everybody on my block, and they knew me. They knew me on sight, and they knew all the children on sight, and my behavior changed when I entered the block. And so, I think there was a very strong sense of community."

For Thelma Lovette, Barbara Suber, Henry Belcher, Agnes Franklin, George Moses, Ken Nesbitt, and others I talked to from the Hill, those close-knit relationships were essential to life. The dispersal of the community and the loss of those connections had ominous im-plications. Thus, a third part of the discourse on the changing city was the African American community's sense of threat, which was cap-tured in the expression "Urban Renewal Is Negro Removal."[16]

But George Evans, writing before the integration of baseball, before the integration of schools or buses, was living in a world that promulgated racist imaginings while prohibiting genuine contact. The power structure offered no forum for Thelma Lovett or any other African Americans to argue for their version of reality. Furthermore, George Evans could speak in that manner with the full backing of white social scientists who, themselves no better informed than George Evans, concluded that African American communities were "disorganized," the technical term for "no social loss." In the words of a leading academic researcher, "The Negro who hesitates to leave Harlem or the South Side is chiefly reacting negatively to the unknown 'white man's world' out there. His own fellow ethnics share no distinctive heritage excepting a rural origin and a common reaction to the rejection by white society."[17]

Tension Building Up . . .

Geographer Harold M. Rose, who has contributed a great deal to our understanding of the geography of African American urban settlement, depicted the ghetto as a triangle sitting on the half circle of downtown.[18] Public health students, when asked to free-associate to this image, came up with a string of dynamic words:

- Paternalistic
- Tipping
- Constrained
- Enveloped
- Disconnection
- Oppression
- Penetration

These words, and many more like them, get at the charged and unstable relationships among the disparate parts of the city. Let us consider the relationship suggested by the triangle of ghetto squatting on downtown. One of the groups interested in urban renewal was the downtown business district, which hoped to entice the rich to move back downtown by sprucing up the decor. "Just think of what would happen to our downtown business district, with all the surplus buying power within walking distance of the center of the community," Milwaukee city attorney Walter J. Mattison enthused in 1944.[19]

In order to convert the downtown to a shopping mall for the rich, it was necessary, the leaders thought, to rebuild it in a glossy and modern fashion. They began this process even before the federal urban renewal process was invented, but their work was expanded and accelerated once federal funds were available. The model of the new world city had been proposed by the architect Le Corbusier.[20] Its dominant feature was a "tower in the park," a tall building surrounded by grass or open space. Cartoonist Jean-François Batelier, observing

Fig. 3.3. Jean-François Batelier. Corbu combine. Modeled after the machines that cut and bail hay at the same time, this machine winnows old buildings and spits out new towers. Compare these images to the images of "empty" and "full" in chapter 8. COURTESY OF THE ARTIST.

the cookie-cutter fashion in which people were bulldozing cities and putting up towers-in-the-park, thought of the idea of a "Corbu combine," shown here in action.[21]

Though downtown business leaders were interested in clearing blight, ghetto areas seemed to offer a two-fer: clear blight and clear blacks. They had at their disposal two mechanisms that ultimately worked synergistically to help clear the land: one was urban renewal, and the other was the federal highway program. Imagine, then, the triangle of the ghetto diminished by the half circle of downtown completing itself by urban renewal, while highway construction took a juicy slice, generally aimed straight down the middle.

Inherent in taking land is the implication that former residents have to go someplace else, as the working people were moved to the periphery of Paris and the Native Americans were moved to reservations. In many cities, there was literally no place for the displaced black people to go. White people who lived in neighborhoods adjacent to the ghetto were completely opposed to any expansion of "black territory," and they organized to protect their turf. Neighborhood groups were formed to exert political, social, and economic pressure against African Americans who sought to move in. Others organized vigilante groups that carried out terrorist attacks. Whites also used physical barriers to prevent black movement out of the ghetto.[22]

To a large extent, planners had control over the directions in which people could move, and the spaces they would occupy. Their thinking was guided by explicit concepts, described in publications for planning professionals, of hiding and marginalizing the poor. Their tools included using highways, massive buildings, parking lots, and open space as barriers; eliminating connecting streets to inhibit travel in and out; and housing people in public housing projects that were cut off from the flow of the city. In this photograph of the Hill District (fig. 3.4), the clear plastic, cut in the shape of the proposed changes, is overlaid on the existing habitat of the Hill District, the tight streets that held no social value for George Evans but were home to Sala Udin. One goal of the construction of wide roads and the civic arena was the creation of a swath of uninhabited territory, a buffer zone, thus achieving a separation between downtown and the ghetto.

While the downtown leaders planned to take land, and thus decrease the size of the ghetto, the arrival of Southern refugees of the Second Great Migration was creating pressures in the opposite direction. We can well imagine the horror and frustration of those seeking to stabilize the fading center city as they watched, not the return of the rich, but the swelling of the numbers of the poor, and the accompanying reality that the squatting ghetto would need to grow. Focusing on the triangle of the ghetto itself, we must add to the penetration at its tip, an insistent swelling on every side.

Four major options were open to American cities at that point. The option that had the best long-term potential for the nation was open housing. That would have meant the end of the residential segregation and the opening of all neighborhoods for black residence.[23] There are very few places in the United States where this occurred.

The second possibility was that white people would leave for the suburbs, thus leaving behind new areas for black residency. This was a frequent solution, with two negative consequences. First, white people had to abandon their own urban homes and urban traditions. Second, white people controlled most of the wealth and most of the institutions of the city. They took their money and kept their power, creating an imbalance that shapes urban and suburban realities to this day.

The third option was for the city to maintain the ghetto boundaries, but accommodate newcomers by building large housing projects within the existing black area. Chicago is the most notable example of this strategy,[24] which was guaranteed to create areas with large populations of very poor people. This concentration of the impoverished was aggravated by the poor design and minimal equipment of the housing projects. In general, they lacked the features that made urban slums a place to get a toehold in the nation's economy. Thus, in the long run, housing projects could only make the poor poorer. As early as 1972, with the implosion of the Pruitt-Igoe projects in St. Louis,[25] city leaders began to disassemble these dysfunc-

Fig. 3.4. Renovations to the Lower Hill. Upper photograph: Photographer unknown. Aerial photograph of proposed renovations to the Lower Hill, 1956. Lower photograph: Photographer unknown. Aerial photograph of completed Civic Arena, 1961. COURTESY OF THE PENNSYLVANIA ROOM, CARNEGIE LIBRARY, PITTSBURGH.

Fig. 3.5. How urban renewal changed Webster Avenue. Upper photograph: Russell Lee. Webster Avenue, looking downtown from the Hill District before urban renewal. COURTESY OF THE PENNSYLVANIA ROOM, CARNEGIE LIBRARY OF PITTSBURGH. Lower photograph: Rich Brown. Webster Avenue, looking downtown from the Hill District, 2003. COURTESY OF THE ARTIST.

tional complexes, a process that accelerated when Congress passed the
HOPE VI initiative in 1992. HOPE VI, originally called the "Urban
Revitalization Demonstration," was a Department of Housing and
Urban Development (HUD) program designed to solve the problems
of badly designed and poorly run public housing projects, which
HUD had named "severely distressed housing." Of course, as with
urban renewal, HOPE VI's bulldozing of broad swaths of urban land
swept away the good with the bad, in the same way that clear-cutting
a forest does far more than harvest trees.

The fourth option was for the city fathers to continue the policies of containment that governed ghetto life. That proved to be a disastrous choice, because, as geographer John Adams has pointed out,
those do-nothing cities violated nature's "law of proportions." That
law states, "Any living organism thrives at only one scale . . . it will
collapse of its own weight if size is doubled, tripled or quadrupled and
proportions are held constant."[26] Adams's study of midwestern cities
found that, though black population was increasing rapidly, housing
was actually being lost. Thus, the ratio of people to housing was doubling and tripling, until people couldn't take it anymore, and civil insurrection broke out. Though somewhat less coherent than the Paris
Commune or the Montgomery bus boycott, those insurrections represented an equally distinct mass movement, this time against the spatial squeeze the community was under. In simple terms, people
burned a doorway into new living space.

The American ghetto revolts of the 1960s were tightly linked to
urban renewal, according to the report of the National Commission
on Civil Disorders, popularly known as the Kerner Commission.[27]
That report, which is a seminal work on segregation in the United
States as well as the classic investigation of the outbreak of civil disorder in the summer of 1967, noted that inadequate housing was the
number-three grievance among people the commission surveyed in
fifteen cities and four suburbs. The report noted that "In Detroit a
maximum of 758 low-income housing units have been assisted
through [federal] programs since 1956 . . . Yet, since 1960, approximately 8,000 low-income units have been demolished for urban
renewal.

"Similarly, in Newark, since 1959, a maximum of 3,760 low-income housing units have been assisted through the programs considered . . . During the same period, more than 12,000 families, mostly low-income, have been displaced by such public uses as urban renewal, public housing and highways.

"In New Haven, since 1952, a maximum of 951 low-income housing units have been assisted . . . Yet, since 1956, approximately 6,500 housing units, mostly low-income, have been demolished for highway construction and urban renewal."[28]

Though the renovations of Paris were often cited by planners who were remaking American cities, few people pondering ghetto uprisings were also thinking back to Baron Haussmann. Yet one can trace many parallels between the Haussmann era and the urban renewal era: government that stifled dissent (the empire in France, the McCarthy era in the United States); remarkable bureaucrats (Haussmann in France, Robert Moses and others in the United States); massive displacement of poor people (moving the poor to the newly annexed arrondissements in Paris, and moving the poor outside of the renewal area or to housing projects within the ghetto area in the United States); and popular revolts (the Paris Commune in France, civil insurrection in the United States).

In comparing urban renewal in these two countries, I find that the distributive property of urban renewal is rarely adequately addressed. One observer of dam building in India made a similar observation and reported, ". . . an officer representing the Madhya Pradesh Government . . . treated [resettlement] lightly. He said in a very casual way that many tribals who were asked to leave their forest homes were volunteering to go and settle down in cities like Bhopal. He appeared to believe that the project was a od [sic] send opportunity for those people to modernise themselves. I am mentioning this because it shows how happy an administrator could be if he can remain immune to the realities around him and does not have to know the feeling of the poor tribals who have to leave their homes."[29]

In India, as in the United States, the failure to appreciate the costs that upheaval places on the poor means that grossly inadequate plans are made for resettlement. Issues of community life, transition to new forms of work, emotional pain of separating from a beloved place: all of these considerations are given short shrift. The frustration of the displaced, then, comes as a shock to the planners who worked from the illusion that the changes were a godsend to the people in the way of progress.

At the same time, comparing France and the United States in their urban renewal efforts leads to another issue. Most people would agree that the French planners greatly improved their city, while the United States was not so fortunate. The French effort worked from the specific concept of the *percée*, with construction following immediately on the heels of demolition. The project included carefully orchestrated designs for buildings and sidewalks that created exciting urban boulevards.

The American planners, by contrast, cleared broad swaths of land for Corbusian parks; had little control over rebuilding, which was sometimes separated by decades from the demolition phase of a project; and placed even more unreasonable burdens on the poor and the people of color than did the French. Indeed, in looking at American urban renewal projects I am reminded more of wide-area bombing—the largely abandoned World War II tactic of bombing major parts of cities as we did in Würzburg, Germany, and Hiroshima, Japan[30]—than of elegant city design.

In searching for a deeper understanding of this complex and agonizing American process of urban renewal, I found it essential to speak to planners and historians. But, even more important, I needed to speak to uprooted people, and especially African Americans, as their experience has been largely overlooked in the historical record.

Chapter 4

. . . MEANS NEGRO REMOVAL

Roanoke is a beautiful American city, situated in the foothills of the Blue Ridge Mountains along the Roanoke River in southwest Virginia. It was first settled as a stop on the Great Wagon Road, a major colonial trail that followed an Iroquois route from Philadelphia, through Harpers Ferry, down through Virginia, and then west through the Cumberland Gap.[1] Roanoke was a "western" town until late in the 1800s. Its rough frontier style confronted grace and culture after the Norfolk and Western Railway established its headquarters there in 1888, and the railroad brought executives and their wives in from Philadelphia, Baltimore, and other eastern centers.

In 1906, the wealthy white women of the area, appalled by unsanitary and unseemly conditions, organized the Women's Civic Betterment Club, under the leadership of Mrs. Lucien H. Cocke, president, and Mrs. M. M. Caldwell, vice president.[2] Their efforts were remarkably farsighted. Among other projects, they sponsored Boston landscape architect John Nolen to develop a town plan for the growing city. Characterized by well-laid-out neighborhoods, and parks along the banks of the river, the plan echoed many of the themes

Frederick Law Olmsted and others were bringing to American city planning. The enlightenment of the white city mothers was not met by equal clarity on the part of the white city fathers: the 1907 plan, "Remodeling Roanoke," which has been recognized in the annals of city planning as a National Historic Planning Landmark, languished on the shelf. Instead, with all the gusto of the American frontier, the leaders of Roanoke focused on making money.

The emphasis on grace and harmony, though defeated at the level of the city, did lead to the creation of remarkable neighborhoods composed of well-designed houses closely spaced on tree-lined streets, within easy walking distance of shops and services. Though each home is uniquely designed, they share common features, such as wide front porches. The close placement of the homes creates a solid backdrop, framing the activity on the sidewalks and the streets. The streets themselves are wide enough for cars, but narrow enough to retain the connection between the houses on either side. An air of serenity hangs over the area. My first night in Roanoke, staying at Mary Bishop's house, I was lulled to sleep by the trills of birds and insects, the rustle of leaves and the closeness of the natural world, yet we were not two blocks from a corner store stocked with daily essentials and a friendly clerk. The New Urbanists, who in the 1990s have issued a challenge to re-create such neighborhoods in American cities, might have taken their inspiration from the remarkable historic neighborhoods of Roanoke. Even after a brief visit, I resonated with the local residents' pride in their city.

Mary Bishop and the Story of Urban Renewal

There are stories within stories, and at the heart of this book about urban renewal lies Mary Bishop's concern with the untold stories of vulnerable people. Her heart is gripped by such stories, and her work won't stop until they are told. She stumbled onto the urban renewal story accidentally. "I had been at the newspaper [*Roanoke Times*] and we would take turns pulling the weekend shift. I was working one Saturday and they told me there was going to be a neighborhood reunion, which is often just a little feature story.[3] There are so many of those. And so I looked into it, and it was the neighborhood Northeast. I knew that there was some Northeast Roanoke still, but I didn't know who these folk were, so I called them, and they told me that their neighborhood didn't exist anymore.

"I then went to see a few people, especially Charles Meadows, who is in the story 'Street by Street,' and he drove me around among all of these industrial buildings, and the post office, and the gas company, and by the McDonald's and the Days Inn. And I had only been in Roanoke two or three years at that point, and he began to re-create for me what was once there, which was totally new to me. I had no idea. And, of course, the interstate coming through. And I remember him driving up by the Roanoke Gas Company, and pointing to a picnic bench out there, and he said, 'That's where my house was.' Of course, the streets had all changed and it was hard for me to imagine.

"But anyway, because of that event, and preparing for that reunion, I saw that something really big was going on. And when I went to the reunion, people said, 'You need to look into this. This is a big story here. Something that nobody remembers very well, and it has never been written about.'"

Getting into the story took a long time. Winning the trust of people was difficult, both because the newspaper had been an apologist for urban renewal and because Mary Bishop was white. Understanding the process was hard, and locating the lost terrain required extraordinary efforts of imagination, even for people who had lived there. But Mary persevered over three years and a hundred interviews. By the end, she had traced the fate of every house in the area, and was able to create an extraordinary map, detailing what had happened to the homes, businesses, and institutions of black Roanoke. "Street by Street, Block by Block" was quite a literal description of what she had accomplished in depicting the process at the level of every building in the affected areas.[4]

Mary Bishop's assessment of the effects of urban renewal offers an extraordinary window into the impact on the people displaced. "We still don't see urban renewal as a destructive force, because it hadn't been written, it had never been said really, except among a few academics a few years ago; people didn't see what had hit them. They didn't see the deep trauma, the assault almost. I am sure that people died as a result of this. I am sure they died way prematurely." In this chapter, I use Mary Bishop's work, supplemented by my own visits and interviews, to tell the overlooked story of urban renewal in Roanoke, which, as far as I can tell, is the story of urban renewal all across the nation.[5]

Mary Bishop's story is subtitled "How urban renewal uprooted black Roanoke." It spans four decades, beginning with the first urban renewal project in 1955, which was called the Commonwealth project, involving eighty-three acres located in a section of the city known as Northeast. Northeast was situated just north of the central business district, and housed a poor but striving portion of the black community. The Commonwealth project was followed in 1964 by the Kimball project, which destroyed the remaining portion of Northeast. In 1968, a third urban renewal project was designated for Gainsboro, the neighboring African American community. Unlike Commonwealth and Kimball, which quickly bulldozed massive sections of the Northeast neighborhood, the Gainsboro project followed a more leprotic process, slowing eating away at the neighborhood until only a tattered shadow remained to remind people of the once-vibrant area. In 1995, when Mary Bishop published her landmark study, to all intents and purposes, the African American community of Roanoke had been dispossessed from its original place of settlement.

The study went block by block, street by street. In the accompanying map, reproduced here, you can see what happened to each and every one of the buildings that dotted the area.[6]

Commonwealth, 1955

As in all urban renewal projects, the Commonwealth area was first declared "blighted" so that the homes and businesses could be leveled for new uses—even the area's hills were bulldozed.

The white power structure supported the process. "It had to be done," former councilwoman Mary Pickett told Mary Bishop, ". . . for the good of the city, for the good of the future. Their kids were growing up in slum conditions . . . That was prime growth land. Some people had to suffer."[7]

Fred Mangus, for decades a member of the city housing authority's board, remembered, "You used to go for a ride on Sunday, and it was pitiful, children sitting out on the curb, dirty. It was a slum area and it couldn't go any way but up."[8]

The African American community, which was largely excluded from the political process, had no opportunity to present its side of the story. Survivors, through their stories and photographs, contended that the city's gross characterization of the area belied its heterogeneity and overlooked its high level of functioning.

Arleen Ollie was nine when her family was forced out of Northeast in 1956. She is a star of "Street by Street," as a happy picture of her as a young girl beside her bicycle adorns the first page of the report. When I first met her, she explained that that picture had to have been taken at 4 P.M. because she had no socks on, and she was none too clean. Her father was fanatical that she be tidy, so her mother would wash her socks and tidy her up just before he came home. The comments about clean socks resonate with the efforts—hers included—to make clear that Northeast wasn't a dirty, nasty neighborhood. Certainly her thoughts remind us of Fred Mangus's justification for bulldozing the area: there were dirty children on the sidewalks.

Arleen Ollie insisted to my husband, Bob, and me, "I did not know anyone, even as an adult, that I would consider living in a shack . . . [one house] could use repairs, but it was not a shack. Everybody had flowers, I mean, the smells—I can still remember the smells of roses. And there was an open field next to the house, I don't even know if my parents owned that property or not, but we played over there. And it had blackberries and honeysuckle, and just a child's haven. We played war games, cowboys and Indians, Tarzan, swinging from the trees, just had a really good time."

"Knitted" was the word one observer used to describe the strength of the community,[9] and Arleen Ollie had a profound awareness of that strength. She described, ". . . a good, friendly, loving atmosphere in my neighborhood, because I had restriction. I could go to the corner on one end, to the streetlight on this end, to the backyard, and to the alley that separated the two streets. I could go *to* the alley. So I was really confined. But those people were really loving and

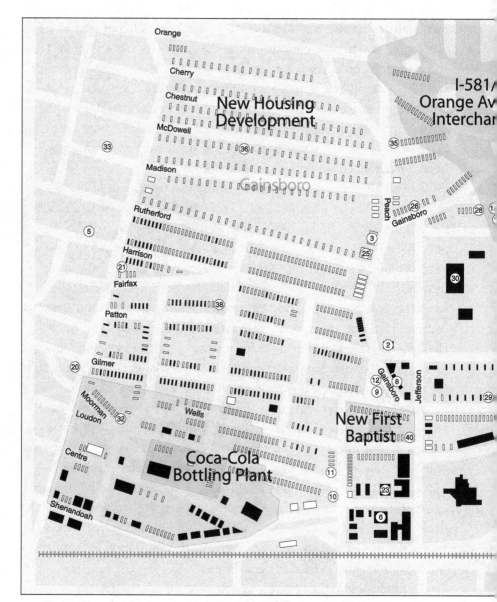

Fig. 4.1. Urban renewal in Roanoke. Adapted by Richard V. Miller from the original map created by Rob Lunsford, and published in Mary Bishop, "Street by Street, Block by Block," 1995. COURTESY OF THE *ROANOKE TIMES*.

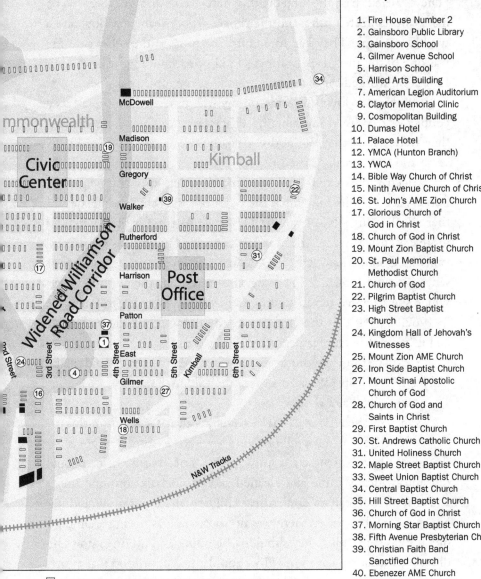

☐ Houses and other buildings destroyed by urban renewal.
■ Houses and other buildings standing in 1995.

Directory of 1950 Landmarks

1. Fire House Number 2
2. Gainsboro Public Library
3. Gainsboro School
4. Gilmer Avenue School
5. Harrison School
6. Allied Arts Building
7. American Legion Auditorium
8. Claytor Memorial Clinic
9. Cosmopolitan Building
10. Dumas Hotel
11. Palace Hotel
12. YMCA (Hunton Branch)
13. YWCA
14. Bible Way Church of Christ
15. Ninth Avenue Church of Christ
16. St. John's AME Zion Church
17. Glorious Church of God in Christ
18. Church of God in Christ
19. Mount Zion Baptist Church
20. St. Paul Memorial Methodist Church
21. Church of God
22. Pilgrim Baptist Church
23. High Street Baptist Church
24. Kingdom Hall of Jehovah's Witnesses
25. Mount Zion AME Church
26. Iron Side Baptist Church
27. Mount Sinai Apostolic Church of God
28. Church of God and Saints in Christ
29. First Baptist Church
30. St. Andrews Catholic Church
31. United Holiness Church
32. Maple Street Baptist Church
33. Sweet Union Baptist Church
34. Central Baptist Church
35. Hill Street Baptist Church
36. Church of God in Christ
37. Morning Star Baptist Church
38. Fifth Avenue Presbyterian Church
39. Christian Faith Band Sanctified Church
40. Ebenezer AME Church

caring and generous, and just good, decent, hardworking people. [They] varied; past the streetlight, where I couldn't go, there was a man who collected junk, and then there was a wealthy widow and a wealthier couple. They had hired him, the man on the other side. He was one of the first black postmen, and I don't know what he did but I think he worked for the railroad, and lived a couple of houses down. But two houses down from me on my side of the street, there was a couple who were really fantastic characters . . . They were drunks, they were winos, they did nothing. So, the whole street was really diverse and it was really close."

Arleen Ollie's experience after the destruction of the neighborhood was quite difficult. Just at the point of losing their home, her father also lost his job as a janitor. Desperate to pay for their new, and more expensive, home, Arleen's parents decided to work as live-in servants in Connecticut. Arleen Ollie and her brother, then four, were sent to stay with relatives. Thus began a long nomadic period, during which she attended ten schools in seven years. Returning to Roanoke in 1962, she felt that the closeness of the community had been lost, and it had not been regained when I met her.

"I don't think anything could happen here that would make [African Americans] work together," she told us.

I asked, "Is that a change?"

"Oh *yes!*" she replied. "I mean, think about it. Going from this really supportive, caring neighborhood—where if someone got sick, they didn't have to send out a message that 'I need some help'; people just automatically came and cleaned and cooked and brought meals and visited, took care of each other's children; there was no such thing as paying any babysitter, there was no such thing as having a child go out and do something they shouldn't be doing and no one knows he did it—to what we have now. How could a neighborhood make such a difference? The people I have lived in the same apartment house with for [the past] five years, I know who the people are mainly because I have seen them, and I have talked to everybody on that block except for one woman. But nobody talks to each other."

One of the serious problems faced by families affected by the earliest urban renewal projects was that of compensation. M. Caldwell

Butler, grandson of one of the founders of the Women's Civic Better-ment Club, who was then a young lawyer starting in practice, repre-sented some of the families who were fighting for fair payments for their homes. Caldwell Butler got to know African Americans and their community at a time when few white people did so.

He told me, "I guess the thing that impressed me more than any-thing else was that these people were comfortable, happy in their houses. They were old houses, had been there for years. They were well situated, in that most of the people worked at the shops within walking distance, almost across the street. At that time a lot of the N&W Railway Shops were over there. So, it was convenient for them. They had lived there all their lives and raised their children.

"They were hardworking people, I think without exception at the time. They were all good citizens. But the thing that I reflect on, I was impressed with their character. I mean they were really honest, hardworking people, and they had a lot of dignity and class. And we worked on a very professional basis. They raised their families well and that sort of thing.

"I was struck by the unfairness of the whole thing, because of the substandard question. But those people, if they had had the same clout to get together and organize a project of this nature in cooperation with the housing authority, they would have taken better care of themselves if they wanted to sell, and that is just something that you couldn't do. But the housing authority did make good use of the property they took, from an economic standpoint. But from a social standpoint, it was horrible. These people were rounded up and spread all over town."

Lawsuits similar to that filed by Caldwell Butler were fought all over the country during that period. As a result, the compensation peo-ple received for their houses slowly increased. Moving expenses were factored in, and consideration was given to the costs faced by renters. Even though the basis for compensation was gradually extended, the payments continued to be linked to individual property rights. Collec-tive assets—the social capital created by a long-standing community—were not considered in the assessment of property values.

Caldwell Butler, horrified as he was by past practice, thought that market mechanisms offered a much better solution for change. "When you were coming here," he told me, "you saw that Lowes [building supply store] over there. Prior to its very recent construction it was a black community with nice housing on the fringes of Roanoke, going back more than a hundred years. When they came along to get that, they bought the land. [The homeowners] got fair prices and were able to move out gracefully, but probably all of them had to move. And, across the street as you come in here on your left, just before you get to the Wal-Mart, there is another black community that is larger and known as Southern Hills. And that was a less affluent neighborhood, but it is a stable people, and they are gradually being bought out by the real estate developers at market prices. The point I am trying to make is that urban renewal is a far more equitable process if the market controls the transaction instead of the government getting involved in it. So, I just wanted to get that off my chest."

It is important to note, before continuing the story, that Caldwell Butler was not unique among white people in Roanoke. James Robertson, a white union leader, shared with me his own experience with urban renewal. He was asked by city leaders to help convince people to move. His work in the union gave him credibility with other working people. But as he observed what the process of urban renewal was doing to the community, he became horrified by it. He withdrew from the process and made his story public, one courageous effort to stem the tide of destruction.[10]

Getting back to the Commonwealth story, I learned that people were told the project was intended to help them—that improvements would be made to the neighborhood from which they would benefit. This turned out to be completely untrue. The land cleared in that area was used for the highway, the civic center, and businesses. No housing of any kind was built on the land that was taken.

Willis Anderson, known to one and all as "Wick," was part of city government during the Commonwealth project. He spent an afternoon telling me about that period, as we sat on a porch by a noisy street on Washington and Lee University's otherwise quite peaceful campus. "Commonwealth," he explained, "was originally designed to be—the original intent was to tear down all the substandard housing and build new housing there for low- and moderate-income people. But a few things happened along the way to change that. First of all, the projection for Interstate 581—which as you know goes right through the heart of the city—581 from Orange Avenue to the river goes through what was the Commonwealth project, and before that of course was a residential area. It was mostly, you know, a low-income residential area. And so, then later it was—because the land was clear and available, that is where the Roanoke Civic Center was built. You know—the coliseum and the auditorium. So you have Interstate 581, the civic center, those two buildings, and the parking area, and that pretty well consumed the land that was part of the Commonwealth project.

"And then across Williamson Road where Magic City Ford is located, and the hotel and so forth, was the so-called Kimball project. And it was consistent with what urban renewal was about at the time. The idea was to clear substandard housing, slums they were usually called at the time, and then relocate the families to better housing. Some of the relocation was to be accomplished through public housing, and that is when the Redevelopment Authority started building the public housing developments."

It was Wick Anderson's opinion that most of the protest about urban renewal came from the landlords who were the owners of the "slum" properties. Mary Bishop thought otherwise. "There is a picture in 'Street by Street' of a whole black audience, listening to the housing authority director explain the Kimball project. This was after Commonwealth. And their faces are, their faces just tell such a story. Their faces kind of say, 'Oh no, not again. The Commonwealth was gone. They promised something that was not delivered, and he's saying it is not going to happen again but how can you know? What is going to happen to us now?' There were just furrowed lines in people's brows. They just looked stricken" (fig. 4.6).

Kimball, 1964

The Kimball project, which started in 1964, was the next disruption for the African American community. Charles Meadows, who lived in Northeast for fifty of his ninety years, had much to say on the topic of community. "In Northeast, there was no poverty because every-body helped one another. When we could afford two pounds of beans, our wives would cook them up and everybody would have a bowl. If our next-door neighbor didn't have a job, we would help them out. We were independently self-supporting as a neighborhood. We enjoyed it, because we knew we had someone to rely on. The sec-tion was so unified at one time, you could start at the Norfolk and Western station and call the names of everybody on every street. We didn't need telephones. You'd just walk out and call somebody's name, or spread the word. 'Hello, Brother John, hello, Sister So-and-So,' hol-lering on both sides of the street."[11]

Mr. Meadows was one of the people I talked with on my first visit to Roanoke. He was an austere man, made bitter by what had hap-pened. He had had a wonderful house in Northeast and not only had he paid off the mortgage, but he had also invested in improvements. He had the house "to where he really liked it" when the city took it away. He was compensated for only a fraction of the worth of the house, and he had to take out a new mortgage when he moved to an-other section of Roanoke.

"I don't own this house," he said, gesturing at the solid and spa-cious room we sat in. "I'm just leasing it until the government comes to take it away." Part of his enduring sorrow was the loss of the tight community—the stroll of "howdys"—that he had found so support-ive and pleasant. The neighborhood was knitted together by having an active street life. "We walked everywhere in Northeast. We walked to the market, downtown to the market. We walked to church, we walked—and every corner almost in the section had a little store on the end of it. So you met your neighbors, you could go there and you could talk until your meat burn up at home if you wanted to." This image made us all laugh. "You could stand out and talk," he contin-ued, "so we just had better relations. We knew about 'em; if anybody was sick, you knew about it; anybody died, we knew about it; any-body went to jail, we knew about it; if anybody got into trouble, or if there was a secret, we knew about it." More laughter. "There was no secret there, everybody knew everybody's business. But we still had better relations."

He pointed to two factors that changed that way of life. One was the loss of old friendships. After being dispersed, people from the old neighborhood got together only at funerals. The second, and perhaps more subtle, change was an alteration in the street activity, related both to a slight increase in the distance between houses, and a marked increase in the use of cars, instead of feet, for transportation. No longer were people likely to walk down the street saying "Howdy" to the right and to the left.

Concretely, Mr. Meadows pointed out, "See that apartment across the street there. I think in the last year, about five different families have lived there. And you know, what few people that own their own homes and are in them, I don't know whether they stay in the house, or whether they work. Their houses look like they closed up. Every once in a while you see somebody pulling up in a car, or they might get in a car and leave, but you just don't see them."

Miss Dolly, Mr. Meadows's friend, added that, in addition to not knowing people, there was no longer a sense of safety. "Northeast, you didn't have to lock your doors, just shut your door and go in the house, go to bed, and go to sleep and leave the front door standing open, just the screen door shut. But here, well, you are not even safe in there with your doors locked."

There was deep disappointment in all that Mr. Meadows had to say, comparing what he had lost and what he had gotten in exchange. Most bitter was his disappointment in the system. The promises that the outcome of the Kimball project would be different from that of the Commonwealth project turned out to be hollow. The land was used for various enterprises, including a new post office. No housing was rebuilt in the area for former residents to return to their neighborhood.

Gainsboro, 1968

The total demolition of Northeast and Kimball was followed by the more piecemeal destruction of the Gainsboro neighborhood, which was called Northwest at the time. Gainsboro had such landmarks as Burrell Memorial Hospital, one of the best-known black hospitals in the South; Burrell Pharmacy, one of the first black pharmacies in southwest Virginia; the Claytor Mansion, a twenty-two-room home that was one of Virginia's largest black homes; the Gainsboro library, organized in 1921 and one of the South's earliest black libraries; First Baptist Church, organized in 1867 and established in its brick building on North Jefferson Street in 1900; and Fifth Avenue Presbyterian's first 1898 church at 303 Patton Avenue, NW.[12]

The great center of Gainsboro was Henry Street and the surrounding area, called "the Yard." A person who spoke to Mary Bishop, but not for attribution, told her, "Henry Street has been glamorized. Henry Street was a street of hustlers. A lot of those places were fronts for gambling, bootlegging." He went on to list the crimes and violence that inhabited the street. "Just realize one thing: life was nice, but life was hard."

It was on Henry Street that Richard Chubb established his counseling business and remembered the bright lights that used to shine there. "Henry Street was a great street," according to Mr. Chubb. "Stores, clubs, *neon*."

On my second trip to Roanoke, I visited the office of the housing authority. Carefully boxed up and stored in their facility was an old neon sign that said DRUGS. It had been saved from an old pharmacy, destroyed as part of urban renewal, and it was waiting patiently for its next life.

I asked Zenobia Ferguson, who moved out in 1976, if she could tell me a little bit about life in the old neighborhood. "Four-oh-two Chestnut Avenue, Northwest. It was just a close-knit neighborhood. The neighbors were, okay, I'll give you an example. My daughter, and she is really my stepdaughter. My husband had her before we got married. I have a son and he has a daughter. But when she went to college she said that somebody took her bag with all of the clothing that she could wear at that time. And she called back home crying. My neighbors across the street started buying clothes for this girl, and gave them to me so I could take them down there to her. That is the kind of neighborhood I lived in. It was just, 'What can we do?' You know? And she wanted to come home, you know. She didn't want to stay at college, but I was determined that she was going to stay there."

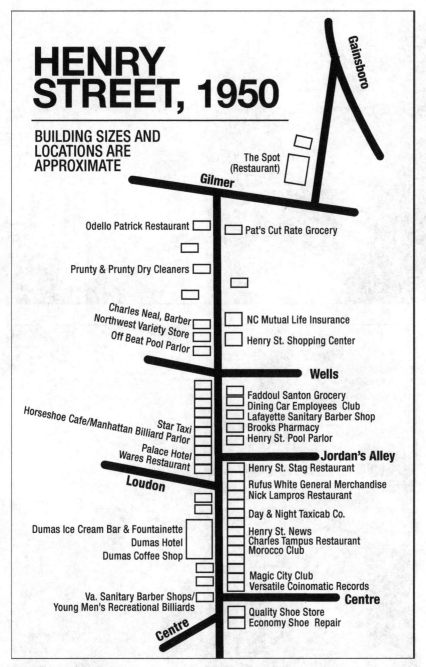

HENRY STREET, 1950

BUILDING SIZES AND LOCATIONS ARE APPROXIMATE

Gainsboro

The Spot (Restaurant)

Gilmer

Odello Patrick Restaurant

Pat's Cut Rate Grocery

Prunty & Prunty Dry Cleaners

Charles Neal, Barber
Northwest Variety Store
Off Beat Pool Parlor

NC Mutual Life Insurance

Henry St. Shopping Center

Wells

Faddoul Santon Grocery
Dining Car Employees Club
Lafayette Sanitary Barber Shop
Brooks Pharmacy
Henry St. Pool Parlor

Horseshoe Cafe/Manhattan Billiard Parlor
Star Taxi

Palace Hotel
Wares Restaurant

Jordan's Alley

Henry St. Stag Restaurant

Rufus White General Merchandise
Nick Lampros Restaurant

Loudon

Day & Night Taxicab Co.

Dumas Ice Cream Bar & Fountainette
Dumas Hotel
Dumas Coffee Shop

Henry St. News
Charles Tampus Restaurant
Morocco Club

Magic City Club
Versatile Coinomatic Records

Va. Sanitary Barber Shops/
Young Men's Recreational Billiards

Centre

Quality Shoe Store
Economy Shoe Repair

Centre

Fig. 4.2. The businesses on Henry Street. Adapted by Rich Brown from the original map created by Rob Lunsford, and published in Mary Bishop, "On Henry Street, Renewed Interest." COURTESY OF THE *ROANOKE TIMES.*

Kimball Worried as Renewal Project Nears

By BEN REAGLE
Times Staff Writer

About 400 residents of the Kimball section—wondering what is going to happen to them if urban renewal comes to Northeast Roanoke—packed a meeting room and the hall at Gilmer School Wednesday night.

It was an initial meeting of the residents with representatives of the Roanoke Redevelopment and Housing Authority and almost all of the questioners asked: What if I don't get enough money for my house to buy another house?

R. R. Henley, the executive director of the redevelopment authority, told them the authority has learned a lot since the days of the controversial Commonwealth Redevelopment Project.

"From the experience of that, we knew a whole lot more than we did before," Henley said. "We've gone a long way with this program.

"We do not intend to shove people out in the street," Henley said.

Henley said federal laws on aiding relocation of families in urban renewal projects have been liberalized since Commonwealth days and that they are

money is allowed in such cases and that this amount may be increased.

"I'd be out in the cold, wouldn't I?" the man said.

A woman wanted to know about the public housing project into which many of the relocated residents would move. She wanted to know if "it would be like Lincoln Terrace"—one residents already built—"with stone floors."

"It will be entirely different," Henley said. He said there would be plastered walls, "innovations in design," covered floors and the buildings would be multi-colored.

A federal grant of $1.7 million for construction of the Hurt Park housing project was announced Wednesday by U.S. Sen. A. Willis Robertson. The Hurt Project would be primarily for residents relocated as part of the Kimball redevelopment.

Some questioners wanted to know if they couldn't sell their property to commercial or industrial users now and get a better price.

Henley said the idea of urban renewal is to offer large tracts of land for such buyers. He said there is "no relationship whatsoever" to the purchase price for residential lots.

Henley (left) Answered Questions at Meeting Attended by Kimball Residents

Fig. 4.3. Photographer unknown. Parade on Gainsboro/Peach Road, circa 1939. COURTESY OF BOBBY SMITH.

Fig. 4.4. Photographer unknown. "Colored Division" of the Norfolk and Western Railway Veterans Association at its Convention at the Lincoln Theater (later the Morocco Club) on Henry Street in the late 1930s. COURTESY OF THE HISTORY MUSEUM AND HISTORICAL SOCIETY OF WESTERN VIRGINIA.

Fig. 4.5. Photographer unknown. Church supper at Greater Mount Zion Baptist Church (#19 in fig. 4.1). COURTESY OF JUDITH MUSE.

Fig. 4.6. Photographer unknown. Worried faces in the news, March 3, 1966. COURTESY OF THE ROANOKE TIMES.

Zenobia Ferguson's daughter carried the hope of her family with her. As with many young people in a similar position, the difference between success and failure was the presence of caring adults. Joycelyn Elders, who served as surgeon general of the United States, related a similar story.[13] Dr. Elders arrived at Philander Smith College penniless and was told that there was no record that she had been awarded a scholarship. Wandering around in a daze, she happened to bump into Reverend M. Lafayette Harris, the ever-watchful president of the college. He asked what was the matter, and on learning of the crisis, immediately straightened matters out. A small intervention, but one that helped shape the history of the United States.

Zenobia Ferguson went on to tell me, "When Burrell Hospital was built, we were so proud. And then the Addison School was built. All those things made us so proud. We felt like we owned something. But then when the community was taken away, and we had to move away from it, it was just sad. It took that feeling of pride away from us." She was the only person in the six cities I have studied who told me that she had found a new community that resembled what she had had. Yet the loss rankled.

Urban renewal ate away at Gainsboro. A few areas were cleared for new uses, but most of the community went into a slow decline due to the impact of the "urban renewal area" designation. Planner Earl Reynolds, Jr., who had grown up in the neighborhood, told Mary Bishop that in applying that label, the government altered the value of the land. Banks stopped lending money, and people stopped investing in repairs and renovations to their homes. "It was just as effective as what we think of as redlining today."[14]

People were afraid to invest because they knew they would not get their money back when the government took their homes. One elderly man, Daniel Jones, complained at a city meeting, "This winter, I'm not aiming to buy that much coal. I ain't spending four or five hundred dollars putting in another furnace in that old house. I want to know what you going to do and when you going to come out and inspect and tell us when we got to move, and that you going to build a house for us. I want to know, because five or six years from now, I don't expect to be living. I'm just actually tired. Lord, I'm not complaining, but I'm just tired. I got an old termite-eat-up home. Take my home. I thought that was the idea."[15]

In areas of disinvestment, contagious housing destruction ensues. The process spreads through an area, with the destruction of a single home increasing the likelihood that those around it will also be destroyed. Fire is the principal mechanism for the destruction of homes in an area of contagious housing destruction. The wonderful Claytor Mansion was the most spectacular, but certainly not the only, victim it claimed over the years.[16] As fire burned out the area, the Claytor family's clinic became one of the only buildings left standing. Finally, it was impossible to use the clinic as a medical office, and soon thereafter, it, too, burned.

Just before my first visit to Roanoke, old First Baptist was lost to fire. On my first visit to Henry Street, the church's charred steeple still led the eye upward, but the sky was claimed by the shiny First Union tower just beyond.

Under the right circumstances, contagious housing destruction can destroy miles of urban habitat. It is easily stopped by effective fire service, garbage pickup, and building code enforcement, but, sadly, civic redlining—that is, the withdrawal of key municipal services—is a part of the redlining process.

As the infrastructure of homes and businesses was destroyed, the community fell apart. The remaining businesses failed, elderly people could no longer walk to the store, and institutions had no one left to serve. Zenobia Ferguson remembered, "It was left barren." The strain on people, especially the elderly, was enormous. "There were some people who got really ill," Mrs. Ferguson related. "They were going to meetings and the next thing, we were going to their funeral. I knew what the people had been through, people who worked from sunup to sundown, and maybe it didn't look like something to other people, but it was their life's blood."[17]

Despite the efforts of area residents, the repeated promises of city authorities, and the expenditure of a great deal of money, Gainsboro was devitalized, not revitalized, by urban renewal. In 1950, there were nine hundred homes, a dozen churches, and 165 small businesses in Gainsboro. In 1995, Mary Bishop concluded her landmark report by

Fig. 4.7. Mindy Fullilove. First Baptist Church, after the fire in 1995.

saying, "Now, Gainsboro is a neighborhood of 190 old homes—many of them vacant—on a few streets and 79 small ranch-style homes and duplexes on redeveloped lots. There is one small office building, several industries, and acres of vacant, weedy lots, many that the housing authority says it can't give away."[18]

Just as the Commonwealth and Kimball projects had failed to deliver on promises on new housing, the Gainsboro project had not delivered on the bright future that had initially been painted. The denuding of the neighborhood left a vast, empty area that was ripe for sale to the highest bidder for the most lucrative uses. All things considered, these were unlikely to include providing housing for poor African American people. Thus, the complete loss of Gainsboro as an African American center seemed to hang over the area as a fait accompli.

A Drive Around Roanoke

On my second visit to Roanoke, in 2001, I stayed at a business travelers' hotel in a new mall on the outskirts of town near the airport. By contrast to the peaceful repose I'd experienced at Mary Bishop's home, the hotel seemed isolated and lonely, situated as it was in a sea of parking lots alongside I-581. As the only way to get around was by car, I rented one and made my way from interview to interview, with frequent stops in the downtown City Market for excellent coffee and out to Colonial Avenue to check email at Kinko's. Zipping up and down the streets and highways, I slowly got a sense of the city.

The City Market is a redevelopment of the historic center, its large brick buildings and splendid square creating a wonderful zone for eating and visiting. Reginald Shareef, a professor of political science at Radford University, described it as a great place to eat with the best jazz in town—the safest downtown in Virginia. I might add the area included a fine bookstore.

The strength and vitality of this area represent the side of the urban renewal picture that gave Wick Anderson so much pride. Part of downtown was made possible by what he described as the "Downtown East" urban renewal project, which he rated an unqualified success. That project took place in an area that was on the fringe of downtown and provided land that was used for what he considered to be significant development—including the Norfolk Southern Office Building, SunTrust Plaza, Trigon Blue Cross Blue Shield, and part of the land for the First Union Tower. "Now all of these," he remarked, "are very significant and important additions to the downtown business core. I am certain that most, if not all, of these buildings would have been built somewhere in the Roanoke Valley, but they would not have been built in the downtown business district without urban renewal."

The land for that project, a good deal of it vacant, he explained, was the site of commercial buildings, some of which were unoccupied. Because there was no disruption of a community, the harm of the project was minimal and the benefits maximal. The increasing densification of the downtown was being promoted by other projects in which Wick Anderson was engaged, at that point because of his role as the chairman of the housing authority. He described three projects, all close to the downtown area: one involving the renovation of a public housing complex, the second a conversion of an old office building to downtown, market-rate apartments, and third, the development of a biomedical park on "underused" commercial land. The emphasis in those projects was investment, all designed to strengthen and extend the functions of the central city area. They had in common that they avoided condemning the property of poor people in order to improve the viability of the city.

Gainsboro lies due north of the City Market, just across a footbridge that connects downtown to Hotel Roanoke. Though it hasn't happened yet, the redevelopment of the Henry Street area will happen soon and it will be critically important to the city, for many reasons. As argued by Reginald Shareef, it will determine the extent of African American social, economic, and political presence in downtown Roanoke. It will also be another point of choice between good and bad design. Good design would extend and strengthen downtown in a manner that could accelerate economic progress in the city by a huge margin.

Taking Williamson Road from the City Market, one tumbles out of the city landscape and into strip malls. This is the former Northeast, and it was in this area that Richard Chubb pointed bitterly to the sparse reuse of land, and said over and over again, "There used to be houses here, now there are only buildings." His phrase sums up a major critique of American urban renewal: that it stripped the downtown of residences and replaced people-friendly blocks and structures with megablocks and megabuildings surrounded by parking lots. In one area, overlapping with the Kimball project, he pointed out to us a post office, a Ford dealership, and a few other structures where a vibrant community once stood.

There is a massive visual and kinesthetic clash between the tight, vertical structure of downtown and the strip mall to the northeast of it. A few blocks farther, and the on-ramps to the highway appear. We are at the point where I-581 bisects Route 460, as unfortunate a use of the middle of a city as I have ever seen.

The area near downtown that was not given over to urban renewal is divided between run-down houses in the pathway of contagious housing destruction and brick housing projects that radiate despair. Mary Bishop worked with S. D. Harrington to produce a second special report, "The Invisible Inner City," which examines the plight of these neglected neighborhoods in minute detail.[19] They ring the urban renewal area, and their decline represents the playing out of contagious housing destruction, a predictable sequel to the clear-cutting of neighborhoods. The report emphasized the problems of abandonment and disinvestment that were causing the rapid decline in the housing stock. Fire had consumed many of the decrepit buildings, and the population of these troubled areas had fallen.

The area of the invisible inner city overlaps with the inner section of African American settlement, the second ghetto that had been pushed to the northwest from its origins in the center of town. By 2003, Roanoke was noted to be one of the most segregated cities in America, and many of the African Americans in Roanoke lived in the redlined zone Bishop and Harrington were describing.[20]

Actually one kind of investment is being made in the area: an investment in services for the needy. People who come to live here are likely to be poor and disabled. For them the area is affordable and convenient—located near public transportation and service providers of all kinds. In fact the area is so attractive to the poor that it draws people from a very wide radius who have nothing comparable in their own hometowns. This leaves Roanoke footing the bill for an inordinate number of troubled people. It also leaves the city facing an ongoing destructive process that will continue to undermine the stability of Roanoke's housing stock, spreading in concentric circles from the original point of damage, the Commonwealth project of 1955.

It only takes a few minutes to drive through the sad "invisible inner city" and to get to a neighborhood that represents "better"

Roanoke. Once there, however, the special grace of the city extends
itself. A quiet kind of enchantment rewards the driver, each corner assembled with care, each street put together with consideration for individuality.

This, however, is all too short. At the edge of the city, malls and
sprawl take over, replacing authentic charm with bright plastic, designed to last no longer than the first mortgage. It is clear that massive
investment is taking place in that zone, supporting the same cookie-
cutter developments that are going up near my home in New Jersey
as well as in every other American community I've had the opportunity to visit. I am no longer in a special place, I am *where*? How do we
name this ubiquitous entity we have installed everywhere in our
country so that nowhere is away from home? At the end of such a circuit I am back in my hotel, dismal not because of age or dirt, but from
disconnection with the beat of the city.

Roanoke, in 2001, resembled most other American cities, and was
nearly identical to those that carried out urban renewal projects.
Highways zipped through the center of town, cutting the whole in
subunits. The core, outside of the vibrant historic district, was rather
vacant, and surrounding that core was a ring of older, neglected
neighborhoods that were slowly dying. Better Roanoke retained its
intimacy and grace, but new Roanoke, which was springing up now
at the edge of the city, sprawled into the new universe made for cars.
The disconnections among the parts, the shocking transitions, and the
clear intention of abandonment marked it not as a unified city, but as
a process of leapfrogging investments.

Urban renewal in Roanoke hung on the thesis that the African
American ghettos were grossly inferior to the beautiful neighborhoods. Midcentury civic improvement, those in power argued, depended on clearing out the slums and replacing them with new
structures that would deepen the city's claim to civic beauty. What
those in favor of urban renewal could quickly begin to claim was that
tax revenues had multiplied as a result of putting the land to new uses.
What no one could claim, driving around the rebuilt areas, is that they
enhance or even meld with the historic charms of a sweet city. In fact,
the ghetto areas were thoroughly in the mode of gracious Roanoke,

their replacements in the style of the strip mall. Roanoke's array of disassembled neighborhoods presents the quintessential issue in American city making.

Assessing Urban Renewal

Wick Anderson, who was part of the power structure that carried out the urban renewal project, had, perhaps, the most positive assessment. He argued that the people who were displaced got to move to better neighborhoods. He said, "I think that many of the people thought, 'Yeah, I am glad to move because nobody else would have bought this place. And while I wish I got more money for it, I'd rather take my money and go buy a better house, and get a small mortgage, or whatever.' There were people who were glad to have an opportunity to move because they felt they were living in an undesirable neighborhood and they wanted something better for their children."

Thus, Wick stressed individual economic advantage in assessing the project. In that same vein, he applauded urban renewal for providing downtown land for the civic center and other enterprises that otherwise would have located on the outskirts of the city or in the suburbs. I asked him to name seven of his favorite places in Roanoke. In response, he spoke warmly on the solidification of downtown. "Some of the specific things that I am proudest of, and enjoy the most, and I think visitors and residents do, too, of course, are Farmers Market and Center in the Square, because Center in the Square includes a regional theater, we have an art museum, we have a science museum, a history museum, a planetarium, all under one roof. And then of course, just outside is the Farmers Market and all the shops and so forth. And lots of special events down there that draw people into town. So I guess that is my favorite part of the city.

"I am also very proud of the Hotel Roanoke and Conference Center. Now, that closed for several years. It was reopened after a very strenuous effort, and even a public fund-raising campaign. This sounds ridiculous to some people, but I gave a thousand dollars, which to me is a pretty big gift, you know, to a hotel that I don't have any ownership in? But it is owned now by the city and Virginia Tech. It is operated by Doubletree." And he continued, naming with pride many pieces that had been assembled to make the downtown a vital, interesting center, not just for the city but for the region.

Mary Bishop had a different summation of the evidence. "Out of my work, I have this image of a person and their connection to home, a wider kind of a home, not just a house to live in, but their surroundings. It's like in the pictures from *Gulliver's Travels,* where you might have lines from the individual. In my image, you would draw a line to the sun, or the way the children's laughter bounces off the schoolhouse wall, and the way the water runs through the neighborhood, the rain, the way the snow lies, and all of those things, being able to look through your porch nook and see your neighbor sitting out on her front porch. All of those things are very comforting to us, and we have not recognized the comfort we get from probably thousands of factors that are involved in that. It is just too big for us to see it.

"People are still so angry about it, and so hurt. To this day, there is an attempt to try to rebuild part of Gainsboro, and there are people who live there now, or used to live there, who are very divided over this. And while there are other factors that help to explain that division, urban renewal is a big culprit in that. There is that lack of trust. . . .

"One, the city just doesn't look the way it would. I mean, if that had not happened, we would have big trees, we would have big old homes, and churches and schools and things over there. We would have a much more pleasant entry into the city than a hot, dry, dusty interstate. They could have done beautiful things with all those neighborhoods. But nobody saw that. They just saw a slum. And it is where black people live. 'Who cares? It is cheaper land. Let's get it. They are not going to offer much resistance. They have no power.' "[21]

This point is dramatically illustrated in before-and-after aerial photographs of the urban renewal area.

"And white Roanoke has lost, too, and I don't know if people realize that. People brought pictures together for us at the family center, and we started looking through their scrapbooks at the houses that are now gone. We could see it in our own newspaper files and stories,

Fig. 4.9. The hollowing-out of Roanoke. Upper image: aerial photograph of Roanoke, 1944. Courtesy of the Norfolk Southern Collection, Virginia Polytechnic Institute and State University. Lower image: Wayne Deel. Aerial photograph of Roanoke, 1995. COURTESY OF THE *ROANOKE TIMES*.

the pictures that we got. We could see that mix of houses. We could see solid, big old wonderful houses, and then you see, right down the street—because every social class was packed in together, they couldn't go anywhere else—you would see smaller or larger, less well maintained places. Well, that all could have been done very nicely. Some houses did need to be replaced, I am sure. But they didn't have to take down the whole thing."

Reginald Shareef, who has conducted studies of the economic effects of urban renewal on African Americans in Roanoke,[22] helped me see the way in which these two different perspectives informed each other. "What happened here in Roanoke is typical of what happened in urban renewal programs that began in the 1950s and sixties throughout the country. What cities and municipalities wanted to do was to develop the inner or the core city, or redevelop it. And most of the development, or the people who lived around the core of the cities, were poor African American people. So, the public policy was that we were going to come in, rehab your neighborhood, put sidewalks in, improve your housing; if you didn't have toilets, we are going to do the sewer line. And so, the promise to improve the quality of life of people who had been disenfranchised historically.

"But the reality of urban renewal was that cities wanted to improve their tax base. And that is my interest. I have always looked at the intersections between public policy and economics. And what happened in Roanoke was neighborhoods were torn down so that commercial developers could develop properties and sell it to private interests. And the city won because it increased the tax base, and the private developers won, because of course, this was very lucrative.

"The only people who lost were the people who were promised a better quality of life. So, in Roanoke [at the City Market] that downtown area now is one of the most vibrant economic downtown areas, and across the railroad tracks you will see all of this development going on, in what was originally supposed to be an improved community. You see a lot of economic development. You see a Coca-Cola plant, and all of these type of things.

"But you don't see a vibrant black community anymore. Those people have been removed. So it gets back to what Moynihan said, I mean urban renewal is basically black removal—what he called in 1966 Negro removal.

"And that is just a brief overview. The long-term implications here have been just a deepening, deepening distrust and mistrust between the black community and the city government. Because government and government officials really pitted neighbor against neighbor during the 1960s and seventies."

These divisions had not dissipated over time, he noted, but rather had seeped into all aspects of political life, derailing African American economic opportunity in Roanoke in 2001. "My argument for the past nearly ten years is, when Henry Street gets developed—because there is no doubt it is going to be developed—who are going to be the entrepreneurs? Who is going to own the businesses? Who is going to own the clubs? Who is going to own the franchise restaurants? And the legacy of urban renewal has been, in my estimation, that the black community has so little trust of city administrators, that for the past five years there has been this ongoing battle not over so much about who is going to own anything, or who are going to be the businesspeople over there, but in airing grievances about past injustices."

As an outsider visiting Roanoke on a small number of occasions, I found it indisputable that African American neighborhoods were destroyed, and nothing like their old vitality re-created in the city. I know, as a psychiatrist, that, at the level of the individual, the loss of neighbors who "automatically came" was devastating. At the level of the community, the loss of the collective capacity to solve problems in order to make progress became a permanently crippling one. Social scientists have established that social loss of that order makes people vulnerable. After a loss, a second blow will hurt more and do its damage more quickly than the first, setting in motion an accelerating downward spiral of collapse.[23] Thus, for the displaced citizens, urban renewal sapped resources and depleted strength in a manner that increased the vulnerability of the uprooted not simply for a few years, but for many decades to come. Perhaps most problematic, at the level of the city, the dismantling of some poor, disenfranchised neighborhoods for the "greater good" pitted one section of the city against the other, and unleashed divisions and hostilities that remain a heavy burden for the city to bear.

Arleen Ollie raised a series of questions she thought were, as yet, unanswered. "I don't think the adults ever talked about this to each other, because they were ashamed they couldn't protect their children. Maybe even that God let them down because they tore down all the churches. I just don't think they ever, ever, ever talked about it. In Mary's article someone made the anonymous statement, 'This is being romanticized. Northeast was just slums and I am glad it's torn down.' I don't believe that can really be many people's feelings, because if it were, then it wouldn't have had such a negative, isolating effect. Because, like I talked about, I couldn't get with the same friends. You know, I couldn't get up in the morning, after breakfast, and run down the street and play with these people. But the majority of them were within walking distance, but I guess the physical distance was more important than I had actually thought about.

"What I don't really understand is, what did the adults think? How did they feel? Because I know my mother used to talk to the woman who lived next door. My father, because he was quiet and didn't do a lot of talking, because he was always working, but I would imagine it would have affected the breadwinner of the family differently than their spouses. Did it cause a problem within their relationship, their marriages?

"I just feel like there is more to this. Because I really feel, generally speaking, blacks withhold their emotions, because even when I grew up, there were certain things you weren't supposed to tell. You know, certain things just stayed in the house. It didn't go outside the house. And then there were other things that could go outside the house but had to stay in the neighborhood. And then there were other, completely different facades that you had to have when you went around whites. So, there were all those different levels of intimacy. Well, not intimacy, but how did they connect or disconnect from being treated like they were bad children?"

These questions linger with me, waiting to be answered.

CHARLES MEADOWS

The following comments are taken from a 1995 conversation with Mr. Charles Meadows. My husband, Bob, and I had the honor of spending an hour at the lovely home of this senior member of the African American community of Roanoke. He was a great teacher, and spoke in a form of poetry, every phrase filled with wisdom and emotion. In order to convey the art of his speech, I have followed his phrasing in setting out this transcript of a portion of our conversation. He asked us why we had gathered, and I said that we wanted to know the connection between rising rates of disease and physical destruction of the black community. He joined me in wondering about this, as any Zen master might do.

Mr. Meadows:

Well it—all—winds down to a very small note.
It seemed to me—, through the years,
and I've been here a good little while,
that when the black community got together,
or they were segregated,
they had to stay in one corner of a city.
There were boundary lines everywhere.
And—for some reason or another they stayed more healthier.
They—were more protective to the families in the neighborhood
and whatnot.

And to my idea,
I mean I'm tryin' to find an answer for your question, now as to the
    cause—
because we can't have a cure until we find a cause,
you know that.
The cause is because when they integrated,
and allowed the black people to go to their schools,
their hospitals and their different places,
they take on a different culture.
Now it might have been, they—
all these years they thought and they—believed
they lived in a better life of everything, the—other race of people.

Black people were just takin' the leavin's and the crumbs and
    the gravy
so as to say.

But somehow or another we—strive,
we like—children in—Daniel and the Hebrew boys and all that.
When we took away the meat, we didn't have the meat,
we strive on what we had and—stay healthy.
But now the great thing about it is that the lack of education,
the lack of preparation they had
that was one key that helped against the black
of givin' you jobs and employment.
If you don't have employment of some kind,
you—can't live, you can't survive.
They took away the dignity of manhood,
because when he couldn't support his family
then he didn't feel like he was a man in the neighborhood
or he dropped from the practice of culture.
Because in his mind he didn't see where he was worthwhile with
    nothin' to support hisself.

It brought about—too many projects and—
where maybe twenty years or thirty years ago,

we didn't have the best of homes to live in,
we lived in such as we had.

But it was home, and it was individual and it—was private.
When you took away everything
he—his livin' and condemned his employment,
there's nothin'—comin' in,
then he had to accept what they offered him,
this project business around here.

And I think when we got in that
it kind of screened 'em out,
that you've got a certain bunch of the same kind all together.
So from there on you begin to contact everything.

Bob:

We were real interested in whether or not you saw that here in
    Roanoke. With the destruction of the neighborhoods—and the
    Northeast, whether or not when people moved they managed
    to stay together or whether or not they got all separated and
    started to fall into the patterns that you described. You were
    around then and saw what happened to a lot of the families;
    what do you think?

Mr. Meadows:

Well I think it was an abuse,
and I think it was—
on the other—words
we didn't—
Black people didn't see,
and they didn't have—
the privilege to find out.

I saw a lot of misery, and a lot of sorrows.

You might say that you develop this area in here for a better
    improvement.

No, no, it didn't do that.

What it did, it made us struggle harder—
to try to regain the footin' that we—
we were satisfied
in a four- or five-room house,
but give me a five- or six-room house
and I don't have nothin' to support it or to—go in it,
what good is it?

The—then I got to turn to somethin'.
In that case, you made it
you changed the minds of people.

In other words the thinking and the—dreams,
all of us have a dream,
and we—work towards that dream
and try to accomplish a certain purpose we make in our minds.

But when you kill the roots of that, what have you got?

Nothin'.

So we were damaged,
we had white lawyers here,
who black people went to to fight the courts to prohibit destroyin'
    our neighborhood
and where we lived and so forth.
He knew what would happen,
but he still pretend he was fightin' the case,
he wasn't doin' anything for us. They—lost just the same,
they—paid him for—to—kill protection for 'em
and he just sold 'em down the river.

He collected the money and set it down what he wanted to do
   right on.

Bob:

Did they ever have hearings, or did they ever have any kind of trials
   to force the city to rethink what it was doin', or—?

Mr. Meadows:

They told lies,
if I might say it that way,
about that whole thing.
The—story they sold to the black people of—
the Northeast—
we got it goin' on now down in Gainsboro.
Those people been promised to have—
renovation and redevelop for twenty years down there.
They have 'em, they've died,
they've got too old.
They—just recently over—there—
I don't know whether you've been by,
whether you're acquainted with the city or not,
to know where the Hotel Roanoke is over there?

Bob:

Yeah, yeah. Mary Bishop took us around this morning.

Mr. Meadows:

Oh you seen Mary?
Well she, I rode with her for two or three years when she started
   writing—

Bob:

Yeah, she told us.

Mr. Meadows:

—and pointed out those things.
She should know.
But over there where the Hotel Roanoke is used to be—
Developments for blacks all over in there.

Now, in the recent year, or year and a half
they changin' the highway and bringin' it right through the section.
Those people asked for it,
and they cried
and out of that four or five of those have died struggling—
heartbreak, I would say,
or depressed because of—what they were losin'.

And every time they decide to do something,
why don't they do it,
why don't they bring highways through the South Roanoke over
    there,
or—the Southwest area where white people live, and all the big—
they don't bring highways through that way.

They cut everything through the black section,
they can use it at any time.
And they hold meetings,
And they all have a big political talk,
"continued good things are gonna happen to you out of this
    movement,
and this is progress."
And who—what the good things,
Who they gonna benefit?

And the black people out strugglin' again,
tryin' to find some way to survive.
You get out and
paint your house

and fix your home up
and build your house out here
and a couple years come through,
and they don't ask you no questions,
they tell you they comin' through there.

And—we probably have like—that thing with
they had maybe six or eight months of discussion
between the—officials downtown
and most time, as you know,
our ministers are the greatest fighters that we have
and we look to them for information
because we feel like they can get to it where we can't.

It hurts for them to bring information as to what we supposed
    to do,
or what they know.

And then for somehow or another they get to them and quiet them
    down.
You go and have a meetin' every six months
and the same progress,
the—movement goes right on.
And that's what I can't understand.

What is it,
what is about us,
what is a weakness about us
that we can never win none of those battles that break our hearts to
    see done.

Our landmarks gone,
no description of what happened.
Nobody cares after they've accomplished their purpose.

Chapter 5

WHEN THE CENTER FAILS . . .

first met David Jenkins in 1994 at Housing Works, an organization providing services for homeless people living with HIV/AIDS. I was leading a focus group with agency clients. David's remarks fascinated me. He said he had lost his community at age eleven, due to urban renewal. But, he emphasized, "I've always been homeless." I was hooked.

David is tall—six-three—and very thin. He was born in 1947, a mixture of black, white, and Native American, and hence has a medium brown color, high cheekbones, and wavy hair. He is openly gay. He has never been married and has no children.

David is energetic and loud. When angry and feeling betrayed by the world, he rants about his misfortunes and the people who have done him wrong. When happy and at peace, he tells obscure jokes and laughs heartily at them. David doesn't walk into a room: he enters. He always has a lot to say, and will generally say it to anyone who will listen.

Saying hello to David can precipitate a discourse on the most intimate matters. He is a bit like a Venus's-flytrap: the unwary fall in, but they can't get out. It can be painful to watch the faces of passersby who had planned to make some form of superficial conversation but weren't prepared for a detailed history of childhood sexual abuse. They attempt to edge away, to escape, but I have noticed that the sort of people who are most likely to make superficially polite remarks are also likely to make firm eye contact before uttering their trivialities. David's capture mechanism is eye contact. He doesn't look away or blink, and so they remain trapped, at least for the period of time dictated by their standards of cordiality.

Some people—though equally trapped by the eye contact trick—find the immersion pleasurable (obviously I am a member of that group). There was no more remarkable example of this than Jeff Becker, a musician and graduate student in social work and public health, who saw to the soul of David's musical talent in a manner I'd never witnessed before. In David's presence, Jeff was worshipful. In Jeff's presence, David quieted, focused, and showed his genius.

Over the years that I have known David, he has never been late, he has never canceled an appointment, and he has never wavered in his loyalty to me and to our project. I've lost count of the number of people who've drifted through my life since 1994, and so it was surprising to turn around one day and realize that David had become one of my "old friends." He was hospitalized briefly at one point, and I realized how much I had come to treasure his presence in my life and how sad I would be to lose him. Though he has been HIV positive since 1981, only after 2000 did the illness begin to take a toll on him. But with that decline, I have taken on new roles in his life, primarily that of literary executor, to make sure that his art lives on.

All of this came out of a conversation that started August 10, 1994, and took on a life of its own. On my side, I was not so much interested in piecing together a diagnosis—though there seemed to be lots of material for making one—as I was in understanding David's lifelong sense of homelessness, as well as his childhood displacement. Having just embarked on my effort to unravel the psychology of place, it seemed that David could help me see exactly how place fit into a person's psychology.

On his side was a need to understand all he'd been through. He told me, at that first meeting, that he had gotten social security disability as a result of a back injury he suffered while living in California in 1989. This gave him money to live on, and, for the first time since age fifteen, he was free of the anxiety of supporting himself. He had decided that he should use the time to sort out the pain and confusion that seemed to dominate his days. "I have to think back on my life and try to understand what has happened to me. You know, when you are always worrying about where the next meal is coming from, you don't have time to think about the past."

It was in the spirit of self-discovery that he plunged into his life's story. "Really. Now let's start. That's a sort of homelessness. I didn't feel at home at home, where my brother and sisters, they were all older than me and I would go to the fields, I would go to the Tinicum Wildlife Preserve, and I would hang out with the game warden and would learn about the birds, you know, like, fragmites, there is that tall—bulrushes they call them but it's actually fragmites—that was the first thing I learned from George Lamb, I think he's with the Rockefeller Foundation now, but I was only like four or five years old then. I used to go out to the wildlife preserve and I remember the first bird, first time I saw an egret, he says—he was driving out and he had a dog named Cocoa and his wife was pregnant and George—his name is George Lamb—he says—he's—he had the city car started—and said, 'David, what's the name of that bird again.' I said, 'I forgot.' He says, 'Remember, the egret gets all wet.'" David laughed at the happy memory of that little ditty.

Over the years, I slowly learned enough to follow the several stories that got started in that paragraph: his dysfunctional family; his place of refuge, the wildlife preserve; and his childhood friendship with George Lamb, the game warden at the Tinicum Wildlife Preserve. David worked hard to help me understand. He spent many hours in conversation with me; he shared his poems, photographs, newspaper clippings, and memoir; he took me to see the important places in his life, like the single-room-occupancy hotel where he was living when I first met him; and he gathered friends and acquaintances for me to meet and interview.

This complex process was designed to help me, but it helped David as well. For example, when I gave him a copy of the transcript of our first conversation, he was quite upset by the realization that he had rambled from subject to subject. He began to make a conscious effort to stick to the subject. That made it much easier for me to understand him, but it also revealed the interesting fact that what had seemed to me like a severe thought disorder was, to a large extent, under his control.

I would not say that anything we did was therapy, but David would say that it helped him. It illustrates a principle in education: the best way to learn something is to teach it to others. By acting as my teacher, David was able to master his demons. This joint effort at dissecting place in David's biography occupied our time at monthly intervals from August 1994 to August 2001, when we agreed we had finished.

The Scenes

Family

David's family scene, so to speak, was quite intense. His main agenda in the fall of 1994 was to write a letter to his family confronting them with the abuse and neglect that had tormented his childhood. It was a blunt, angry letter filled with pages and pages of accusations. He raged as he talked about it, and each draft seemed to stir up more and more anger. I didn't think that it would improve family relationships, for who could face such a blast of condemnation? But David has survived by dint of his independence, and does what he thinks he should do. He believed in the letter. After months of work, he sent it off. No one responded—how could they?—but it was said, at last, and to David that meant a great deal. In the space of recovery that he was giving himself, it was time to speak of the horrors that had been visited upon him.

David's family consisted of his father, Gus, his mother, Alfonza, and eleven sisters and brothers. Gus Jenkins died when David was four, but as he often beat David, I don't think there was much tenderness in the relationship. David didn't speak of missing him. Alfonza suffered from depression and alcoholism. Whether these were present before her husband's death is unclear, but they were quite important problems afterward. Alfonza was extremely abusive to David, beating him with an extension cord, forcing him to do noxious chores, humiliating him often and publicly, and remaining ignorant of the ways in which he was being abused by others in and out of the household.

David's brothers and sisters understood him to be the family scapegoat and generally joined in belittling him. David, in his memoir, wrote, "Mother would say, 'David is bad.' 'You ain't never gonna be nothing, why can't you do like the other kids?' Brothers and sisters would say, 'Oh, that's David, always bringin home snakes and frogs and stuff, git dat stuff out of here.' 'That'—the word underscored by my sisters and brothers—meant the object farthest away from them, like, 'That's my brother, oh, that's David, just David he likes those "things." ' They used the word 'that' to indicate that they did not include me or welcome me as part of them."

The family's perception of David's sexuality was a part of their scorn for him. David wrote, "One day I was hit in the head by a Coke bottle and received stitches at Philadelphia General Hospital. I was crying. A sister-in-law living in the house, with some glee in her voice and laughing while ironing some clothes, said, 'You ain't nothin but a little girl.' Some time later, after we moved to the city, I heard one brother-in-law chuckling and saying to another brother-in-law, 'Oh, he ain't nothin but a faggot.' "

In addition to physical and psychological abuse, David endured sexual abuse at the hands of an older brother and other men from the local community. David wrote in his memoir, "I can count on two hands the few times that I've done sunshine, blotter or purple haze in my late twenties, but I cannot count the times I was raped from age four to twelve. It was practically every day and always the same persons or neighbors. I didn't understand it, no feeling for it, but did it, thinking that maybe this man loved me for doing that, even though I was told girls were for boys and when we grow up men married women just to have babies."

The House

The family house, at 8217 Botanic Avenue, Philadelphia, Pennsylvania, was not a home for David, and he noted, other families members may have felt similarly. They tended to say, "Meet me back at the house" rather than "Meet me at home." It was built high enough off the ground to be protected from floods that threatened the low-lying area when there were bad storms. The building was a large cube, divided in half. David's family lived in the north half, and their neighbor in the south half. On the back of the house was attached a "shed kitchen," complete with icebox, gas stove, sink, kitchen table, and window.

The large backyard had many parts and bordered on the equally interesting yards of neighbors. In one part of the yard, Gus Jenkins had built a cesspool. David remembered, "Boy, the smell of that in the summer, plus mosquitoes that would bite the hell out of you while breeding in the urinated water puddle on top of the ground. I never checked to see how many times each year the tank truck came to empty the cesspool." In another part of the yard there was the garbage can. This was, according to David, ". . . full of maggots at the bottom, so many maggots that if you shook the can (which I was always eager to do) it looked like a huge ball of moving rice!" Next to the garbage can was a vegetable garden, planted with okra, cabbage, collard greens, beets, sweet potatoes, and tomatoes. David noted, "I hated to go and pick tomatoes because of those humungus green worms with a big stinger on the tail."

Tinicum Wildlife Preserve

In my estimation, those green worms are the only one of nature's creatures that David didn't want to know better. His brothers and sisters were not wrong when they pointed out that David was always bringing things home. All through the years I've known him, David has always come back from Elmwood or Eastwick, the neighborhood bordering the preserve, with things—a turtle, tall grasses, whatever he could carry.

David spent many, many hours at the wildlife preserve, tutored by George Lamb and by the marsh itself. He waded in the waters, reveled in the tall grasses, and pined to adopt every animal he could stuff in his pockets. He played at the intersection of purity and pollution, with the freedom of country childhood within the borders of the city.

According to the display that I saw at the visitors' center of the John Heinz Wildlife Preserve—David had a great deal to say about the discarding of "Tinicum," which was the name of the local Native American tribe—the Tinicum marsh was steadily whittled away over the course of the twentieth century. In 1901, most of its original 5,700 acres were intact. Eastwick—what David calls Elmwood—occupied twenty blocks on its eastern edge.

Lying by the river at the edge of the city, it served for a brief period as a popular resort, but the push of railroads and highways, infill for farmland, and the advance of industry, changed the shape of the land dramatically. By the 1950s, when David was growing up, infill along the Delaware River had created a land bridge between the river and the wetlands. Eastwick had grown as a community. Approximately 1,660 acres remained. The Army Corps of Engineers pumped soil dredged from the Schuylkill and Delaware rivers into the marsh, which provided land for the municipal airport.

Changing land needs led to the Eastwick urban renewal project, cited as one of the largest in the nation. One small bit of the 2,500 acres that were to be cleared was David's neighborhood. At the same time, the encroachment on the wetlands continued, partly by the extension of the city and partly to provide land for the airport to grow. By 2000, when the Heinz Visitors' Center prepared its exhibit, it sadly informed visitors, "Today, only 450 of the original 5,700 acres of wetlands in Tinicum Marsh remain. Of these, 190 acres have been cut off from tidal flow."

Elmwood Neighborhood

By the time David was growing up, the resorts had left the land around the Tinicum Marsh, and noxious factories, such as an oil refinery and the Fells Naptha Soap Company, had taken their place. Black families, drawn by the availability of work others scorned, ar-

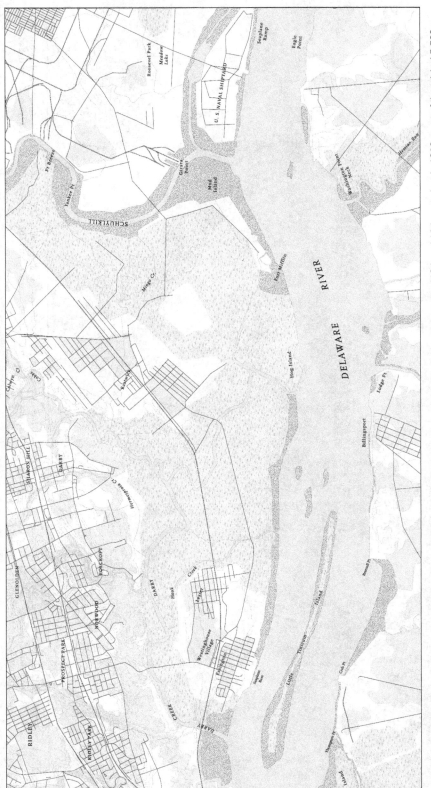

Fig. 5.1. Tinicum Marsh, 1901. This map is displayed at the John Heinz Wildlife Refuge Visitors' Center, and has the caption "18th and 19th centuries: In 1890, most of the original 5,700 acres of native wetland of Tinicum Marsh remained intact." Notice, also, the beginning of the neighborhood of Eastwick (also known as Elmwood). Created by Keith Helmatag, based on maps of the United States Geological Survey. REPRODUCED WITH PERMISSION OF CHERMAYEFF AND GESIMAR, INC.

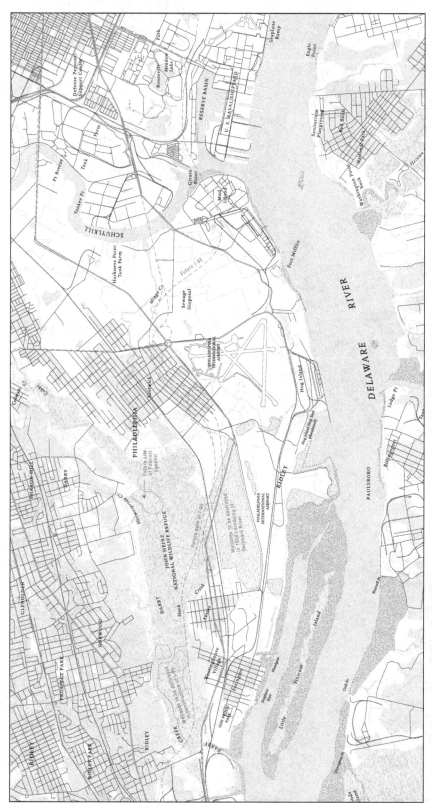

Fig. 5.2. Tinicum Marsh, 1942. At the John Heinz Wildlife Refuge Visitors' Center, this map has the caption, "By the 1950s, less than 1,660 acres of native wetlands remained in Tinicum." At that time, the Eastwick neighborhood was slated for destruction by one of the largest urban renewal efforts in the United States. Created by Keith Helmatag, based on maps of the United States Geological Survey. REPRODUCED WITH PERMISSION OF CHERMAYEFF AND GESIMAR, INC.

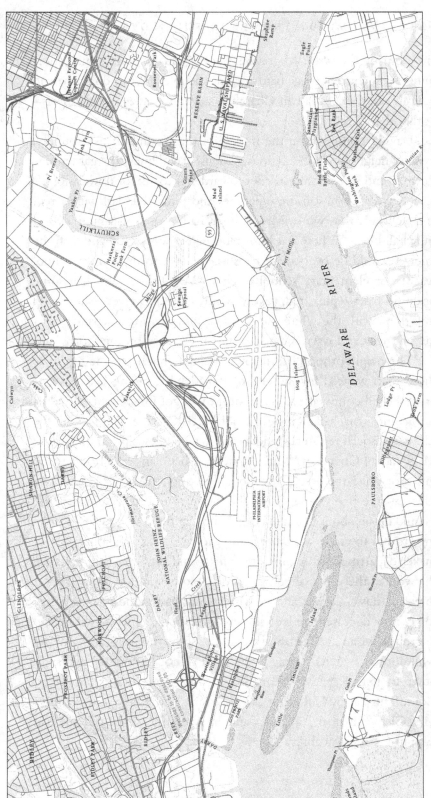

Fig. 5.3. Tinicum Marsh, 1997. At the John Heinz Wildlife Refuge Visitors' Center, this map has the caption, "Today, only 450 of the original 5,700 acres of wetlands in Tinicum Marsh remain. Of these, 190 acres have been cut off from tidal flow." The Eastwick neighborhood is largely gone, replaced by the airport and its service areas. Created by Keith Helmatag, based on maps of the United States Geological Survey. REPRODUCED WITH PERMISSION OF CHERMAYEFF AND GESIMAR, INC.

rived during the Great Migration. They gradually built a small community of churchgoing, hardworking people. "We didn't have no radicals out there," Nathan Chapman, a leading citizen of the neighborhood, told me.

David's house was in the middle of the community, surrounded by kind neighbors with fabulous gardens. David knew the gardens intimately and went from gardener to gardener to ask for flowers for his teachers. Mrs. Johnson grew peonies and pink, red, dark velvet red, and yellow roses, while Mrs. Palmer had a one-of-a-kind hybrid snowball bush. "When that bush bloomed it was so full and lush she knew I would be over to ask for some to take to my Sunday school teacher or elementary school teachers. Mrs. Palmer also had some beautiful roses—pink, red, yellow, white, maroon, velvet—she would mix them with the white snowballs or just give me a separate bouquet of roses and warn me not to hurt my fingers on the thorns."

The neighborhood had its own social hierarchy. At the top were those who worked for the city of Philadelphia or the U.S. government. David commented, "That meant you got full benefits upon retiring and you had a big-time job." To describe the top of the Elmwood social register, David gave a detailed description of Mr. and Mrs. Nathan Chapman. "Mrs. Harriet L. Chapman was a brilliant and gifted organist, the best Elmwood had to offer, a stone-cold jewel if I ever saw one. She was tops in all the 'city part' of Philadelphia, as well. I could go on about her credits; that you can find out yourself by asking around town. As well as playing the world-famous John Wannamaker department store pipe organ for grand occasions and holidays, she worked there as a salesclerk. So you know being our church choir director, music teacher, and an Eastern Star past grand matron (sorry to say now deceased), indeed she was a blessing to anyone who heard her music while she lived. She taught me some things I'll never forget while others weren't paying attention. I've got her piano style right down to 'Jesus Keep Me Near the Cross,' her favorite song, or 'We've Come This Far by Faith.' Just ask me to play either and you will hear Mrs. Chapman in my fingers, dancing across the keyboard. She had faith in my musical ability."

David went on to shower an equal amount of praise on her husband. "Back at home, Mr. Chapman worked for the City of Philadelphia. He worked at the morgue. Anyone and everyone who died in Elmwood of natural causes or not had to pay a visit to 'Big Nate' before the mortician picked the body up. Mr. Chapman's job was important because he knew something about the person who died. He was a good source of information, boy, if he ever really talked! He is still living today, working in his church with the senior citizens and I believe a trustee and deacon at Elmwood Community Methodist, at Forty-sixth and Chester Avenue, and is also a Mason . . . So that's a shining example of how important a married couple like the Chapmans were to the Elmwood community and two of many people I admired and knew."

David's description of community life gives a fascinating glimpse into the overlapping networks that existed in a small black community. Though individual churches were the nucleus of life, organized exchanges of ministers and choirs and other forms of interchurch socializing made the churches, as a group, the bedrock of the larger community. David explained, "All black churches had different auxiliaries, such as the nurses unit, Willing Workers, pastor's aid, junior and senior ushers, trustee board, deacon board, deaconesses, junior choir, senior choir, young adult choir, and the gospel chorus (old folks). Then there were the Sunday school teachers. When any of these groups would celebrate an anniversary or the pastor would visit another church to speak (on the down low) outside of the pulpit, the congregation would talk among themselves before and after the service (most of the time over food afterwards) and exchange any information of what's been going on, with what or whom, politically or not, in Elmwood."

Everyone performed services for the church, and often people filled multiple roles. David commented, ". . . it was not uncommon for one person to be a member of a number of different auxiliaries in the church at the same time. It helped carry important information from one group to the next, sort of like a beehive." People often comment—as Arleen Ollie did—that in the old days they often received help without even asking for it. The bee analogy is quite interesting, because bees' communication was quite enigmatic until the dance of the bees was decoded by Karl von Frisch. David offers a window onto the interactions that permitted nearly wordless communication among a tight-knit group of people.

There was much goodness to be had, and David knew enough to distinguish the good from the bad. He summed up his experience of Elmwood by saying, "Outside of being beat by my mother every chance she would get, or being molested by a male neighbor, or just outside my family period, Elmwood community life was beautiful." It is a complex thought, one that captures much of what David and I pondered over a long period of time. Vicious scapegoating in his family, and sexual abuse outside the family, left David's sense of intimacy twisted and stunted. By contrast, the unrestrained love within the tight circle of the neighborhood gave him a sense of optimism that has never deserted him. The enormous endowment of love he received from the neighborhood—"*everyone* tried to give me as much love as they could"—did not undo the curse put on him by his dysfunctional family. But it did create a buffer that prevented the abuse from becoming the entirety of his world. This buffer gave him reason to live while he healed as best he could. The story of Sleeping Beauty comes to mind, in thinking of this balance of curses: the good curse that can't undo the bad, but can create time for the Prince to come along and make things right again.

The Loss of Elmwood

When David was eleven, the Elmwood neighborhood was condemned by urban renewal, under the aegis of the Philadelphia Redevelopment Authority, and the land cleared for new uses. David and his household, which consisted of his mother, one brother, and one sister, moved to West Philadelphia, an area that was rapidly turning from white to black. The move was very difficult for David. In the early days, he would often run back to Elmwood and sit by his old house and cry. He missed the fields and the wildlife. One good aspect of the move, he noted in his memoir: "No more rape!"

Many neighbors from Elmwood settled in the area near David's family. They moved some of the churches. One, St. Paul AME, was still located in Elmwood in 2003.

"Near" is not the same, however, as "the way it was." People had to adjust to a much more urban life.

In my first interview with David in 1994, we had gone into this story in some detail. At the time, he sputtered with rage, as he recounted what had happened. "But you know the old folks, when we moved to the city, it didn't dawn on me—I was like twelve—and guess who so-and-so, Miss so-and-so died. So all the churches that was out there, they had to move and everything was all spread out, our whole community was ruined. The old folks, every week there would be three and four funerals a week, at all, People's Baptist Church, at our church was Beulah, New Hope, Calvary Baptist church, all the churches that were out there, the only church that didn't have to move was the Catholic church, the white church right there on Tinicum Avenue . . ."

David was getting quite agitated. I asked him if he was always this agitated or if thinking of the past still made him sad and angry. He replied, "Yeah, angry is the word. There is this, it's just like, there's so much that I could have done, if I knew then . . . what I know now. Them white folks at the development authority, I would have kicked their tired asses right back into the city, 'cause they wouldn't have took that property, not from my community, but see, those black people didn't know any better. They couldn't do anything, their hands were tied, they didn't have no city, they didn't have no pull. [So] they died. They couldn't handle it."

The Undoing of Kindness

Urban ghettos were vilified as places of shame and dysfunction. Though filled with the poor, though incorporating red-light districts, though inhabited by con men and robbers, residents taught me that those neighborhoods were places where people shared with one another. People had in common experiences of migration from the South. People had in common the pressures of daily life. People had in common the struggle to survive in the face of racism. And though such pressures might turn people against one another, in those places it made for a great deal of kindness.

The kindness had multiple sources. One source was the church, and particularly the churches imported from the South, which had a history of being the kindly bulwark against oppression. Those churches sponsored youth achievement, permitted adults to relax, and provided the sustenance that made weekly life possible. The community-building of the church—feeding the congregation, caring for the sick, watching over the children—bled into the community-building of the neighborhood. The church women became the tireless workers of the political organizations, the parent-teacher associations, and the unions. They brought to those tasks not simply the motivation to be kind, but, of equal importance, training in the acts of kindness.

But there were other sources of kindness. The gardeners, who planted crops in small backyards, had produce to share. The men of many professions who managed the streets minded the wild children, to limit as much as possible their descent into harm. The musicians and dancers and athletes gave content to consciousness: ideas to think about and access to the tools of creation. My father, who traveled a great deal in the late 1940s and early 1950s, described arriving in a new town, going up to another black man and saying, "Where's the ghetto so I can get a taste?" Inherent in his question are the assumptions of the urban ghetto: its existence, its salience to a random black man, its bar, and the common "taste." In the currency of the ghetto, a bottle of whiskey was an offering of kindness, in much the same way as a hot meal.

Kindness worked through the collective as both buffer and glue. It was a force for tolerance and respect: it was not a guard-all shield. Kindness did not stop child molesting, it did not stop wife beating, it did not prevent children from torturing each other, it did not prevent unemployment. It did ooze into the interstices to ease the pain of all these things. David Jenkins, though abused by many, was kept afloat by the kindness of neighbors. "Mrs. Sloan was an excellent cook, and if I was at her house at dinnertime she would say, 'David, pull up a chair and eat with us.' She knew that I would get in trouble with my mother, so she would call my house and say, 'Alfonza, David's going to

eat with us. I'll send him home right after dinner.' I loved her cooking, and then I wouldn't be hungry." David still laughs about his childhood cleverness at cadging a hot meal out of a kindly neighbor. Yet
who doubts that she knew exactly what he was doing and what she
was doing, as well?

Kindness declined after the rupture of community. Arleen Ollie
of Roanoke noted that, when she graduated from college in 1995, no
one was glad for her. In the old days her Roanoke neighborhood
would have celebrated what she'd accomplished.

What happened to the kindness? Why wasn't it re-created?

Certainly, after urban renewal, individuals remained kind, and organizations continued to nurture rituals of concern. The field of dis-
persion, however, appears to have altered substantially. In the compact
space of the ghetto, a tight field of activity was created, through which
acts and words might pass quickly. It was possible to know of someone's pain or glory, and to respond as needed. Actions toward others
were permitted and expected. They were extended with the consent
of the community, and received in that same vein. This passage
through the field of the community, with the consent of the community, meant that the sense of kindness was everywhere, at least within
the community.

The shattering of the field, which is a principal outcome of urban
renewal, had an enormous effect on kindness because kindness was
passed through the field. In the aftermath of urban renewal, individuals were preoccupied with making a new life, and perhaps they could
not be as kind as they had been previously. At the same time, given the
loss of the field, the kindness did not extend as far as it had before. The
buffering effect of the kindness was lost, and the negative behaviors
and attitudes that had always been present were given greater scope.
Given the other difficulties that were to come, the decline in kindness, however small, triggered a downward trend in kindness over the
ensuing decades.

The stories take us in several directions. Arleen Ollie's family
moved to a nearby neighborhood that had previously been all white.
They bought a house next door to a white family. On the day they
moved in, the wife died. Arlene's mother went to pay her respects and

ask if there was anything she could do to help: she was, in other words, being kind. The husband said that her help wasn't needed and closed the door in her face. His refusal to let her be kind was an act of prohibition that prevented the field of kindness from being reestablished in a new place. For people who moved to previously white neighborhoods, such experiences were not rare.

In the projects, the experience was different. Sala Udin of Pittsburgh remembered many lessons in neighboring that accompanied moving to the Bedford Dwellings housing project. All of the families in that project shared responsibility for the common spaces. Families took turns cleaning up the garbage room and the laundry room. If a family was careless in its duties to others, its members would be censured by the other families, as well as charged a fine.

Yet the intensification of bonds within the projects did not necessarily bode well for the surrounding neighborhood. Pittsburgh projects, like those in other places, were designed to create an interiority of the housing development and a break with the surrounding area. Hence, the field of kindness was limited by physical barriers that marked the project as a unique entity within the neighborhood. Because of this interiority, when the kindness in the projects collapsed, the decline was rapid and bitter, with meanness consuming the net of relations.

Smaller institutions—notably the church and the family—sustained kindness within themselves. But as kindness was no longer the same kind of universal language or value, divergent paths appeared. The celebration of meanness that appeared in gangsta rap in the 1990s grew out of the decline in kindness that appeared in the aftermath of urban renewal. David's life, when I met him, was lived in that field of meanness.

Hell Hotel

In September 1994, David invited me to visit him at the single-room-occupancy hotel where he was living in New York City. Such hotels had been set up for homeless people, as a temporary solution to their housing problems. Because people lived in a single room, without a kitchen and often without a private bathroom, occupants of these places were still considered "homeless" in acknowledgment of the fact that they had moved off the street but not into a real home.

Hell Hotel was built as a monastery, and the rooms were small, with thick, solid walls. Residents were usually sitting on the stoop when I arrived, a motley, disheveled bunch of people, drinking beer and being loud to pass the time. The same kind of behaviors obtained on the inside. It was years before David knew me well enough to share the details of the drug dealing and drug using that went on there, though it was obvious from the beginning that the residents were inches away from catastrophe. People I met mostly drifted back to the streets and to more active levels of drug taking. David was emphatic that that was not going to be his fate.

I proposed to David that, while waiting for better housing, he try to make himself feel at home there. I'm quite sure that, had I really understood the roses and the turtles of Elmwood, I would never have so blithely suggested Hell Hotel could work on any level. But David took my advice to heart, and immediately began to search the streets for the materials for the transformation. As he was living in the Garment District, fabric was easy to come by. So were light fixtures. Soon, he had created a curtain that divided the cell into three areas, a foyer, bedroom and living room. I had never seen anything quite like that before: the creation of space where there was no space. He draped the light fixtures with gauze, and taped photographs from his professional life on the walls. He had produced a homey-looking place. It was a long time, though, before he decided he was "home," and home certainly wasn't Hell Hotel.

Visit to Elmwood

In the spring of 1995, David took me to visit Elmwood. Though there was no community left, we would see what there was to see. I was supposed to speak at a conference in Philadelphia, so the plan was that David would go down with me. I woke up at 4:52 that morning, jerked out of sleep by the alarm clock. It was raining fitfully, and I thought for an instant I wouldn't have to go. But David was not worried about the rain. We took the 7:15 train, and I slept most of the way, largely to escape the incessant chatter of my companion. We walked from Thirtieth Street Station to Reading Terminal Market. David was flooded with memories almost from the beginning. He bought a soft pretzel from the first newsstand we passed. As we walked farther down the street, he began to wonder who he would see that he would recognize. "David—David Jenkins? How you've grown!" he joked.

At city hall he pointed out where his mother would leave him while she went off to buy liquor. Around the corner was the spot of an interracial gay bar, the Ritz. "In those days people dressed up—shirt and tie and it was very closeted." At the Reading Market he searched for a special stand with Lebanon bologna, but it wasn't open that day. We ended up buying sandwiches at a hoagie stand, and David regaled the saleswoman with stories of how hoagies were made in other parts of the country. On the way up to Philadelphia Community College, where I was to give my talk, we passed more spots of importance—his old art school and the hospital where he was registered (but not born). He was pleased with my speech and had good comments to make. He gathered up literature to give to people who needed it, and we set out for Elmwood. This involved the subway and a trolley, which took us through badly deteriorated neighborhoods. At the last stop of the trolley, we got off and followed a young man under the highway, through a railroad fence, and up to a roadway. We later saw the young man washing car windows on a corner.

We walked to David's neighborhood. It was hot and humid. The rain had stopped and it was a beautiful June afternoon. The air was filled with wonderful smells, dominated by honeysuckle and underpinned by the fetid marsh aroma floating in from Tinicum. White fluff, which David identified as cottonwood blossoms, floated through the air. We came to a wonderful complex of gardens. One—which David said was built on "the little field"—was being tended by an Italian man and his wife. We stopped to chat with them and he posed for a picture. He had been a peasant, in the United States since 1966, and spoke English with a thick accent. His tomato plants were a marvel. David was angry, though, and wanted to get away. "That's my father's land," he muttered to me.

We continued our walk through an area that was part woods, part fields. We came to an old house and a small, old woman who demanded to know our business. David explained who we were. She said who she was—Delores Rubillo—and David realized she was a former neighbor. He exclaimed, "You're still here!"

"That's obvious," she snorted.

It was, I thought, an extraordinary moment for him and one that deepened his sense of the futility of his loss. She had, as he wished *he* had, battled for the land and won. She had the whole neighborhood in a deed of trust, and nothing would be developed in her lifetime. She scoffed at the people who had taken the $5,000 and left—they had no principles, no moral fiber. She explained she was a harpist and had stayed in grand hotels all around the world. "But there's no place like home."

She waxed poetic when I asked her what "home" meant. "People know, you know where you are—" and leaning in to me added, "you are safe in the dark." I really liked that image.

She shared her memories of what Elmwood had been like, a rare interracial community in which everyone got along. "If a kid got in trouble, you'd tell his mother and he'd get a beating." David liked that, as it was a point I'd made in my speech. We talked for a while, standing there in the semiforest around her home, and then we continued our walk.

The most dramatic moment of our trip was arriving at the spot where David's house had been. It was a simple field. The larger trees had been there in his youth and he was shocked by the girth they had attained. David plunged into the undergrowth, quite absorbed in the effort to find signs of the past. "It would be easier in winter," he commented, "so I will have to come back."

He was suddenly upset. "You have to take me back now."

I convinced him that we should see the rest, so we walked a little farther, past where the school had been, where the churches had been, where there was nothing but fields and trees, a gentle breeze and the hum of a highway. At one point we stopped and he said, "This is where we graduated. It was a day like this."

I was flooded with thoughts of June, of hot days when you long to get out of school, of June afternoons when mothers are starting to make dinner, and kids are playing in the welcome heat. All around us birds were singing, and I basked in an utterly pastoral peace.

It was the kind of knowledge that lets you measure loss.

As we walked back, David related old nightmares he used to have of being run over by the trolley.

The Times Square

In the fall of 1995, David succeeded in moving to the Times Square, a highly regarded, supportive housing development on Forty-third Street, near Eighth Avenue. Gilded and shiny, the pretensions of its grand lobby struck me as more ominous then the rowdies on the steps of Hell Hotel. I worried, too, about its size. In my view, the Times Square had at least as much pathology per square inch as Hell Hotel could boast, but ever so many more inches. I worried for David that he had put himself in a worse position by trading up. David, however, was thrilled. He had a wonderful room, looking south over midtown, and he moved in happily.

It turned out that there was some truth to my fears. The horror of the Times Square was not at all like that of Hell Hotel. Where David's old place had been openly brutal, in the new hotel things happened silently. People died in their rooms and were discovered days later, or fell off the roof, no one knew how. It was spooky in its horror. To add insult to injury, the Disneyfication of Times Square started soon after David arrived, adding jackhammers and construction dust to the other indignities of the place.

Where David could post a bold poem on his door at the Hell Hotel, it was harder to keep the ghosts out in his new place. His use of drugs and alcohol went up, until residential treatment was required for him to get stable again. His T-cell count started to fall, and his viral load started to rise. Illness followed.

In sad pictures there are always bright spots. One such was Cary Medwin, a social worker who happened to be a feng shui adviser as well. She was one of those intrigued by David. She offered a feng shui consultation, and helped him reorganize his room. It made such a

Fig. 5.4. David Jenkins in 2002.

change in David that I immediately asked if she could help me. Karen Furth, a photographer who worked at the Times Square, became a good friend and supplied David with cameras he used to document the transformation of Times Square from the unique perspective of his fourteenth-floor home. David always seemed to be working to get his career going, and his house/home in order.

Healing

Healing is a peculiar process because it is hard to say what it is that makes us feel better, or why it happens when it does. Through a period of slow deterioration in his health, David actually began to heal some of the psychic pain he had carried for so long. This became most evident in 2000, around two events: a family reunion and the death of his mother.

The family reunion was the first event. A large group of people—David's therapist, his probation officer, his spiritual adviser, his support group—worried that David would go to Philadelphia and disrupt the family reunion. David shared their concern. But, as it turned out, he was able to manage it. He was relieved to be able to be there in an appropriate manner. And his description of the event demonstrates a marked shift from the disjointed, agitated manner in which he expressed himself in 1994.

He told me, "[Friends] were concerned about what I might do, including my probation officer, if I go down to Philadelphia to this family reunion. That I don't turn it out. I mean actually, literally and figuratively, tell those people what a piece of my mind is about or get in a fight, but they worked with me, and some of them prayed with me, and other people put me on their altar, and my support group—and I got there and handled everything. I saw it a different way, like I was supposed to see it . . ."

Not only did he not turn it out, he stood up and made a wonderful toast honoring the three family matriarchs who were present.

Shortly thereafter, he was tested again. He was called by his sister to come immediately to Philadelphia, as his mother was dying. Again, his story was clear, and the emergence of balance and calm remarkable.

The call came, as such calls usually do, at the tail end of a busy day. David borrowed money for the trip from the hotel's petty cash. The bus was late leaving Port Authority, so David did not get to Philadelphia until 10:25 that night. He told me, "I rushed to the nursing home. Nobody was there. I got in, signed in, went upstairs, and nobody was there. Mind you, I haven't eaten all day, and I'm flying! I get in my mother's room and—this is at Haverford Avenue over in West Philly, St. Ignacious Nursing Home—and I just know they would all be waiting for me, to have that last prayer—Mindy! The last prayer with your mother! Darling! Those Negroes left me! And they went home! No one waited till I got there, or to see if I was all right. What this book is about is the dysfunctional family? I see now. This is really terrible.

"So I just stayed there . . . I just went to my mother, and I told her, and I whispered in her ear. I said, 'Go to the light, go to the light.' I said, 'Mother, this is David, go to the light.'"

A nurse came in and asked if he was David. David asked her how she knew, and the nurse replied that his mother had been calling his name constantly. David was awed by this. He continued to tell his mother to go to the light. "I said, 'Girl,' I said, 'Listen: GO TO THE LIGHT! Get up out of here!' I said, 'Mother, listen. You're finished here, your time is up, now is the time for you to rest. That's all you have to do is rest. So go to that white light, and walk in it, and you'll be happy for the rest of your life, cuz you're finished. I'm all right, this is David. I'm doing real fine here. I've got a book coming out and you've got to help me with it when you get on the other side. You got to turn everything around on these people,' I said. 'But go to the white light.' "

David spent the night at his cousin Barbara's house, and enjoyed talking to her and to her sister about the family and its issues. On returning to the city, David learned that his mother had died just as he left. In a sudden shift, he felt loved by her, and most proud that he could guide her in her last moments.

David and I didn't get back to Elmwood until March 2001. Marian Banzhaf, a Revson fellow working with me to understand David's story, accompanied us. We drove down first thing in the morning to meet with Nathan Chapman, "Big Nate," and his daughter, Zara. We had a long conversation with them, and learned a lot about the Elmwood community. Mr. Chapman's memories confirmed David's, but from an adult perspective. The community he described was much larger than the community that remained in David's mind, perhaps on the order of ten thousand people. Mr. Chapman had a detailed map of the community in his head, and would often refer to places by including their cross streets.

We explored the industrial nature of the community, and the large number of polluting plants in the area. Fifty years ago no one worried about that. More recently the community had become concerned about exposure to cancer-causing agents. After lunch, Mr. Chapman took us out to see a section of the community that still existed, as well as St. Paul AME Church, which had never moved.

After we said good-bye to our host, we set out in search of David's house. As we drove down the street, we were shocked to see a parking lot on one side, and a large Hertz rental car location on the other. We got out and walked around, trying to digest what had happened. We tried to locate Mrs. Rubillo's house, but there was no way to access the place where we thought we would have found it. The evidence pointed in a clear direction: Mrs. Rubillo had died, and the deed of trust had ended. After a long struggle, the land of David's community had finally been claimed for other uses. David stood looking at the place where his house used to be and tried to make a joke: "where it 'Hertz' to rent a car."

David and I made a third trip in August of 2001, just before another reunion of his family. We spent most of an afternoon at the wildlife preserve. Many of the creatures that had lived there in abundance—turtles, frogs, and birds of all kinds—seemed to have gone somewhere else. It was smaller and more challenged than David remembered it. We met some bird-watchers who let us look through their telescope at some massive old turtles sunning themselves on a log.

David used the analogy of a turtle to describe himself to a class of graduate students that helped with the task of understanding David's life.[1] "Imagine," he said, "thousands of little turtles are born in the sand and they struggle to get to the water. Lots of bigger creatures want to eat them. Somehow a few little turtles make it. Then they are in danger from creatures that live in the water. Still, some survive. When you see a big old turtle sunning himself on a log in the middle of the Tinicum Wildlife Preserve, think what he has been through in order to survive."

In April 2002, my team helped organize a conference on community mobilization for trauma recovery, post 9/11. David joined the working group I led. At the end of the hour-and-a-half discussion, as we were getting ready to leave, David asked, "Can I say something?"

I said, "Of course."

"What I just wanted to say," he told the group, "is think of the children. I was a child when I lost my community. I now have lived at the Times Square for seven years—I haven't lived anywhere for seven years. I have always felt insecure, and I just kept moving. Please think of how anxious the children are right now. We want to help them be as secure as they can be."

A few days later, a study of children in New York City schools confirmed David's thought that the children were anxious. What was remarkable about the study was that it was not simply children in the area closest to Ground Zero who were affected by the attack, but rather children all over the city.

About that time David decided to return to Philadelphia. He couldn't face life in midtown any longer, and he had struggled to no avail to find affordable housing in other New York City neighborhoods. His illness had progressed, and it seemed time to be at home. Once again, I was skeptical, but, as always, David did what he thought was right.

"I'm home," he told me shortly after the move was completed. "It took a long time, but I'm home."

Chapter 6

. . . WHAT WILL HOLD?

African Americans of all social classes were confined to the ghetto under the rules of segregation. Urban renewal blew away houses of the rich and houses of the poor. Urban renewal initiated a destructive process that radiated from the center of Newark, New Jersey, outward through the surrounding suburbs. My sister-in-law, Patricia White Fullilove, grew up in Newark, and her life has been spent in the long shadow of the Housing Act of 1949.

Patty is the daughter of Clifford and Mary White. Clifford White, an important undertaker for the black community in Essex County, was adored by his family and his community. "Just a good person, you know what I mean," Patty often said. Mary White, a nurse, showered the world with welcome. She was the kind of nurse whose simple touch on your fevered brow eased pain and permitted sleep. Patty and her sister Sharon, who is ten years her junior, were raised in an atmosphere of reason and dignity.

In her early years, Patty lived in a two-family house, with her grandparents on the first floor and her family on the second floor. She said of that house, "I loved it because I could go up and down. Plus, it

Fig. 6.1. Aaron Fullilove.
"Patricia White Fullilove."
COURTESY OF THE ARTIST.

was a neighborhood. Everyone knew everyone, and if anything happened, the whole neighborhood was out on the street. And it was the
kind of neighborhood that, if somebody saw you doing something
wrong, they would call your mother or your grandmother. It was a
multiracial neighborhood when I was little, and by the time I left, it
was all black. We had a big garden in the backyard, so big that my
grandfather used to rent part of the garden to neighbors so they could
have their garden. It was just a great place to me. We could leave our
doors open at night, unlocked. You could leave your bike out at night,
and nobody would ever take it."

Patty went to Newark public schools, where she excelled and was
recognized for her musical talent. She competed for admission to Arts
High, which was the first performing arts high school in the country,
and boasted such famous alumni as Connie Francis, Wayne Shorter,
Savion Glover, and Tisha Campbell. Patty majored in music, taking
courses in harmony, theory, and music appreciation that were as rig-
orous as college courses.

Arts High was, and remains, a remarkable institution. Students were admired because of their talent, and individuality was nourished. Though New Jersey high schools were quite provincial at that time, Arts High was an oasis of tolerance. In fact, it was such a unique environment that even young gay men could feel free there. Friends from Arts High have remained a key component of Patty's social network, shaping her life experience in many ways. One small example: Patty has lost many friends to the AIDS epidemic. Another, maybe even more important: it was at an Arts High dance that she met Harold Fullilove in 1962.

Patty and Harold quickly became best friends. He was two years ahead of her in school. After he left for college, the friendship blossomed on weekends when he would come home from college. Patty remembered the Fulliloves' neighborhood as lively; it was home to black people of all income levels, as well as some Jews who had been part of a much larger Jewish community that had inhabited the area in earlier years. Near the Fullilove house were the homes of other friends, Kathie Barcliff, Reggie Jenkins, and Richie Bland among them. Walking in the neighborhood on a Saturday after marching in a parade, Patty and Reggie passed the Fulliloves' house at 24 Waverly Avenue, which housed Harold's family and his father's surgical office; Reggie's family home at 683 High Street, where his father maintained a medical practice; Dr. Shelton's home, where he had a dental practice; then Wigham's Funeral Home and the St. James' Church. "You were walking in a really nice area," Patty concluded. Indeed, a substantial black middle class had settled in the neighborhood's fine houses, using their gracious space for the business of business, as well as for the business of community and family life.

Twenty-four, as the house on Waverly Avenue was known among the Fulliloves, proved a hospitable place for courtship. Whether it was while "studying" in the basement, or chatting under the wide stairs on the first floor, Patty and Harold fell in love. Patty remembered one of those moments that are quite funny in retrospect. "Harold and I had gone out on a date. We came in the back way through the kitchen, and Mom [Fullilove] is standing there with the mop in her hand because she had just finished mopping the floor. When we walk in the

door, so does their dog. And the dog goes just like a commercial—
there are black footprints all across the floor. Mom looked at Harold
and called him a name I can't repeat. I was mortified, because, of
course, I wasn't close to her then, I was just dating her son."

Patty only applied to two colleges, Boston University, because she
wanted to go to college in the Northeast, and Douglass College, then
the women's college connected to Rutgers, because her father
wanted her go to college in New Jersey. Patty got her wish to go
to Boston University, and she was gratified that it "looked just the way
I pictured it."

When Patty left for college, her parents moved to another house
without telling her. "In fact," Patty remembered, "for a whole week I
tried to get them and I got no answer, and then they finally called and
said, 'Oh, we've moved out of there.' And that was strange."

The new apartment was in a three-family house on Goldsmith
Avenue, more spacious than the previous apartment, but the house
was shared with neighbors, not family, which made a difference.
"With Sixth Street, this was my house. This was *my* house. Every bit
of it was mine, even though it was my grandparents' apartment downstairs. This was our family house." I believe that the friendliness of 24,
and the presence there of her new family, made 24 seem more home-
like than did the new apartment.

At college, Patty studied hard and made many friends. She became part of a tight circle of black students that included those at
MIT and Harvard. She was engaged in the effort to increase minority
enrollment at the university, and participated in a sit-in after the death
of Martin Luther King, Jr., a BU alumnus. Patty was able to get to
know the Boston branch of Harold's family, and slowly became the
person who kept the distant relatives in touch with one another.

Thus far, Patty's life was almost idyllic. She was loved, admired,
successful. She was diligent, forthright, and politically correct. She
was, in sum, prepared to live happily ever after. But life was quickly
getting more complicated.

First, there was the 1967 civil insurrection in Newark, three days
of terror that left many people dead and many homes and businesses
in ruins.

That same year, Harold was drafted. He was sent to Vietnam in 1968.

At about that same time, urban renewal claimed the Fullilove home on Waverly Avenue, forcing the family to relocate to 53 Lincoln Park, a grand mansion that was too cold to substitute for the cozy Victorian that had been their home. The Barcliffs, Blands, and Jenkinses were caught up in the same spate of urban renewal, either because their homes were taken or because their neighborhood was destroyed. Many of the homes, including 24, stood empty for years and years. The proposed highway was moved to another location, and finally cheap town houses were erected. "These town houses are just stuck together and it's just not what was there. You don't have that sturdy, neighborhood feeling," Patty commented.

Despite insurrection, war, and urban renewal, Patty focused on her future with Harold. "I knew in my heart he would come home from Vietnam and I would spend the rest of my life with him," she said. This ability to focus on what she knows in her heart has proven, I believe, to be her most important asset.

Patty and Harold got married soon after his return and spent the first year of the rest of their lives in Kentucky, where he was finishing out his service to the army. The eight months in Kentucky were unique in many ways. Patty had nothing to do, so she cleaned all day. In describing this period in her life, Patty was hesitant. Honesty compelled her to say it wasn't *all* good, but the habit of never speaking evil of anyone stilled her tongue. Harold jumped in to give her permission. "Oh, say it. Everybody around there was basically stupid."

Patty admitted the strain it placed on her. "Everyone was stupid. It was very, very difficult. We were the only college-educated folk around. I remember saying to someone, 'Did you see It Takes a Thief with Robert Wagner?' And I remember a couple across the street said, 'Oh, we don't understand that.' And that was the end of the conversation. That was very difficult." Just as she had when Harold was away at war, Patty kept her focus on the life they were building together, a shared life in which she found deeper and deeper pleasure with each passing day. Just as she had spent the year while Harold was in Vietnam planning her wedding, so she could pass the time in Kentucky think-ing about graduate school at Columbia University.

For Patty, the move to Columbia and the Upper West Side was the real emergence into adult life. "A reason I think we liked it so much was that we were doing our own thing. We were going to grad-uate school and we were paying for graduate school and we were making our way. That too was a big thing. We had no support from Mom and Dad [White], or Mom and Pop [Fullilove]. If we messed up, it was us who messed up, but if we did okay, it was us, too. I think that is another reason why I really liked it. It was home. This was ours."

After Harold finished his law degree, and Patty her master's in ed-ucation, they moved back to New Jersey, settling first in the Colon-nades, the Mies van der Rohe apartments that tower over Branch Brook Park, and were built as part of one of the first urban renewal projects in Newark. The Colonnades was a very successful project, with roomy apartments that had great views. Because the Colonnades had been a part of all of our lives, this part of the history prompted an exchange of memories.

Patty opened by saying, "The Colonnades was nice because it was big. And a lot of people we knew were having children when we were having children."

Because both the buildings and the apartments were big, I asked Patty, "When you say it was big, you mean the apartment was big?"

"Big living room, nice kitchen, two bedrooms. You know, real nice kitchen. The living room was big. There was a big bathroom," Harold offered by way of explanation.

Bob pointed out another advantage: "It looked out over the park there."

"Yeah. And then we had a cleaner's downstairs, a Laundromat downstairs, and a store downstairs. And then David[1] lived there, so we could see him," Patty said, adding to the list of items.

Bob emphasized the merits of the building, saying, "Yeah, there were a lot of people in that building. Back in the day, it was like the place to live. It was an upscale address. I used to tell people my brother lived there. 'Oh, really? Oh.' I remember it took forever to build. Remember? And then when it finally opened up, it was like, this is the event that the whole of Newark is waiting for."

The Colonnades, though built to be part of the revitalization of Newark, flanked the Columbus Homes, one of the city's major housing projects. Instead of forming part of a vibrant city neighborhood, the two housing communities were socially and structurally disconnected. As hard times hit the city, the residents of the Colonnades became a target for robbery by nearby poor people. It didn't seem to be a place where Harold and Patty could raise their growing family.

After five years in the Colonnades, they moved to a house in the upscale section of Orange, New Jersey. Orange is my hometown, and I went to two years of grammar school on Patty and Harold's street. In my day, the area was alien territory: all white and very gracious. I remember the street's tall sycamores from my childhood walks. The crunch of fallen leaves still feels like wealth to me: I love to visit Harold and Patty in autumn and step on their leaves.

Their house, built in the 1930s for executives who commuted from Orange to offices in Newark and New York, was designed to be solid and comfortable, and even spacious by the measures of that decade. It had amenities—dining room, sunporch, master bathroom, garage, full basement—and large shade trees that have continued to grow, and wide sidewalks made for leisurely walks to school or for playing hopscotch afterward. It held the growing family close, but with just enough space that Harold could be alone now and again. Patty and Harold defined a house style for a new age. Lacking money and time, they simply left the house to its own devices, and focused on their children.

When I first met them in 1982, Patty's domain extended east from the kitchen, Harold's west from the sunporch/TV room. This meant that the children were under constant supervision. The charismatic Butch, enigmatic Aaron, and cherubic Gregory were bouncy boys, yet, under this two-overseer system, chaos was kept to a minimum and homework to a maximum. Sports were encouraged, church was not optional, and good manners and standard English were nonnegotiable.

Dinner fell midway between order and laissez-faire. When Bob and I were there, a time would come—say 7 P.M.—when Patty would say, "I'm going to the store for a second. Want anything?" A while later she would return—say 7:45—and would start to cook, relating as she broke up chunks of iceberg lettuce, the stories she had collected while buying food or renting a video. At 8:15, dinner would appear, and the family would collect, organizing chairs, dishes, and silverware in a manner that remains slightly mysterious to me. For a brief interlude, stories of all kinds would fly around, accompanied by a few "yum"s and a lot of laughter. The "Mom-he-hit-me" whine often heard in American households was decidedly not a feature of these meals. There was, instead, a "we Fulliloves are GREAT" hum that energized each and every one there. Patty has assured me that this was "company manners" and indeed she spent plenty of time managing in-fighting when there were no other relatives present.

Virginia Woolf would say, and rightly so, that Patty was the angel of the house, the quiet, self-sacrificing woman whose nearly endless giving made other people's accomplishments possible: her husband's brilliant law career; her sons' good character and reasonable scholarship; and her larger family's sense that there was goodness just outside their own home circle to which they could have access as needed. Patty said of her approach, "My mother taught that you don't just marry a person, you marry a whole clan. I have always felt that all of Harold's family was my family, too."

What Patty has helped me understand about her life is that this style is more pragmatic than one might assume. How does one raise three rambunctious black boys to a manhood of which one will be proud? Just as the war in Vietnam hung over her engagement year, so urban renewal hung over her childbearing and parenting years. The collapse of Newark sent ripples through the whole of Essex County, and Orange is not spared. Though her immediate neighborhood is solid, just five blocks to the east contagious housing destruction is eating away at the territory. Given the sad state of Orange schools, middle-class parents hesitated to move to the big houses that surround hers. Now, as the houses are being sold to poorer people, they will be split up for apartments and the inevitable decline will arrive at Patty's doorstep.

But if the decay of housing is a few years away, the collapse of manners has run ahead of it. At the time Harold and Patty had to decide whether or not to send their sons to Orange Middle School, there was serious fighting between the African American and Haitian American youth. People said to her, "Send your children to the school because it will help in our struggle for school improvement."

"But I hate to experiment—I only get one chance with them," Patty said to explain her decision to move them to St. Benedict's Preparatory School in Newark. Though the school was topnotch, and not far from Harold's courtroom, it was also not far from housing projects awaiting the wrecking ball, and urban blocks returned to a sad form of pasture. Mary White explained, "We just drove them every day. We acted like we were helping—they never thought it was for their own safety—and so they accepted it. Of course, that's what you can do if you have resources."

I can't help but reflect that, in 1954, my mother felt completely safe putting my best friend Sally and me on a bus from Orange to Newark. Sally was then five and I was four. We were to be met at the other end by Sally's father, Dan. Patty, by contrast, had to keep her sons off the bus until they were adults. It required a high level of involvement on her part, but it was pragmatic to be so involved, as it kept the boys on the narrow path to productive adult lives.

The same pragmatism infuses Patty's teaching. She has, by dint of years of work and great talent with young people, built up enormous personal power. She walks the hallways of the school where she teaches with great authority. The deference that is a part of being an angel of the house slips away. It is she who arranges, directs, coordinates, and guides. Though there too she is beloved, more important, she is in charge. Hers is, however, authority without ambition, a rare combination, as people who have some power often would like more. She doesn't lack ambition, she explained to me. "I'm a perfectionist," she revealed. The achievement of perfection in a demanding profession like education would have taken more time than she had at her disposal. She saw herself as a full-time teacher and a full-time mother. The question emerges: Who would Patty have been had the neighborhood—and not she alone—been responsible for the safety of her children?

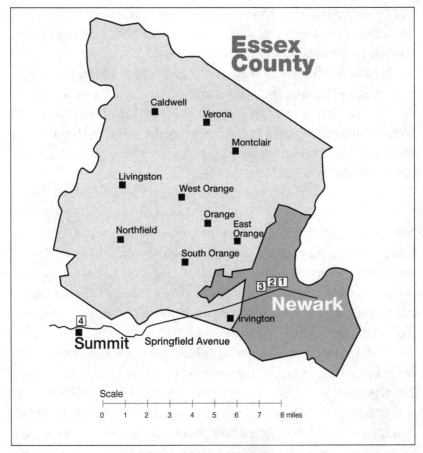

Fig. 6.2. Map of Essex County. The numbers along Springfield Avenue refer to the location at which we took the photographs that follow in Figures 6.3, 6.4, 6.6, and 6.12. CREATED BY RICH BROWN.

The Transect

To understand the strain in Patty's life, it is important to look at the relationships among the towns of Essex County, New Jersey.

Rodrick Wallace, my mentor in the study of urban environments, has applied the ecological tool of "transects"—a narrow band that cuts through a swath of land—to the study of cities. Major roads are not only trajectories of travel, but may also be used as transects through the urban terrain, displaying the contents and status of the land on either side. In Newark, this is a form of horizontal archaeology, revealing layers of history as we move from block to block, allowing us to read the evidence in brick and asphalt of the city's urban renewal program and its long-term effects.

Newark's urban renewal effort was gargantuan. Under the leadership of Louis Danzig, the Haussmann of Newark, the program was designed to clear nearly half the land in Newark, and displace one in seven residents. For years, Danzig's agency, the Newark Housing Authority (NHA), worked at reorganizing the Central Ward, the major black neighborhood in Newark.

Monsignor William Linder, head of New Community Corporation, helped me to understand the history and strategy of urban renewal. As he put it, urban renewal proceeded in two waves, clearing a series of interesting and vital working-class neighborhoods. In the first wave, the city built housing projects designed to concentrate the black population. In the second wave, they pursued "institutionalization," replacing the residential area in the center of the city with colleges and universities.

Working hand-in-glove with urban renewal was highway construction, which created a barrier around the black ghetto. "Route 280 was done to stop the movement of African Americans north, and that is a very wide highway, ten lanes. And if you go to the South Ward, [Route] 78 cut right across, really, and again is an extremely wide highway, particularly at this point where there were the most homes.

"And my feeling was that that was to be the Great Wall. You know, railroads and highways sometimes can stop movements of people, and can separate people. They saw it in the East Ward here because we already had the Pennsylvania Railroad, which is Amtrak now. And the Ironbound [which was divided from the rest of Newark by the railroad] developed totally separately from the rest of the city. When the rest of the city was going down, the Ironbound was coming up."

He argued that the Great Wall combined with vigilantism to funnel displaced African Americans west along Springfield Avenue. "Now, I've looked at migration patterns from a couple of parochial schools, and you don't see people of color going too far. They really were afraid. In that time, Irvington would have been white, believe it or not, and only had two blocks on the Newark line that had any kind of people of color. And people were very hostile going that way, so they tended to move west, but not really far. They tended to follow the main street. They would have gone up Springfield Avenue, South Orange Avenue. But they are going to run into dead ends very quickly. The west part of Vailsburg would have been white, and actually had white vigilante groups, so they couldn't move that way. They wouldn't have tried to skip over into another community. So, there was really not much room to move."

A final piece of the Newark urban renewal story, emphasized by Monsignor Linder, was its ruthlessness. "There were no resources. There was no government help for moving. And then, of course, they got very low appraisals on houses, because they were in the African American community. So what people got for them wasn't anything you could use anywhere else to relocate."

New Buildings in the Center

Against this backdrop, Rod Wallace and I set out to see Springfield Avenue, beginning at its origin off Market Street. The angle of the two great streets is a monumental point in the urbanism of Newark. A statue of President Abraham Lincoln sits there, with courthouses and other official buildings hovering behind him. New buildings on either side, in a variety of styles and visually unrelated to one another, undo the potential power of the vista. On the other hand, we are seeing investment: investment in new businesses, in education, and in housing. Walking just a little ways up the street, a major housing development sits on the right, carefully set back from the street, and walled off from passersby by an iron fence and a swath of grass. A lot of money has been spent in the first few blocks, but without producing the vibrant backdrop for city life that Monsignor Linder remembers in days gone by.

The Newark Prairie

And then the investment stops, and we enter a vast open area, an urban prairie of neatly trimmed grass extending north and south of Springfield. It would be an overstatement to say that it goes as far as the eye can see, but for a city dweller it's quite an expanse of open land. Vast housing projects once occupied this terrain, but they have been demolished in recent years because they were deemed dysfunctional. The land will be used for many purposes, among them, new public housing buildings.

Fig. 6.3. Photograph 1: Traveling along Springfield Avenue. Jennifer Stevens Madoff. New houses.
COURTESY OF THE ARTIST.

Monsignor Linder had a lot to say about the housing projects, which were built in the first wave of urban renewal. By his estimate, half of the residents in public housing in Newark were living packed together in the center of the Central Ward, 26,000 people in all, representing about 5 percent of the city's population. The buildings themselves were not designed to support so many people with so few resources. "They were basically poorly designed, particularly Stella Wright and Scutter Homes. They were designed by 'politically right' architects, which means that they paid into the campaigns. And you know, they were not very imaginative, and they were really about minimal construction." The federal HOPE VI program provided funds to tear them down, fifty years after they were first put up. The prairie will only last until new money comes along.

Fig. 6.4. Photograph 2: Traveling along Springfield Avenue. Jennifer Stevens Madoff. Urban prairie.
COURTESY OF THE ARTIST.

Fig. 6.5. Springfield Avenue, looking downtown. Upper photograph (1957), photographer unknown. COURTESY OF NEWARK PUBLIC LIBRARY. Lower photograph (2003), Sara Booth. COURTESY OF THE ARTIST.

Civil Insurrection

As buildings reappear a few blocks later, we can look to the east and see the skyscrapers of downtown Newark.

Another grassy triangle catches our attention. It is a marker to the people who lost their lives during the days of insurrection in 1967.

The riots are part of a critical piece of urban renewal history: the effort to bring the newly formed New Jersey College of Medicine and Dentistry to Newark. The college wanted 150 acres of land, and was interested in a site in suburban Madison. Danzig and the housing authority pressed hard to get the state's new medical school to settle in Newark. They offered to clear 150 acres of the Central Ward in order to meet the school's demands for land.

The outcry from area residents was forceful. People were well aware of the meaning of yet another urban renewal project: the medical school project was the fourteenth project directed at the Central Ward. The black community in Newark was large, and had a relatively sophisticated political organization, though corruption in city government, political divisions within the community, and the generally chaotic nature of Newark all served to undermine the effectiveness of the community's political arm. That is not to say that people didn't wage a forceful effort against the city and the state's effort to railroad the plan through the approvals process.

At a large public hearing on June 12, 1967, held to review the designation of the area as "blighted," an exceptionally clear picture of the debate about urban renewal emerged. Representing the official point of view were the executive director of the housing authority, the director of urban renewal, the director of relocation, and representatives from the Newark departments of health and welfare, fire and police, and inspections. The opposition was represented by George Richardson, speaking for the Committee against Negro Removal, along with several members of the Central Ward community.

Louis Danzig spoke for the Newark Housing Authority, arguing that urban renewal was the only tool that could create jobs, education, recreation, religion, health care, and entertainment, all "to make life worth living."

George Richardson, a civil rights activist, former Democratic assemblyman, and a founder of the Business Industrial Coordinating Committee, presented the major counterargument. He opened by saying, ". . . any urban renewal project, planned or contemplated, that will uproot 22,000 Negroes, without any planned new housing to be built . . . will never be completed in Newark."

The wide-ranging definition of "blight," Richardson correctly noted, and as Danzig himself was well aware, could apply to a vast number of neighborhoods in Newark. Richardson called it "a gimmick that the City of Newark and the Housing Authority has used to bring about plans and programs they deem necessary . . . any other area that the Medical trustees of the College wanted for the

Fig. 6.6. Photograph 3: Traveling along Springfield Avenue. Jennifer Stevens Madoff. Marker commemorating deaths during the Newark Riot. COURTESY OF THE ARTIST.

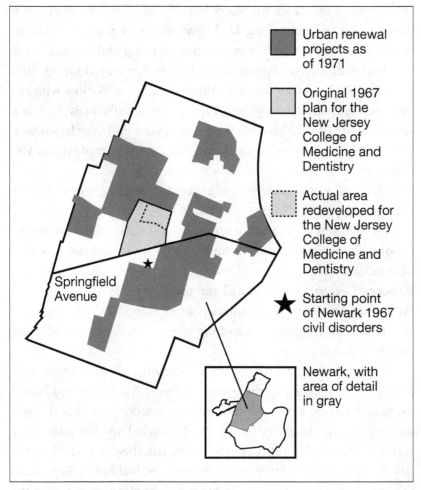

Urban renewal projects as of 1971

Original 1967 plan for the New Jersey College of Medicine and Dentistry

Actual area redeveloped for the New Jersey College of Medicine and Dentistry

Starting point of Newark 1967 civil disorders

Newark, with area of detail in gray

Springfield Avenue

Fig. 6.7. Urban renewal in Newark. MAP CREATED BY CYNTHIA GOLEMBESKY AND RICH BROWN.[2]

site, . . . the Planning Board would have been asked to declare that area blighted and the Newark Housing Authority [would] have come before you with all the statistics necessary to show that this area was blighted." In a series of important points, it is essential to note that although the plan would have a major impact on the black community, that community's input had not been considered.

While the representatives of the Newark Housing Authority continued to argue for the good that it would bring to the city, the citizens continued to express their anger. James Walker, an opponent, said, "[The city planner] really does not care. He will take his salary and he will leave for Short Hills, to Madison, or wherever it may be and the only thing he knows about Newark is when he comes into Newark on the bus in the morning and he would say, 'Look at what those niggers done, look what they done to their property.' We know, we live with those conditions. We live with the roaches, with the bedbugs, the rats . . . on a daily basis. You talk about blighted. YOU have blighted it. It is your property. It was you. You had the right to go in there and make some sort of repairs. You don't care."

That night civil insurrection broke out in the ghettos of three U.S. cities.

The tensions around urban renewal—and the tensions around the nation—did not stop the city from pushing forward the authorization of the clearance of the Central Ward for the medical school complex. Rebecca Doggett, who worked for many years as an organizer in Newark and was one of the founders of a group called Tri-City Citizens Union for Progress, spoke of the weight of loss that was affecting people at that time.

"As the sixties came into play it was clear that those factories were leaving and relocating to the south. And so it was harder and harder for people to find work, and to have that mobility that they thought they were going to get by coming to Newark. They lost jobs—they couldn't follow the jobs and so they were left, they were stuck in the city. By the time of the riots, this disinvestment had been going on. So the displacement because of the medical school was sort of like the straw that broke the camel's back. It was like adding insult to injury. They'd lost everything else and now they were going to even lose their homes, and a vibrancy to the community that others may not be able to see.

"I mean, those were neighborhoods and the people knew each other for years, took care of each other's kids, went to school together. So, even with the tenements, they were still neighborhoods where, you know, at least for a few blocks people knew each other and maybe, you know, four blocks away they didn't. They kind of had the wrong turf.

"But they were clearly neighborhoods. The stores were there, the residents were there. The displacement meant they were scattered. There was no way they were all going to be picked up wholesale and just moved into another community where they were all going to be together. So they knew that they were going to be losing friends and family and all kinds of connections that they had in that neighborhood."

In protest of that loss, civil insurrection broke out in Newark, as it did in 167 other cities that summer. While many accounts exist of what happened—running the gamut from "black people rioting" to "police rioting"—it is clear that the three days of confrontation represented the same clash of interests that had been evident at the urban renewal hearings only a month earlier. Black people living in the Central Ward were essentially helpless to control their destiny. In the confrontation with urban renewal, they were unable to stop the taking of their land. In the confrontation with authority, they were unable to fend off the massive invasion by police and the National Guard. The insurrection was a desperate attempt to grab some control over the community's future.

The Moving Front of Disinvestment

Monsignor Linder was emphatic about the link among urban renewal, insurrection, and a dispersal of displaced Newark residents. "I mean there was a direct correlation. We relocated people, and remember, we were relocating a good number of people without any relocation resources, so there was nowhere for them to go. You begin to see the doubling up of families; you begin to see people moving out of Newark."

The insurrection won some concessions from the government and white flight freed up badly needed housing. But those gains needed to be nurtured and developed, economically, socially, and culturally. It is apparent to Rod Wallace and me, as we continue down Springfield Avenue, that no substantial investment has been made in the area for a long, long time. We pass vacant lots, where buildings were burned out, and old buildings in urgent need of pointing and paint.

Monsignor Linder remembered that, in the aftermath of the riots,

"We began to see more and more property being abandoned. We saw more and more renters who weren't paying rent, so there was no investment in the house; and we began to see houses finally reaching the point that no one could live there. Next, we had fires, lots of fires, significant fires, because they were basically wood-framed buildings built around 1910."

The poorest people, who were slowly chased out of Newark by the rampant fires, moved to Irvington, East Orange, and other nearby towns, overcoming racial barriers by their sheer numbers. The weight of problems the displaced people brought with them crushed those surrounding cities. In the words of Monsignor Linder, "Irvington is

Fig. 6.8. Photographer unknown. Newman's Market. COURTESY OF THE NEWARK PUBLIC LIBRARY.

Fig. 6.9. Photographer unknown. Children at the Wedding. COURTESY OF THE COLEY FAMILY.

Fig. 6.10. Photographer unknown. The Leaguers float, Newark 300th Anniversary Parade, May 1966. Gift of W. G. Hetherington and Co., Newark, 1967. COURTESY OF THE NEW JERSEY HISTORICAL SOCIETY.

Fig. 6.11. Helen M. Stummer. The making of a prairie. Upper photo: Irvine Turner Boulevard in 1977.
Middle photo: Irvine Turner Boulevard in 1988. Lower photo: Irvine Turner Boulevard in 1997.
COURTESY OF THE ARTIST.

now African American. Irvington is worse than Newark, or equal to Newark. East Orange is African American. Years ago, they won that National Beautification or whatever award they give for beautiful cities; they wouldn't get it now. I think Orange has been impacted. South Orange—and everybody said South Orange is never going to change—has changed significantly. You begin to see more and more people in South Orange selling and moving out to the Chathams and the Summits. So basically where we had a low-income population concentrated, we now have it spread out. And we have just destroyed maybe four cities. I think you can go as far as Short Hills, and you feel the impact on real estate."

Rod and I read this history in the buildings as Springfield Avenue passes through Irvington. Though more prosperous—and more in-tact—than the buildings in Newark, their scruffiness is still noticeable, and the contents are dollar store rather than deluxe. In our *chercher-le-dollar* trip, it is some miles away from the center, and four towns later, that we find the prosperous downtown of Summit, New Jersey. Though the street is still called Springfield Avenue, I am sure Summit officials would be most upset at me for linking it in any way with the sad avenue that starts at Market Street in Newark. In the thinking that accompanies this unequal distribution of wealth, the good (hence rich) place and the bad (hence poor) place are disconnected. In the ecological archaeology of the trip Rod and I are making, the two ends of the street are more tightly linked because of their separateness than they would have been in a freer system.

It is a curious consequence of a geography made unstable by un-even investment: without money, buildings burn, and people move, taking their despair to the next neighborhood. Only substantial in-vestments across the whole terrain of Essex County could stabilize the area. Patty's house in Orange, which in my childhood seemed so secure, sits just at the leading edge of collapse. Urban renewal took the Fullilove family home at 24 Waverly Place; the long shadow of that process is poised to take its Orange replacement. Summit, after all, is only a few miles—or a few years, depending on how we measure dis-tance—farther along.

Fig. 6.12. Photograph 4: Traveling along Springfield Avenue. Mindy Fullilove. Upscale stores in Summit.

The Music

In the context of the unstable transect that is ordering her existence, Patty manages by maintaining her focus on the joys of life. This seems to entail that she stay on a straight-and-narrow path. "Pragmatic per-fectionist" seems an oxymoron to me, but it perhaps explains why she draws so little attention to the many sides of herself. At no point at any meal or any other kind of family gathering did I ever hear Patty take the spotlight. The Fulliloves are people of accomplishment and they take delight in sharing what they have done. Unlike the rest of us, Patty keeps her achievements to herself. She chats about the comings and goings of friends and neighbors, the exploits of her family, the shows she saw on television, lines of conversation that gloss over the complexity of what she is doing on any given day.

Music is, of all the parts of her life, the most complex and the most profound.

Her singing life occupies Wednesday nights, and those Saturdays and Sundays her group performs. Patty expressed gratitude for the time to sing. "It's so good of Harold to let me have the time for my rehearsals every week—he knows how much it means to me." It is hard for me to imagine my accomplished sister-in-law saying that in the year 2002, and on thinking about it, I find myself struggling to understand what "time" means in the life of this family.

Patty sings with the Essex Chorale. In the midst of that group, she is not the authority, not the angel, but a babe-in-arms, surrounded by very senior and very accomplished musicians. She is a recipient of a tradition that dates back 150 years in African American history to a time when accomplished urban blacks claimed classical music for their own, and used that knowledge to transform the raw emotion of the spiritual into concert music. The musicians of the Essex Chorale are likely to have perfect pitch, sight-read effortlessly, count music flawlessly, and add to that the something more that raises singing to a fine art. They bring to the work a lifetime of discipline in choral traditions.

I went to their performance of Handel's *Messiah,* largely because I had just realized the extent to which music defined David Jenkins and Patty Fullilove, two people who otherwise seem to have nothing in common. The concert took place in the Christ Episcopal Church in East Orange, New Jersey. Bob and I parked our car on the side street to the east of the church, where burned-out buildings and empty parking lots surround East Orange High School. It was a grim sight on a winter day, and painful to think of what had been as compared with what now was. The pews were packed, mostly with black people in their middle years. The first time I heard the *Messiah* performed was in East Orange, many years ago. Then, the audience was all white, except for me. On this occasion, I wondered where this largely black audience had come from. I wrote myself a note, "Who *are* these people?" I enjoyed thinking about the audience as much as I enjoyed the concert. I was so intrigued, I asked Patty if I could go to rehearsals with her. She was delighted with the idea, and I arranged to meet her a few weeks later at 8 P.M. at the church.

The chorale was preparing for their winter concert of Negro spirituals the first time I went. The rehearsals took place in the parish hall of Christ Episcopal Church. Church halls resemble one another in form and function, but may be rated by sun and size. The entrance to the parish hall was up a short flight of stairs—not a basement church hall, so sun was likely; this, in my view, indicates a superior church hall. A sign posted on the door noted that there was a soup kitchen on Saturdays, while another indicated the times to come for free clothes.

Entering through the heavy old doors, I turned to the right, and entered the parish hall. I found myself in a large, high-ceilinged room that easily accommodated the forty or so singers in the group. The room was decorated with the kind of cheery, proselytizing posters that church groups and health officials make, the kind that only get posted in places that aren't particular about their decor, and that stay posted until the Scotch tape dies and they sag off the walls. Occupants of the room were urged to live with a fiery desire to serve God, to try harder, and to take care of their health. Several tables were located near the walls, and coats were laid tenderly across them, exquisitely parallel to each other, as if to make some sort of hieroglyphic. I looked at the coats often during the rehearsals, wondering what their message was.

I was glad to see Patty there, and she introduced me to various people, all of whom asked if I were there to audition. I explained that they didn't want me, as I can't sing at all, and they all politely said, "Of course you can." Given the exquisite nature of their own voices, which they knew perfectly well to be exceptional, I was not entirely sure why they said that. Pity, perhaps, for the nonsinger.

The chairs for the singers were set up on three sides, with the piano making the fourth side, just in front of a small stage hung with red velvet curtains. The sopranos sat on the west, the tenors, baritones, and basses to the north, and the altos to the east. The piano was in the south. In front of the piano was a small music stand. Dr. DeCosta Dawson, founder and musical director, called the group to order.

The Essex Chorale is composed of older men and women. Most looked worn. Some were prompt, others arrived throughout the first hour of the rehearsal. They walked slowly across the room. There was nothing feeble about them, however. They were alert and engaged. They were adept. Dr. Dawson corrected phrasing, pitch, speed, the confluence and disengagement of voices over and over, until even I knew the songs and their pitfalls as the concert approached.

The day of dress rehearsal I sat in the first pew watching a ragtag group line up for the run-through of all the songs. Usually, people arrived from work, but this was dress-down Saturday, sweatshirts and jeans. People of all weights, heights, colors, outfits. I was thinking that there was a certain despair in a dress rehearsal, a certain how-can-it-work? Just at that moment, Dr. Dawson, who had been fussing and correcting and polishing, suddenly said, "I'm not going to interrupt you anymore—we'll just run through it." The songs started to flow one after the other, the disjointed pieces surging to connect and to communicate.

The audience of me was suddenly transported out of the mode "preparation" and into the mode "performance." The songs were talking to me. The sorrow songs, Dr. W.E.B. Du Bois called them. One, in particular, crushed me: "Gonna leave this world some morning, gonna lay my burdens down some morning, gonna journey away to God." The repetition of the gentle undulation in a minor key was so insistently mournful, I felt myself falling into its despair. I have heard that affection for death only once, and that man killed himself. "What about life?" I wanted to shout.

I was suffocating listening to the song. When it was over, I felt, perhaps for the first time in my life, that I had met slavery, that my ancestors had sent a message that these kind, worn people had delivered to me. "No," I promised those long-gone songwriters, "I will not let it happen again."

James Weldon Johnson, the great poet and author of "Lift Every Voice and Sing," also known as the Negro National Anthem, wrote in the preface to his collection of Negro spirituals, ". . . it was wholly within the possibilities for these songs to be virtually lost. The people who created them were not capable of recording them, and the conditions out of which the music sprang and by which it was nourished have almost passed away. Without the direct effort on the part of those to whom I offer this slight tribute, the Spirituals would probably have fallen into disuse and finally disappeared. This probability is increased by the fact that they passed through a period following Emancipation when the front ranks of the colored people themselves would have been willing and even glad to let them die."[3]

The Essex Chorale would not let them die, I knew, and I was suddenly deeply grateful to Dr. Dawson for ensuring my heritage. I was so caught up in my sudden awareness that I thought, as all the newly converted do, everyone should hear these songs sung by the Essex Chorale so as to feel them as I had.

On the day of the concert, the audience—mostly of that certain age, mostly black—assembled in the sanctuary for the concert. The chorale was elegantly dressed, men in tuxedos, women in long black gowns enlivened only by a tasteful single strand of pearls. The concert was as precise as it was formal. The audience knew the chorale, knew the songs, and listened critically for what the particular performance would offer. The concert did not offer to sweep people away. One woman, swathed in a magnificent fur coat, commented to a neighbor, "It's just the right combination of virtuosity and reverence."

"And pain," I wanted to say, but in a way, that was not the point of the concert. I thought, actually, that the audience had missed the best part, the slow immersion in the songs that I had gone through. For me, each arrived like a friend, and I awaited favorite parts with anticipation. There were surprises: solos I did not know were part of the program, and pieces of songs that came together in unexpected ways. I couldn't get over my favorite, "Rockin' Jerusalem." A friend found me a wonderful version on CD and I played it constantly, working it into the graduation speech I was to give at my daughter Molly's commencement.

In the parish hall afterward, Patty introduced me to various judges, doctors, lawyers, educators, and other accomplished people. "Ah," I said to myself, "now I know who these people are." It was a "have" crowd: this concert was done for them. It was a valued touchstone of their culture, of their roots.

Events as City

My daughter Molly attended a college that lacked a student center. The lack of a central gathering place had many effects on student life, and contributed significantly to the distress they experienced at that school. I spent a week there as a "parent-in-residence" and complained constantly that I couldn't buy a cup of coffee after 2 P.M., a small but nontrivial way of describing the lack of ordinary amenities.

Molly worked with many friends to understand and improve college life. One of the ideas that she came up with was this: in the absence of a *place* to gather, people created *reasons* to gather. Thus, she surmised, events were the "student center." A possible solution to some of the loneliness of the campus was a calendar of ritual events that was strongly embedded in the college culture. Actually, at that time, the calendar was quite erratic, and events happened or didn't happen according to the enthusiasm of the student body. Because the lack of a student center contributed to a campus-wide student paralysis, many lacked the strength to implement the only possible cure. It created a vicious cycle. Molly, at the point of planning her last "event-as-student-center," professed great fatigue. The need to create events is a burden on those who have the will to respond.

While talking to Patty about the burned-out, postapocalyptic terrain that surrounds Christ Episcopal Church, she was silent for a moment. It seemed clear that she had screened it out of her consciousness. "You have to keep your spirits up, otherwise what would happen?" she finally said.

This led me to the thought that as Patty was traveling to rehearsal, she was traveling to an event. For her, as for Molly, the reason to gather had replaced the place to gather. The inhospitable, damaged city still had gathering places of all kinds. Within that shelter, people made good times. It took enormous effort, but people were willing to do it, to keep the community going, to keep spirits up.

The problems with events-as-city extend beyond the burden that this places on the event-makers. The most serious problem is that events tend to be created for some and not for others. The Essex Chorale sings for the "haves," not out of any wish to exclude, but out of patterns of cultural separation that make going some places possible for some people, but not for all.

The great gift of the city is that of propinquity: anybody can meet anybody on the streets of a great city. Once the streets collapse, or the market is bulldozed, or the parks are fenced, or the beach erodes, people lose the ways and means of public intercourse. The ensuing separations follow social fault lines that divide populations by class, race, religion, age, culture, or whatever else suggests to people what they like. The street is not about "what I like," but going to a concert is. In that lies the profound structural difference imposed on social relations by the collapse of the city.

The "haves" at Patty's concert, like Patty, have talent, education, wealth, and family support. What they do not have is the "right to the city," the freedom to move anywhere and everywhere. They are not, as in the past, restricted by Jim Crow laws. Now, they are restricted by danger and by difference. In this tense atmosphere, the "haves" must protect what they have, as Patty had to protect her children by driving them to school. This creates a form of isolation—whether it is expressed in the gated, moated housing complex or not—that blocks the creative, generative energy of the city from flowing forth. The divided city is a subjugated city.

And Patty—who by right of birth, goodness, talent, and beauty was meant to live the fairy tale of happily-ever-after—has had to work every day of her life to keep her focus on the glass half full.

Chapter 7

UNCEASING STRUGGLE

Over dinner in the lively Pittsburgh neighborhood of Oakland, Tamanika Howze started to tell me about why she continued to live on the Hill, loving the neighborhood even though it lay in tatters all around her. She followed up with this email message:

"I'll try to explain. This issue of Diss-placement goes back to my childhood. I remember so well what was going on. I saw chunks of the Hill taken, destroyed, and in some places replaced with other structures. I remember hearing people talk about different parts of the Hill, like the Crawford Grill and the Hurricane. Places that I wanted to be a part of because of how adults described interests and involvement. Some of these places seemed to be like rites of passage—I knew that when I got old enough I would be able to go inside the Hurricane to really hear the music that I'd been listening to from the street. I was so excited for that.

"I recall as a teenager people from the University of Pittsburgh coming to the Hill interviewing teens about living on the Hill, about our homes, our life there and giving $5.00 for the interview. I remember Bob Pease from the Allegheny Conference coming to our

youth group and speaking about how we would not be able to recognize the Hill in 20–30 years. I did not fully understand at the time
what he meant. But he knew the plan.

"I hold on because in simple terms, I really like living on the Hill.
It is HOME for me, it is my roots of good and not so good memories. But it is mine. I feel that it is a battle to stay on the Hill. A battle
that I want to fight and be the victor. They took, stole, cheated, lied
and bulldozed their way. We have lost so many battles, I don't want
them to totally win.

"My thoughts about staying on the Hill are not unique. I talk to
people all the time who don't want to go and are willing to sacrifice
something. For some it is living in substandard conditions, for others
it is looking past the drug dealing, lack of basic community securities,
etc. The Hill is home at the heart for many people. Granted I could
buy a home in many other parts of the city and suburbs if I so choose,
but I don't.

"It's crazy and ridiculous to some. The teach-ins [held in 1998]
added greater understanding of the depth of Diss-placement. Diss-
placement is about many things. For sure it is about 'dissing' the people. The people often times with no voices or power to stop the 'plan.'
Pittsburgh is by no means unique in this movement, but it is a part of
a similarity that so many communities are and have been faced with.
Diss-placement is about many things. But clearly it is about $$$$,
power, control, exploitation and oppression of a group of people who
often have no real voice.

"There are pockets of people who organize, but what really does
the organizing bring about? Too often the organizing comes too little
too late. There is not a week that goes by that I don't hear conversations about people wanting to stay, even in the daily midst of violence,
neglect and despair. They are willing to stay, wanting to stay but wondering if they will be able to stay because of the rapid housing development. So Diss-placement continues without real regard to the total
lives of the people. Perhaps an organized movement with some power
will arise that can help other communities avoid the pitfalls that other
Diss-placed neighborhoods and communities have succumbed to.

"There are so many ramifications related to it. I lived in Homewood from 1966 to 72 or 3 and it never felt like home. I made many wonderful friends, was deeply involved in the community but it was not home. My mom felt the same way and she longed for the Hill, really longed. She and a number of others of her generation felt hurt by the upheaval. I could go on . . ."

I have met many people in the cities I visited who remained committed to the old neighborhood in one way or another. Though there are some who stay because they have no way to leave, many are like Tamanika Howze, looking for ways to win the battle.

In Roanoke, for example, Evelyn Bethel and her sister, Helen Davis, formed a committee to establish a Gainsboro historic district. This effort started when Evelyn became aware of a highway connector that was projected to cut through the area.

After speaking with the traffic engineer, she remembered, "I was really astonished and saddened . . . I came down Jefferson Street, rode down Gilmer, up Patton, and back around. I must have driven it for about forty-five minutes. I said, 'That's a shame.' And I remembered incidents and people from my childhood, and I happened to see the steeple and the church of old First Baptist and St. Andrews, and the thought occurred to me that if those two dwellings are historic, and the houses were what held the people that supported those institutions, well, then surely the whole area must be historic. So we decided to pursue that option, and we requested historic designation in three phases."

The efforts of Evelyn Bethel's group were successful in limiting the destruction from the proposed highway, and winning a historic-district designation for the area. These victories helped to ensure some continuity between the past and the future. On a visit in 2001, I was happy to see that a historic-district marker had been erected. But even more impressive to me were the magnificent Christmas decorations that enlivened Evelyn Bethel's and Helen Davis's house. Though much of the surrounding area is still urban prairie, they were declaring victory over despair by focusing on the joy of the season rather than the despair of the past.

In another effort, Dr. Walter Claytor, a member of a prominent Roanoke family of health care professionals, pressed a lawsuit for

Fig. 7.1. Mindy Fullilove. The Claytor Memorial Clinic, destroyed by contagious housing destruction.

compensation for the massive losses sustained by his family. The family's twenty-two-room mansion, a landmark building for African Americans in that period, and their medical clinic were both destroyed by the creeping process of contagious housing destruction (shown in figure 7.1).[1]

In 2003, the courts ruled that his lawsuit had been filed in a timely manner and ordered a board to examine compensation. Though the city promised to appeal the case, it was an important victory. In fact, word of the lawsuit led the Virginia legislature to pass a bill putting a five-year limit on condemnation proceedings. If condemned property had not been taken in that period of time, the condemnation order would have to be lifted. This would prevent a repeat of what the Claytor family had endured: waiting twenty years to learn the fate of their property, while the property slowly lost all its value.

Newark community organizer Rebecca Doggett told us about the role community organizers played in rebuilding the city after the insurrection in 1967. "I think the organizations help, because usually it's the community-based organizations that are there to do what they can. I mean, sometimes, if they're organized enough, they can stave off massive dislocations. Or if they can't stop it, at least they can shape it. And that's what happened around the medical school area. People in the area were able to kind of reshape it and negotiate some terms of their own for dealing with the changes that they were going to have to deal with.

"Most time, if the organizations are neighborhood-based—and the people are leaving—they lose the people. I know there are a few that packed up and left with their folks, largely because most times where people are displaced, they're dispersed. They're not relocated as a village, so to speak. So it makes it hard to keep track of them.

"But some of the old-time organizations in Newark, anyway, stayed with it and just started working with the newcomers. The most immediate reaction that we had back then was to try to come up with an alternative, an alternative that tried to address public policy as well as deal with the immediate needs that people had. And I guess that's always been my focus, trying to develop programs or organize programs that would address people's needs but at the same time would hopefully force the issue on some kind of public policy."

The housing program that she was involved in starting was sponsored by Tri-City Citizens Union for Progress, an organization started by black activists and churchmen from Newark, Jersey City, and Paterson, and dedicated to "the common cause of Black empowerment."

Working at that cutting edge where projects inform policy, Tri-City undertook the rehabilitation of all the houses on a single block in Newark. In their model project, Amity Village, Tri-City was able to demonstrate: 1) the role that housing rehabilitation could play as part of a package of housing programs; 2) the potential for housing cooperatives to be established in poor neighborhoods; and 3) the utility of including a settlement house to provide essential services, including child care, tutoring, and other kinds of support for families that had recently been uprooted. As opposed to urban renewal, which was bent on replacing "blighted" neighborhoods with institutional structures, Tri-City demonstrated a range of techniques for creating and strengthening the "village-within-the-city."[2]

Rebecca Doggett reflected, "I think that what happened in Newark—the fact that people rallied and were able to get a whole new approach to housing evolving out of that crisis—was a real testament to people in Newark, that they had enough grit and staying power to fight that out. And to win and actually see the housing go up. It took a long time, but it's there.

"Now, of course, the medical school takes credit for it!" she added, with a laugh.

That the medical school took a positive role in later years is a remarkable part of the story of what happened in Newark. Stanley Bergen, the second president of the New Jersey College of Medicine and Dentistry—which is now known as the University of Medicine and Dentistry of New Jersey—officially offered an apology to the residents of the Central Ward. Bergen, in a statement without parallel from other white leaders of that period, said, "Although it was intended that the evacuees be compensated for the value of their land and homes, with relocation costs included, the fact that the community had been neglected in these significant policy decisions—decisions that affected their domiciles and their livelihoods—represented a serious breach of trust by both the mayor and the negotiators representing the state of New Jersey. The community read the actions as a gross lack of sensitivity concerning human rights and control over individual destiny."

This respect for the community as an independent entity, capable of self-determination, was the basis for an institutional policy of partnership. From Rebecca Doggett's perspective, "[The medical school] really has been a real force in the local community there. They're not just the medical school and the main hospital in Newark. They do a lot of community-based work. They do a lot of outreach. Their building is used a lot for community meetings and sessions and so forth. So I think that that whole crisis has really changed the way they might have worked in a community like Newark. It's really not an isolated fortress. It really has become an institution of the community . . . It came from a hard lesson back then, but it has stuck and it's still paying off, in terms of how those universities expand, what kinds of projects they get involved with . . .

"So I think a lot of that came out of those early fights in the sixties and seventies when the institutions were sensitized to their responsibility in a local community. Even though it didn't start out that way, but I think it's ended up that way. And people who grew up in

Newark in those days still have real fondness for Newark. Even people who weren't in the Central Ward, people from other parts of Newark, still talk about those days, when they lived in neighborhoods and really knew their neighbors and had friends and people kind of looked out for each other and so forth."

"And they talk about it in a way that it doesn't exist today," commented Jennifer Stevens Madoff, the interviewer.

"Right. They're talking about something that doesn't exist anymore," Rebecca Doggett agreed.

Struggle in the Hill District

The Lower Hill was bulldozed in the late 1950s as part of Pittsburgh's urban renewal effort.

The neighborhood was replaced by the civic arena, which was designed with a retractable roof so that the fans of light opera might appreciate it out-of-doors. Sadly for the light opera crowd, the retractable roof was plagued by wind. Eventually, the civic arena became the home of the Pittsburgh Penguins, the local professional hockey team. A large area of land surrounding the arena was also cleared but never developed. All of these developments—turning over the land for uses important to white people, creating a buffer to downtown, and destroying people's homes, then letting the land lie fallow—contributed to alienation between the African American community and the larger city.

The residents were dispersed to other parts of the Hill, either to private housing or to public housing projects, as well as to other black communities in Pittsburgh, including East Liberty and Homewood. Richard Saunders, a black photographer who was part of the Pittsburgh Photographic Project, took these two photographs in April 1951, during the demolitions that cleared land for the Bedford Dwellings, one of the housing projects in the Hill.[3] The unhappy woman in figure 7.3 has an expression that mirrors that of the woman being displaced in Paris, captured by Honoré Daumier, nearly one hundred years earlier. The site of the demolition is shown in the second photograph.

Fig. 7.2. Harold Corsini. Audience at Civic Light Opera. June 1950. COURTESY OF THE CARNEGIE MUSEUM OF ART, PITTSBURGH.

Many of the businesses and organizations were unable to move, including the majority of the beer gardens and clubs where jazz was played. I have not found a scholarly treatise on this issue, but I imagine that the leveling of 1,600 African American communities by urban renewal played havoc with the national jazz circuit. Obviously, the clubs in white areas were not affected, but the black clubs and spots—located in urban ghettos—had played a vital role in the music and very few of those venues survived the bulldozer.

The plaintive comment of a Mrs. Borowski, interviewed as part of a study of the West End, a Boston neighborhood bulldozed as part of urban renewal, takes us to the heart of the matter: "It's just like a plant . . . when you tear up its roots, it dies! I didn't die, but I felt kind

Fig. 7.3. Root Shock in Pittsburgh. Compare this set of photographs to those of root shock in Paris (fig. 3.2), and root shock in New York as a result of 9/11 (fig. 8.5).
Upper photo: Richard Saunders. Relocation of a Hill District family. April 1951. COURTESY OF THE PENNSYLVANIA ROOM, CARNEGIE LIBRARY OF PITTSBURGH.

Lower photo: Richard Saunders. Wrecking crew at Bedford Avenue and Morgan Street. April 1951. COURTESY OF THE PENNSYLVANIA ROOM, CARNEGIE LIBRARY OF PITTSBURGH.

of bad. It was home . . ."Then, she continued, offering the best advice she could, "Don't look back, try to go ahead."[4]

Most of the people I met during the course of this project had had the same idea not to look back, but ahead. Sala Udin, in response to my question about how he felt at the time his family was displaced by urban renewal, replied, "Happy. And anxious. Anxious because we were going into an unknown area. Happy because the old conditions of the housing that we lived in were being replaced by new facilities. Sad also that the old, old, *old* friendships that bound people together were being broken. So, it was a bittersweet experience, where you were kind of sad that you were losing old friendships, but at the same time kind of excited about the idea of moving into a new experience and meeting new people. At least that's what I think younger people felt. Older people might not have had that same excitement about the new that younger people had."

Sala Udin's family moved to the Bedford Dwellings housing project, where they had the comforts of adequate heat, hot water, and new appliances, as well as new duties to keep common spaces working for all. The newness was part of a hope for the future that buoyed the community. Yet, in his view, the community, which had been in decline before urban renewal, continued to decline from its substantial economic, social, and political losses. "And at the same time, there were local battles being waged here against racism and segregation, de facto segregation in the City of Pittsburgh, in terms of hiring and business opportunities, segregated public facilities, and there were people here that were taking those challenges on. There were picket lines against department stores that, one, would not hire black people, secondly, would not allow black people to try on clothing, and thirdly, that treated all black people that came into the store as suspects, thieves. So, that kind of battle was being waged by some of the organizations that survived the demolition: the NAACP, the Urban League, with strong support from the churches.

"So, there was a kind of freedom fight going on in the rest of the Hill District, what was left of the Hill District. There was some old lines that had been drawn in the sand at Crawford Street, even to the point where people rented a billboard right there at Crawford and

Centre, and sent a message to the City of Pittsburgh and to the [Urban Redevelopment Authority], 'No more demolition. Build affordable housing.' So, there was a sense of fighting back.

"But also a sense of losing. We weren't winning, we were losing . . . And we had some hope, especially in Dr. King. And when Dr. King, the father of love and nonviolence, became the victim of hate and violence, the bottom fell out of the hope, and whatever was left of any symbols, of white ownership, of enterprise in black communities, got burned. Without regard to the inconvenience that resulted. Without regard to the blight that would be left in the community and the marginalization that would occur because people so feared even entering the community.

"That's hindsight. That's stuff that you know twenty years after it has happened. It's not something you know when you've got that Molotov cocktail in your hand and you're looking at this shoe store that's been owned by these white people, and all these other stores, all up and down Centre Avenue from Kirkpatrick to Crawford Street. The only ones we owned were a couple of bars. And so, that kind of anger just exploded. Just exploded. And, it was like, 'What the hell? Why not. What the hell. Burn this shit down. Burn their shit down. We use it, but we don't own it. Burn it down.' "

At a remove of forty years, Sala Udin had concluded that urban renewal was an accelerant in the inexorable decline the community had experienced during the second half of the twentieth century. Critiquing his own earlier enthusiasm, he pointed out to me, "We didn't know what impact the amputation of the lower half of our body would have on the rest of our body until you look back twenty years later, and the rest of your body is really ill because of that amputation.

"The sense of fragmentation is a new experience that we can now sense, that we didn't sense then. We were all in the same location before. Now we are scattered literally to the four corners of the city, and we are not only politically weak, we are not a political entity. We are also culturally weak. And I think that has something to do with the easiness of hurting each other. How easy it is to hurt each other, because we are not that close anymore. We are not family anymore. You are a stranger. You are from another part of town. And, all of that, I think, contributes to a broken culture, broken values, and a broken psyche, and weakness in this city. And it all resulted from the blowup of the community into different pieces, scattered around the city."

Articulating Displacement

The unceasing organizing efforts, led by community-based organizations, had struggled through the years to find ways to influence policy and rebuild the neighborhood. On top of the destruction of the Lower Hill, an enormous proportion of the housing in the Middle Hill had been lost to contagious housing destruction. Even the Upper Hill, traditionally the wealthiest part of the community, had begun to show signs of wear. These vast changes are captured by comparing photographs from the 1950s with those taken in 2002.

Leaders of the African American community thought that my work on displacement would give them a new leverage point in their struggles. Like Tri-City's effort to articulate a new kind of housing redevelopment, the Hill District leaders wanted to stop housing destruction and to implement community-strengthening policies. I became a partner in that effort, contributing to their organizing efforts my knowledge of displacement and my skills as a public health psychiatrist.

Bob and I first went to Pittsburgh in January 1997 at the invitation of Don Mattison, then dean of the Graduate School of Public Health at the University of Pittsburgh. Having read my paper on displacement—which had just been published in the *American Journal of Psychiatry*[5]—he recognized that the issues raised would be relevant to a Pittsburgh audience uneasy about HOPE VI.

Bob and I spoke to an interested group. The positive response surprised me, as many people in other places had been dubious of my ideas. Della Wimbs, Terri Baltimore, and other Hill District leaders gathered afterward and asked if I would come back to meet with people in the community who were about to experience displacement.

That offer sounded too good to be true, but, in fact, a few months later a large delegation of African American "power" women escorted

Fig. 7.4. Contagious housing destruction. Upper photograph: Russell Lee. Side streets near the 100 block on Kirkpatrick. April 1951. COURTESY OF THE PENNSYLVANIA ROOM, CARNEGIE LIBRARY OF PITTSBURGH. Lower photograph: Mindy Fullilove. Side streets near the 100 block on Kirkpatrick, 2002.

me around on my "community day." I had never had an entourage before, but I thoroughly enjoyed it. Much, much later I realized it was not
so much an entourage as my security detail: Pittsburghers are not exactly the most welcoming of people, but the large group around me
said, "She's family, don't mess." When I realized this, I started to demand
that they go everywhere with me, but by then they just laughed and
said, "It's okay. You know we wouldn't let anything happen to you."

At that time, the Hill District was on the brink of a major intervention to clear "blight": HOPE VI, the federal program designed to
demolish "distressed housing projects."[6] In the Hill District, they were
set to level two major housing projects, Allequippa Terrace and Bedford Dwellings. These housing projects were slated to be replaced by
mixed-income housing in the mode introduced by the New Urbanists, i.e., walkable neighborhoods, houses with a mix of styles linked
by a pattern book, human-size buildings, and strong fronts directed at,
and close to, the street. However, the new housing would not be a
one-for-one replacement of the old projects; former residents would
have to meet eligibility requirements in order to rent or buy in the
new spaces; and new building would follow the demolition of the existing housing. Dispersal of the population seemed inevitable.

The thinking and the process around HOPE VI were identical to
the ideas and processes of urban renewal forty years before. To make
the problems worse, some of the people losing their homes were
those who had first moved to the projects as a result of the destruction of the Lower Hill.

On the day of my visit, I focused my efforts on reframing the
coming displacement. The concept of "distressed community," it
seemed to me, was a concept that blamed the victim. The factors that
went into deciding that a community was "distressed" were really
measures of the quality of management, factors like the proportion of
rents that were paid on time. Renters can only fall behind on payments if management is sloppy.[7] Yet people were to be forced from
their homes because they were a "distressed community." This kind of
stigmatizing label is bad for the psyche. I saw my job as protecting the
emotional health of the residents by asking them to remember and
preserve all the good that had happened in those buildings. Dividing

the audience into small groups, we worked on the task of listing good things that had happened as well as ways people might preserve their memories.

I had, at that point, been studying displacement for some years, but the events I was studying had taken place in the past. Suddenly, I

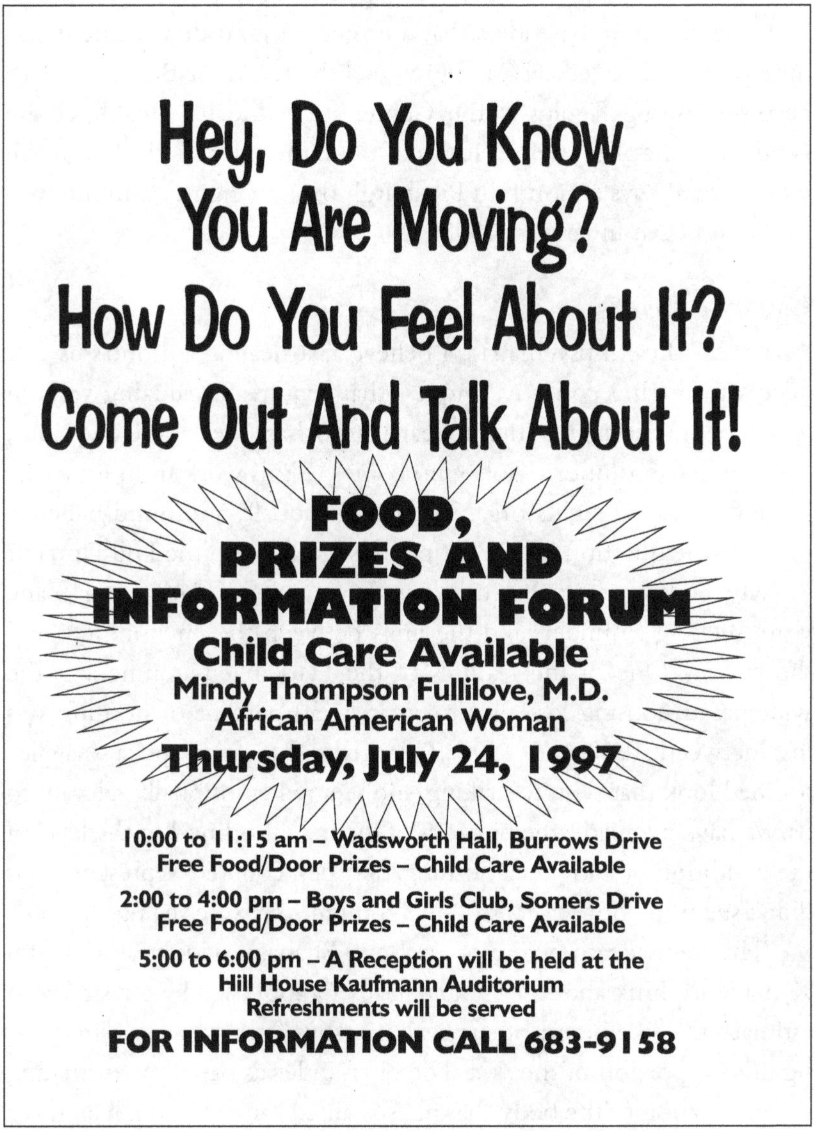

Hey, Do You Know You Are Moving?
How Do You Feel About It?
Come Out And Talk About It!

FOOD, PRIZES AND INFORMATION FORUM

Child Care Available

Mindy Thompson Fullilove, M.D.
African American Woman

Thursday, July 24, 1997

10:00 to 11:15 am – Wadsworth Hall, Burrows Drive
Free Food/Door Prizes – Child Care Available

2:00 to 4:00 pm – Boys and Girls Club, Somers Drive
Free Food/Door Prizes – Child Care Available

5:00 to 6:00 pm – A Reception will be held at the
Hill House Kaufmann Auditorium
Refreshments will be served

FOR INFORMATION CALL 683-9158

Fig. 7.5. Leaflet distributed to residents of Allequippa Terrace and Bedford Dwellings.

was confronted with future displacement, and I wanted to prevent the hurt I knew would follow. My concern was deepened as I met people and visited their neighborhood. I wished that I could return to see what would happen and to be a part of the solution.

My visit made the newspaper.[8] Community leaders were pleased with the impact it had had. Philip Hallen, director of the Maurice Falk Medical Fund, was closely engaged in these events and agreed with the community leaders that a project around displacement was timely. The Falk Medical Fund provided the funds for Bob and me to become visiting faculty at the Center for Minority Health, at the Graduate School of Public Health of the University of Pittsburgh. We spent several days a month in Pittsburgh over an eighteen-month period that began in January 1998.

Creating a Process

As a public health psychiatrist, I believe that healing a group's psyche occurs through a collective process that requires organizing ways in which people come together to learn facts, share ideas, raise questions, and search for solutions. Bob, who comes to this work from his background as a civil rights organizer, has an equally profound belief in process. The question was: What process would help the Hill District?

My research team has conducted research in Harlem for many years, seeking to understand the links between the environment and the person. One of the features of the Harlem environment is the widespread housing loss—approximately 30 percent of housing was lost between 1960 and 1990. This gives the landscape a snaggle-toothed look that is quite striking, and seemed emotionally relevant to us. We have mapped large portions of the neighborhood, at the level of the condition of individual housing, but such concrete representations didn't seem to convey the issues we thought we were seeing.

The tragic death by fire of Dr. Betty Shabazz, widow of Malcolm X, made us think about the "burn index," a tool used by physicians to estimate the likelihood of survival after burns that have destroyed a significant portion of the skin. The burn index is based on estimating the proportion of the body that has sustained burns in which all three layers of the epidermis have been destroyed, or third-degree burns.

People who have sustained third-degree burns on upward of 70 percent of their body are unlikely to survive: infection can easily set in, and bodily fluids rapidly leak out. The organizing mechanism of the skin is dreadfully important to maintaining life.

We reflected that the loss of housing had many similarities to the loss of skin. The movement of noxious influences into a neighborhood and the movement of necessary facilities out of a neighborhood were accelerated by the loss of a house, and the loss of more housing increased the risk that the community would be overwhelmed by bad elements and would fall apart. We called this "the Community Burn Index," and we suggested that the complete demolition, without replacement, of a house should be considered a "third-degree burn." The number of blocks with third-degree burns, divided by the total number of blocks, gives the Community Burn Index.

Prior to our arrival in Pittsburgh, the Community Burn Index was simply a research tool. But, Bob and I wondered, might it help people to think about what was going on? We thought it would, and we thought that, if people had a more precise language for their issues, they would be in a better position in the decision-making process. As it was, there was no real effort to engage people in any discussion of the decisions that were going to change their lives. One example: a survey of residents in one housing project had asked if they wanted their buildings rehabilitated or demolished. Seventy-five percent favored rehabilitation, yet the buildings were going to be demolished.

Through conversations with Terri Baltimore and other Hill District organizers, the idea of a teach-in took shape. I proposed that we use the Community Burn Index as a way of helping people think about the community.[9] At that point, Tamanika Howze shuddered and asked me, "Are you saying my community is dead?"

There was an awful moment of silence. I had to ask myself if that was what I was saying. I had no answer. I knew that the Hill wasn't "dead" in the way a person dies. The Hill is made up of many people and many memories, and certainly the community lived in its remaining residents, and the hearts of its expatriates. But I also knew that the Hill of Henry Belcher's youth was lost to us forever.

Everyone in the room sat quietly.

"Is this idea too upsetting?" I asked, as I was definitely losing my nerve. "We don't have to do this mapping. We don't have to use the Community Burn Index if it feels wrong or overwhelming."

Della Wimbs's firm voice calmed us all. "We had to face the pain when Mindy first talked about displacement [in January 1997]. This is the same pain—facing what we have lost. We can do this, and we must, if we are to create a better future." Everyone agreed. The first teach-in would be on the Community Burn Index.

For me, a very important part of the teach-in was that it became the official beginning of my studies with Michel Cantal-Dupart, a leading French urbanist. Bob and I had made his acquaintance in 1993, at a conference called *"Colloque Triville."* The conference brought together civic and community leaders from London, New York, and Paris to talk about AIDS, homelessness, and addiction. Cantal, in giving the plenary address, made the eye-opening analogy that "Doctors know that one does not treat a boil on the skin without treating the whole body. The same may be said of the city: we cannot resolve the problems of a neighborhood without dealing with the totality of the city."

That statement shifted my thinking from its focus on AIDS as a problem *within* minority communities to AIDS as a problem of cities. I was eager to learn about cities from Cantal, and, when Bob and I were invited to come to Pittsburgh, we asked if he might come as our consultant. Cantal was duly invited to come in late April, coinciding with the first teach-in.

Teach-In #1: The Community Burn Index

On April 18, 1998, our colleagues in Pittsburgh organized the first teach-in. We started the morning at the Dolores Howze Treatment Center, on Wylie Avenue.[10] Prior to the teach-in, Anthony Robins, the postdoctoral fellow working with our project, had put together an enlarged version of the city planning office's block/lot map—that is, the kind of map that shows all the building lots with the outline of the buildings placed on each—for the twelve-block area circumjacent to our meeting place. He had also created clipboards and assignment sheets for five groups. Each group was to go out and survey a set of blocks. The group was to assess each lot on the map and assign it to one of several categories: new, oldie but goodie, wearing out, or severely deteriorated. Vacant lots were inspected for their contents. Groups were encouraged to note other things that they saw along the way. Each group was given a Polaroid camera and took pictures as they circulated. An interesting feature of the groups was that each was composed of a mix of people, some familiar with the Hill but others with little knowledge of the area.

My group set out together, but soon broke into two parts, one enthusiastically engaged with the process, the other straggling behind with a bit of attitude. In the lead of my group was Rebecca Webb, a woman who knew the Hill well. We walked down the first street with no problem, marking all the houses. I noticed that as I was judging the houses, I came to feel like I knew them. I also noticed that the old-timers had to look just as carefully as I did. Knowing the area, in general, often meant that people ceased to see the details.

One very interesting event emerged on our walk, which did reveal something about insider knowledge. There was a street marked on our map, but try as I might, I couldn't figure out where the street was. There was lots of open space between the street we were marking and the general direction of that second street, but there was no street. As we got closer, Rebecca Webb, our leader, showed us that the "street" was a sort of *ruelle,* a little street that was semiclosed and overgrown with grass. As we walked a little ways down the street, she stopped and said, "My aunt used to live here," in a tone of half surprise that made me think it was not something she had thought about in a long time. Writing this four years later I have vivid images of the grass on that *ruelle,* and of a sign for a long-gone street half hidden among some trees.

When the groups had completed their inspection, they returned to the Dolores Howze Treatment Center to work on the second part of the process: transferring the data from the group maps to the large map containing all the sections. I had spent some hours at Pearl Paint on Canal Street in New York concocting an elaborate tape system to indicate the condition of buildings, as well as locations of resources and dangers. As the large map took shape, the strips of tape gave it color and texture.

Everyone gathered together to examine the map. Large blue X's stood out, because many of the buildings that had existed when the base map was made were now gone. People commented on many small observations they had made. Residents of a group of new homes, for example, had not yet planted their lawns, giving a sense of temporariness. Little abandoned streets were found tucked away throughout the area. A working factory was pointed out, in what looked like an abandoned building. Murals decorated buildings, giving charm to the area. Historical buildings, including the New Granada Theater (which is also the Pythian Temple), also gave character and charm. Lots, strewn with garbage and hypodermic needles left by intravenous drug users, posed a danger to the area. In general, the wide-open spaces with neatly shorn grass gave an open-air feeling, at great odds with the urban character of the stores and row houses.

One exchange stands out in my mind. A woman who lived in one of the doomed housing projects—who was one of those who'd been a semiresentful straggler in my group—said, "The developers tell us not to be sentimental about where we live."

I replied, "But of course you should be sentimental about where you live—it's your home!"

A smile crossed her face: it seemed my remark vindicated her own thoughts on the matter. She nodded in assent. It was the most crucial intervention I was to make in all the time I was there.

Cantal, who thought he wouldn't want to say anything at the teach-in, changed his mind and asked to make some remarks. He emphasized that this was a community of working people and that people living in the Hill District worked in other parts of the city. "How did they get there?" he asked. "You must find the paths to the rivers."

The older people present immediately began to explain the connections and pathways, such as the incline—the railroad that went up the side of the cliff—which had connected Cliff Street to the Strip District. Many of those connections, including the incline, had since been lost, cutting off the Hill District from the rest of the city.

The teach-in lasted only a few hours, but in that time, we created an enormous shift in our ability to see and to imagine. I learned something about the difference between interiority and exteriority when it comes to what we see. People who are insiders to a place stop seeing it. It is a handy part of human consciousness that many things—including the scenery we look at every day—slip out of awareness into the vast pool of rote activities and knowledge.

People who are outsiders to a place see it as a landscape. They are inhibited from seeing what they're really seeing, but in their case it's not because it's new. Rather, we have another handy mental device for decoding places we've never been to before and that is stereotyping. On encountering a new landscape, we go through our internal slide show of landscapes we've seen before. When we get to a good match, we say, "*This* is *that*." Much of how we categorize landscapes depends on rather crude cultural cues, such as "deteriorated house" means "nasty." Oddly enough, neither the insider nor the outsider has the foggiest idea what he is looking at.

The mapping exercise forced all of us—insiders and outsiders—to look carefully, not from rote, not from stereotypes, but in the real moment, now and together, jointly decoding what we were seeing. A seemingly abandoned building that is really a working factory—that is only decoded with the help of an insider. The beauty in a vista—that is brought out by an outsider who is still aware enough to be looking in the distance.

This stayed with all of us as we proceeded through the year, informing many of our subsequent steps. At the end of the year, when we produced a scrapbook to document our project, Tamanika Howze, who was initially so shocked by my ideas, wrote in my book, "I look at my community in a new way."

A detailed article in the *Pittsburgh Post-Gazette* gave excellent coverage to our event, and quoted Cantal at length. "Here you have a neighborhood that is very close to the center of town, but has been pushed aside and virtually disappeared. Things are very damaged. But in the few houses that are left, one finds elements of the real history of this community. One can easily imagine redoing their facades. If the old is not cared for, the new will fall victim to the same lack of care and commitment. If nothing happens to rebuild the houses that are there already, will they build walls around these new ones? Even new houses are insecure. If they wish to rebuild this area, they must put something back that will re-create a sense of security. They must include the future, the past and the memories that people have of this place."[11]

An editorial in the *Post-Gazette* commended the mapping exercise for providing correct information for planning a future in which continuity and change were balanced. They noted, "If city officials, who were not involved in conducting the inventory, are wise, they will make use of the results."[12]

Power of Place

We decided that a conference would provide an excellent culmination of our year of work. We planned to have Cantal return and make a major address. I prepared a speech on community-building, using the example of Jane Addams and her work at Hull House.[13] We invited several community storytellers to participate. But the highlight of the conference was a repeat of the Community Burn Index, in which we took all the conference-goers by bus to several areas in the Hill District, where they examined several blocks for the condition of the housing as well as the resources and the dangers. We encouraged all of the teams to talk to community people, as an additional way of having a window onto what was going on. In addition, organizers had informed area residents that visitors were coming and would appreciate the opportunity to talk to them.

This turned out to be a very special event. The conference, called "The Power of Place: To Make a Neighborhood Home," was attended by two hundred people, who were a cross-section of Pittsburgh. We held the conference at the Carnegie Museum of Art in Oakland. The confluence of white and black people in that lovely space was of great importance. In a spirit of togetherness, everyone got on the buses and went off to the Hill.

The trips were full of adventure and interest. One group met a man who'd made a beautiful fish pond for $23. Another group was escorted by a local character, who was informative and entertaining. My group met a man who'd lived in the neighborhood for years, keeping his house and garden in meticulous order, while watching the houses erode on either side.

Cantal might have had the most fun. He was determined to find the incline, which we'd learned about at the first teach-in. He got off the bus and started to run in the direction in which he'd calculated it to be. The rare sight of a white man running *into* the ghetto was startling to all there. I thought it astounding that he went directly to the spot where the incline had been: it was one of many small events that provided empirical proof of Cantal's mastery of the science of cities.

People returned to the Carnegie Museum in great spirits, having, as before, gotten to know the Hill in the pleasant company of strangers. For everyone, this encounter was new, and it opened new insights and promoted concern. A major shift after the conference occurred in the commitment of a number of predominantly white organizations that, as a result of the day, became interested in codeveloping gardening, mural painting, and many other activities with residents of the Hill.

This kind of connection, bringing the Hill and other parts of Pittsburgh together, was underscored by Cantal as the fundamental solution to the problems of the area. He sent a final memo to the members of our project, which included a series of maps, each looking at the Hill in the context of the city. He emphasized the roads that crossed the Hill, and provided access to south and north Pittsburgh, as shown in figure 7.6, top. This provided me with a concrete example of the point I had heard him make in Paris in 1993, that in order to solve the problems of the neighborhood, one had to think in terms of the whole city. The resurrection of the Hill lay, in Cantal's assessment, in the revitalization of the linkages that ensured that the Hill was once again integrated into the fabric of Pittsburgh.

"To make the Hill live again, they must restore the spirit of the inclines. Because in the evening, when people went home from work, they rode the inclines up to their homes. In the morning, when they left for the factories and the mines, they descended via the inclines.

When you see old photographs of the Hill, you understand instantly that the Hill was above the pollution—it's really amazing!" he said to Bob and me, some years later.

The Fight for Home

In 1997, when I first went to meet people in the housing projects, there was no question but that Bedford Dwellings and Allequippa Terrace would be leveled to the ground.

By June 2001, the last bit of Allequippa Terrace had been demolished, and new-style buildings were going up.

By contrast, not a stone of Bedford Dwellings had been disturbed. Prior to the teach-ins, there had been no genuine community participation in planning for the HOPE VI process. Gradually, a group of old-timers—people in Bedford Dwellings who had moved there from the Lower Hill, people who lived in nearby houses, and businesses that were located in the area—began to fight. Those groups, which had battled for years to make the area a decent place to live and raise their children, now faced a new round of displacement.

As the residents began to assert their wishes, the process shifted. A new plan was developed. Houses would be built on sites in the adjacent area. People would move, and then the projects would be demolished. It was a remarkable shift in the power dynamics. From my perspective, as a psychiatrist, it was a shift that made all the difference in the world. Rather than more root shock, people would actually experience a move to better living conditions. Better homes, rather than displacement.

During the same period, Denys Candy, a community organizer who had been a part of the teach-ins and the conference, learned of a new "Riverlife Task Force" that was being started by the city. He went to the Hill District Consensus Group to see if there was interest in getting this river project to include the landlocked Hill. The group agreed, based on their hope that links to the river might increase economic opportunity. The Riverlife Task Force was receptive to the idea, and the "Find the Rivers!" project—drawing inspiration from Cantal's advice at the first teach-in—was started, designed to link the

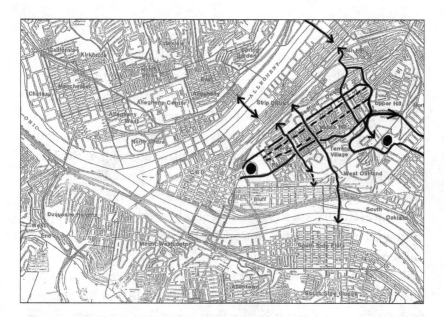

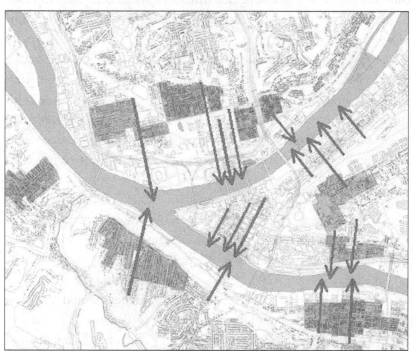

Fig. 7.6. Reconnecting the parts of Pittsburgh. Top map: Michel Cantal-Dupart. Reconnecting the Hill with other parts of Pittsburgh. Michel Cantal-Dupart attached the following comments to this map: "Map 4 embodies the essence of what must be done [to revitalize the Hill]. The geography of the Hill complicates things but already the restitution of the traces of what once existed on these slopes is there in the form of a park which needs only the building of a few foot bridges [*passerelles*] and the creation of a garden. At present this undeveloped space is open to all sorts of mischief [*délinquances*]. Thus I would propose first and foremost a path which would go down Kirkpatrick Road as it is the southward connection to the southside flats." COURTESY OF THE ARTIST. Bottom map: Riverlife Task Force plan for connecting Pittsburgh neighborhoods to the rivers. COURTESY OF RIVERLIFE TASK FORCE/CHAN KRIEGER ASSOCIATES.

Hill to the rivers once again. In 2003, the "Find the Rivers!" report clearly shows the Hill linked to the rivers and the rest of the city.

Cantal, in his speech at the Power of Place Conference, noted that "home" is the center of the world. When people are forced to move, they don't give up the center that they had. Rather, they add another center to it. Tamanika Howze, in her adamant claiming of the Hill as her home, teaches us the same lesson, in another way. David Jenkins's rage at the parking lot that was built over his home—"the place where it 'Hertz' to rent a car"—is yet another effort to explain the enduring connection that is not erased by the bulldozer. Because the link endures, Tamanika Howze, David Jenkins, Evelyn Bethel, and Walter Claytor continue to fight for a world that seems lost to outsiders. One might say they are tilting at windmills, but from time to time they win important battles that ease past and present injuries. These gains are neither trivial nor imaginary. To regain one's roots is an essential task.

I once had the opportunity to walk around northern Manhattan with Erika Svendsen, an urban forester. She pointed out numerous signs that street trees were struggling for life, and all had to do with the state of their roots. "If there's a problem with a tree," she informed me, "look at the roots." Most of the trees were trying to grow from holes much, much smaller than the leafy crown. "The tree just can't get enough water," Erika said. In some cases, the roots were bulging out of the ground, not to show off their beauty, but on the way to death. The bottom line of my urban forestry lesson was that the tree cannot achieve its full height, massive trunk, and glorious crown without a flourishing, healthy root.

In England in the 1700s, it was the custom among the rich to create instant gardens. To fulfill these wishes, gardeners would tear trees out of the ground for reimplantation in the garden-to-be. Capability Brown, a leading gardener of his day, used a particularly brutal method of wrenching trees out of the ground, but not everyone was pleased with the results. According to gardening writer Charles Elliott, "One writer spoke derisively of [Brown's] 'vigorous and short-hand method of tearing trees up by the roots.' Pontey, writing in 1828, is skeptical about the practice of moving full-grown trees, 'as the business is extremely tedious, and hazardous also; and after all, in cases of success, such trees for several years grow so slowly as to remind one of the 'stricken deer.' "[14]

Trees yanked from the ground lose important parts of their root system. The delicate root hairs, which connect the root to the earth, are largely stripped off, as are the tips of the larger and deeper roots. When their delicate roots are injured by such rough treatment, trees struggle to get water and nourishment. They pass through the chancy period of root shock. Like any organism in shock from drastic physiological change, a tree in shock hangs between life and death. Trees need their roots.

People, too, need roots. Human communities, like the tree, cannot produce their "crown" without the massive network of connections that move nourishment from the earth to the entire organism of the group. The evil of urban renewal is that people were stripped of their roots, and forced, without aid, to struggle through the period of shock to replant themselves as best they might.

People, injured by root shock or other traumas, do not give up. The human will to live is an extraordinary force that keeps people going through the worst of times. Will, however, cannot repair all the damage trauma can cause. And so people go forward with the sorrows of their tragedies and joys of their triumphs to make a new life from the good and bad stuff, or as Tamanika Howze put it, "my roots of good and not so good memories."

ERNEST THOMPSON

This short story was written by my father, Ernest Thompson. It describes a meeting with his mythical hero, Homeboy, on John R. Street in Detroit, and their ensuing debate about the best strategy for helping the ghetto. This is a story of time travel, for Homeboy brings wisdom that my father would only have in the future. Therein lies its bitterness and its hope. What is so important to the issues I am discussing is Homeboy's urbanism, which saw the ghetto in the context of the city, and which embraced the street as the best site for debating the future. As the crowd says, "Man, that big cat's bad!" In the description of Homeboy, you will hear bits of many black heroes of the day, prominent among them Paul Robeson, who had befriended my father from the time he first moved north.

As for me, this story held a revelation. I realized, one day, that my father had not invented the dazzle of John R. Street, he had lived it. But I couldn't experience it, as the John R. Street he knew, like so much else, was long gone.

"Homeboy Talks to Train in Detroit"

By Ernest Thompson

I shall never forget the night I ran into Homeboy in Detroit. It was a summer evening in 1951. I had just come to town on the antidiscrimination work I was doing for the union and to prepare for a convention. As soon as I checked in at my hotel, I gave in to the air of expectancy that had seized me as soon as I landed at the airport. I started down John R. Street with my dreams of black progress running through my head. As I passed the hospital, the nurses in their blue and white uniforms seemed to be on the same cloud with me. I soon found myself standing in front of The Flame, and I heard a familiar voice calling, "Train, Big Train!"

I turned and saw the bright lights of the nightclub playing on the features of Homeboy. As Homeboy greeted me, he seemed even warmer and more magnetic than ever. I had known him for a number of years. I was lucky. When I first came from down home as a teenager, Homeboy took a liking to me. He knew, without my telling him, of my boyish resentment against Jim Crow. He spent many hours teaching me, a farmboy, about how the white man had brought us to the cities as a source of cheap labor beginning with World War I, and hemmed us into black ghettos which Homeboy said were forged around black urban dwellers like a ring of steel.

After I'd been up here a while, he told me, "Man, never forget that your hope and your source of strength lie with your people here in the black ghetto. Don't try to run as some of the uppity Negroes are doing. One day, when this ghetto grows strong, as black men and women wake up to their vast potential in the very ghettos that they are now hemmed into, you'll be glad you stayed. For on that day, we'll be ready to break the back of Jim Crow."

Thus, it was natural for me to believe with those who said, "Homeboy is more than a natural man. He is the symbol and the legend of the bond between men and women in the black ghettos everywhere." He became to me and others who knew him what John Henry was to earlier generations of black men and women who helped build our great country with their hands and skills.

Homeboy saw how tense I was. "We haven't relaxed together since before you started running around with the unions. Let's go into The Flame, I hear Willie Bryant's playing."

We went in, and were able to get a table. Seated around us were some whites who had come to the ghetto to enjoy the best in music and entertainment. Joe Louis entered with a party and was seated at the bar. But the glamour of our surroundings barely touched me. What struck me as a miracle was here I was with Homeboy.

Homeboy said, "Man, I got some serious talking to do. I hear you are coming here to help organize a convention of Negro labor."

"That's true, but how'd you find out?"

"Pay that no mind. It is not important how I found out, but it is important to talk to you about my favorite topic, the black ghetto. That's why I was waiting to see you, Train."

After the show we walked out into the summer night. Homeboy must have liked the atmosphere of the crowds on the street, because he insisted we stand around. "Train," he said, "you seem convinced it's time to pool the experience of Negro workers in the cause of equality. I hate to tell you this, man, but if you do not base your efforts on the ghetto, you will lose."

"Why you say that, Homeboy?"

"Train, is it true that you base your hopes of winning the struggles of black labor on the unions and the full support of the Left?"

"Yes, what's wrong with that? This is the missing ingredient the cause needs, because, as you can see, nothing's happening."

"That missing ingredient you're talking about sure would be great *if* you were gonna get it. Just think of it, black labor hitting hard, backed by organized labor, with all-out support from the Left—old Homeboy would be happier than you for better days for the ghetto could not be far off. But your ingredient will not be put together. You're on Cloud 79, Train. Let me tell you again, man, if black labor does not embrace the black ghetto like a mother her child, your hopes will be shattered. There ain't gonna be no days when the big white labor leaders will sit by and let you draw organized Negro labor into a powerful force. They do not want Negro labor organized: they would demand too much. You wait and see. They will overpower you before your objectives are announced. The idea alone is too much for them. By the same token, Train, the Left doesn't care to see Negro labor seriously organized. They'll throw you some curve balls, man, that ol' Satch Paige never even heard of. Train, the Left might even go after you."

Homeboy's last remarks shocked me and I protested. "Homeboy, wait a minute."

By this time, a crowd was listening to our discussion. A bystander remarked, "These cats are bad, the cool cat's got him."

I looked at Homeboy, and was about to suggest that we carry our discussion elsewhere. But he seemed pleased that the gathering was there to hear us talk about the ghetto on one of its main stems. "Homeboy, our way is the only way open at present to start a much needed push. The fight for full equality of the ghetto is in the hands of middle-class intellectuals, and political and economic control is in the hands of the white man who is reaping the harvest. Negro labor has won its leadership spurs in the eyes of the ghetto and you and I know that the black middle-class is unwilling as yet to make the push. The professions are eating high on the hog. A few more white-collar jobs have trickled down. They ain't thinking about challenging the man for economic control of the ghetto. It's up to us, black labor, to start the ball rolling. Answer that, Homeboy!"

The crowd was yelling approval, and I thought I had Homeboy cornered with my arguments, so I added quickly before he could answer, "Furthermore, I see no reason why the unions and the Left will not be compelled to support the justice of our cause."

Homeboy shot back at me, "There's a lot you don't see, Train. That's why I'm digging you on the specific point of a ghetto-base, rather than a union-base. That's the only true base for black labor, if it wants to make the push and stay in the fight. Man, let me hip you. You and others have glamorized your new opportunities in unions. What you have done, and what you can get the unions to do has been blown all out of proportion. I told you you was up on Cloud 79. The day you tell me or other people that black labor can base itself on the unions and not the ghetto, you will be blowing smoke on Cloud 79. You ain't no different from Zachariah, Train. Come down from there, man, come down now."

I tried to get in a word as silence fell over the crowd. But Homeboy continued to pour it on. "Let me take you a little further. One day, messin' around Ford Local 600 in Dearborn, I peeped in and there sits Bill Hood, sittin' at his desk with great dignity and pomp. And that cat could do justice to that dignified performance when he wanted to. When he left that office, though, he could not forget that there lived not one black man, woman, or child in Dearborn. When he got to Detroit, he was reminded that there was not one black woman clerical worker in the Ford administration building. Yet what could he get the union to do about this?

"By the same token, when Hood rolled into Cleveland and New York and Chicago, you cats rolled out the red carpet and said, 'Here's our man Hood! How great can we get?' Wasn't that blowing smoke on a cloud, Train? Dig yourself, Train, if you own up. How many times have you said, 'How great can I get?' Flyin' around the country in planes, arguing with the big whites in the front office, discussin' with the big white union leaders. Train, after twenty years in the foundry, you ought to know better."

I could only say, "Homeboy, you scored."

The crowd roared approval, as Homeboy affectionately put his arm around my shoulder and said, "I got a few more things on my mind. Let's talk about it over some ribs."

As we walked down John R., the crowd that had gathered was still expressing approval of Homeboy for championing the cause of the ghetto. I heard one man say as we passed, "Man, that big cat's bad, ain't he? He's rough, that cat's with us."

Homeboy and I went to a little place on John R. for our ribs. While we waited, we listened to some numbers on the jukebox, the last one a blues by Dinah Washington. Homeboy smiled. "That was in memory of when I first ran across you. Train, there's one thing I want you to keep in mind, that's what I said tonight. You will surely see it down the road. If you forget it, you will fail. But if you can continue to hold on, and not lose sight of the ghetto, you will be a real part of the greatest battle of our times: the all-out struggle for justice, dignity, and equality."

As we parted, dawn was breaking on John R.

Chapter 8

HUMAN RIGHTS IN THE CITY

When all the fancy rhetoric about "blight" is stripped away, American urban renewal was a response to the question, "The poor are always with us, but do we have to see them every day?" The problem the planners tackled was not how to undo poverty, but how to hide the poor. Urban renewal was designed to segment the city so that barriers of highways and monumental buildings protected the rich from the sight of the poor, and enclosed the wealthy center away from the poor margin.[1] New York is the American city that best exemplifies this transformation. Tourists on Forty-second Street now find much to admire. The skyscraper beauty of New York, its remarkable diversity, and its astounding pace fill the casual visitor with awe. "This is beauty," he concludes.

Even five years ago, visitors to Forty-second Street might have stumbled into homeless people. But poverty and early death are now an ugly secret of the City of Canyons. Forty-second Street is rolling in Disney, while the poor in the South Bronx or East New York suffer from the nation's highest rates of AIDS, violence, incarceration, and other life-threatening conditions. Weak and vulnerable, the poor neighborhoods, cut up by disinvestment, lie in shreds, ruined and un-safe habitats for human beings. The poverty margins remain the city's bank: after 9/11, cuts in services to those areas were the first sources of revenue to repair the beauty of downtown Manhattan.

While it is meant to appear that the two worlds are completely disconnected—one prospering, the other sinking—the highways and monumental buildings are an illusory protection. The virulent AIDS epidemic in the South Bronx translates into the suburbs of New York having the nation's highest *suburban* rates of AIDS.[2] The destruction at the margins echoes back to the center, threatening its existence in a most fundamental manner.

The ecological reality of connection leads me to pose the follow-ing questions: Is Forty-second Street beautiful if Willis Avenue in the South Bronx is not? Is Forty-second Street beautiful if its beauty was paid for by the destruction of people's homes? Is Forty-second Street beautiful if homeless people are chased from the area?

Indeed, what do we consider beautiful?

In assessing how urban renewal reorganized American cities, we have many frameworks available to us. Certainly a human rights framework would lead us to conclude, without equivocation, that sys-tems that house the rich in splendor at the cost of putting the poor in squalor are unjust systems. Ecological frameworks, which would ex-amine the environmental costs of the premature destruction of vast areas of urban habitat, would lead us to answer, just as firmly, that these processes are unjustified. But somehow, we judge beauty by standards that have nothing to do with equity or sustainability. People can un-derstand the science of ecology, yet choose as their family car a gas-guzzling small truck they consider "beautiful."

Aesthetics of Equity

The effort to link beauty and justice is the life's work of Michel Can-tal-Dupart. I first had the chance to work with him while Bob and I were visiting professors in Pittsburgh. His work is unique in bringing ecology and human rights together with the classical French tradition of beautiful cities. Cantal defies the dominant practice of hiding poor people in areas of squalor. His practice is devoted to planting equity in a breathtaking landscape. He works from the radical thesis that beauty, if shared, can end poverty and injustice. Over some years of studying his work—including many trips to France to visit his projects—I have deciphered what I've come to call the "aesthetics of equity" in the manner in which he assembles ecology, human rights, and beauty into the spaces and places of the city.[3]

Principle One: Respect the Common Life the Way You Would an Individual Life

The first thesis of this aesthetic acknowledges that a precious resource is created any time people live together in a place. Though he is a master of the creation of design—hence able to assess an object on its merits—Cantal looks first for function. Walking down a street in Harlem, I pointed out the neighborhood's disarray, but he pointed to a red balloon left over from a child's birthday party. "Look," he instructed, "at the ways in which people are using the space."

In learning a new neighborhood, he searches for the net of human relationships, which he views as a sacred entity, the Higher Power that is helping each and every person survive and thrive. He is not thrown off by a sidewalk ballet that diverges from Jane Jacobs's tidy Hudson Street. He can find the thread in a prison or a resort, and he appreciates one as much as the other. "In making their cities and their lives better, people start with what they have," he emphasizes, and hence values all human relationships.

Principle Two: Treasure the Buildings History Has Given Us

Just as his work starts with an appreciation for the networks people have created, so too he starts with a deep respect for the historical processes that have led to the set of buildings existing in a particular place. Cantal searches for the history and culture of a location, absorbing the ways in which people expressed their common life through architectural forms and city spaces. In our walks around cities, I have noted that he searches constantly for words to convey what he sees. "Empty" and "full"—the English words—became quite important as we sought language to compare an old bastide we had visited with a Paris suburb cut by highways in the modern fashion.

Bastides were an early form of free city, built during the Middle Ages. The bastides were built at the boundary of land whose ownership was contested by England. Places in that danger zone were offered to house people who were landless because they had been excommunicated or were for other reasons seeking freedom. The form of the bastide was democratic. The houses were tightly linked together around a central square, with farmland extending from the backs of houses outward. Among the bastides I have visited, the square form of Armagnac stands out, simple and beautiful. The center of Armagnac is an arcade around a central square. From anywhere in the square, all is visible, all is approachable.

Long ago, an architects' myth tells us, people lived in caves. One day, lightning struck and caused a big fire to burn. The people were drawn from their caves. As they drew close to the fire, the warmth enchanted them. They decided to keep the fire going and to build houses to stay close to it. As they built, they watched each other, and they developed language so that they could talk about that which they were creating.[4] And thus, the first house was built as part of the first city, and that first city was a bastide.

Cantal and I are like those first builders, inventing a language for cities. "The bastide of Armagnac," Cantal tells me, "is full." He draws a schematic of the place from the official city map. The plan's dark spaces make manifest the occupation of space, an arrangement of forms that has survived hundreds of years because it is so effective in providing a spatial foundation for human community. It is equitable, sociable, appealing, and approachable: all attributes that lead to stability.

Cantal talked with great excitement about Bagnolet. When we arrived, I thought there had been a mistake; perhaps we had fallen into a black hole that had taken us instantaneously from Paris to New Jersey. I thought France didn't have cities that could rival Route 1. Especially by comparison with the bastide of Armagnac, Bagnolet was overwhelmingly complex, with multiple levels of roadway passing overhead like some future city squatting on the remaining echoes of a charming past.

On our first visit, we parked on the street and, fighting the wind, crossed an overpass to a shopping center decorated in shiny plastic. We wound our way through crowds of shoppers to emerge, one level down, on a deserted street, surrounded by hotels. Wind at our backs, we pushed forward, suddenly leaving the wide section of the main street for its narrow continuation in an older, once beautiful piece of

Fig. 8.1. Urban space, full and empty. Upper photograph: Mindy Fullilove. The central square at the bastide of Armagnac, All Saints' Day, 1998. Lower photograph: Mindy Fullilove. Between two squares in Bagnolet. July 2002.

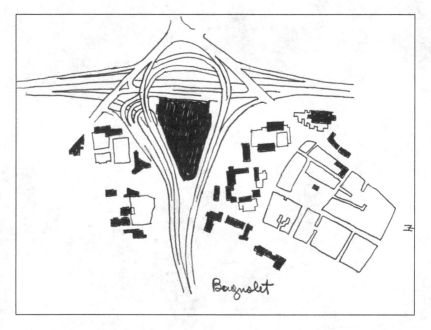

Fig. 8.2. The organization of the city, full and empty. Upper drawing: Michel Cantal-Dupart. The fullness of the bastide of Armagnac. Lower drawing: Michel Cantal-Dupart. The emptiness of Bagnolet. COURTESY OF THE ARTIST.

France. Maps flapping in the wind, Cantal paused to say to Sybile, his assistant, Bob, and me, "It is so simple. We just have to make the connection stronger between that part of the street and this. Then the two centers of the town will be joined."

I looked around at the boarded-up shops, and an empty, lifeless plaza, and I couldn't see it. It was not the first time that Cantal and I have been tuned in to different realities on a single street. But I don't think I had ever felt so helpless or so hopeless about the future of a place as I did at that moment in Bagnolet.

"No," I thought to myself. "You are *crazy*, Cantal. This place is ruined, like New Jersey, just cut to pieces by highways, littered by the ugliest versions of modern buildings imaginable, and scarred by the abandonment of its history and its charm. *This* is hopeless. Everybody had just better move out."

Listening to myself, I realized, "I'm starting to sound like an American planner."

The goal of the evening was to attend a meeting in which residents of Bagnolet would talk about the city with Cantal. The meeting was to be held in a little trailer, which deepened my conviction that I had reached the end of the line and there was no hope there. Forget a "there."

My skepticism was overcome, however, by the people who eagerly crowded into the trailer to talk about their city. My "What?" was squashed by their love and connection. They knew what I didn't know: that this was a real place with a real history. People had done things there that mattered. They were radicals, trying to make a place that was ahead of its time. A book of old picture postcards was perhaps most revealing. Their pictures included a proud shot from the 1930s of the Socialist youth group, trying to help children become citizens of a better tomorrow for all people. I learned that their town square was named for Salvador Allende, the democratic leader of Chile, deposed by a military coup supported by the CIA. It mattered that the town become strong again, because it was a town that mattered. Simple as that. It was in the faces of the people in the room, the open, confident faces of these people of all ages.

I went back to Bagnolet in September 2002, and walked around again, this time better able to grasp the form that Cantal had talked about, the modern square around the Métro station, and, just a few hundred yards away, a second, older square in front of city hall. That the square was filled with a flea market to one side and the weekly farmers' market to the other helped me understand why people loved the place. Lunch at one house, coffee at a bar, and more coffee at another house hammered the concept home.

Imagine that there is a start of a town, a bastide, perhaps, built around a square. Then some layers are added, and, after a while, someone gets the idea to have another square. This goes on in all directions until there is a jumble of squares that may or may not relate to one another. What is to be done?

The solution to the "many centers" problem lies in improving the connections among them. The passerby must be able to figure out how to move among the jumble of squares. We need images that compel transition, promote flow, and permit movement from one place to another. We need a permeable city, safe not because of its walls, but because of the engagement of its citizens, each and every one a guardian of the public piece/peace.

What is so important about Bagnolet is that Bagnolet is the present of nearly every American city of any size. We struggle to make meaning in the midst of "empty." When Cantal drew "empty," it was in stark contrast with "full." Yet, despite the fundamental unattractiveness of the twisted, weird landscape of Bagnolet, Cantal's interventions start with what is there: the highways, the two squares, the committed people.

Principle Three: Break the Cycle of Disinvestment

The third thesis I have identified is that the urbanist must break the cycle of disinvestment. In America, we have come to use the expression "broken windows" to refer to the process of downward decay and disinvestment that ensues when a broken window is not fixed.[5] The neglected window serves as a green light for undesirable activities, which are more costly than fixing the window would have been. These activities, in turn, lead to further destruction. In the end, the place is stripped of its capacity to support life and becomes "dead," as brown fields or toxic waste zones are dead: they can live again, but the costs will be quite high.

The decline of Gainsboro in Roanoke is an excellent example. Disinvestment was initiated by the city's identifying the area for urban renewal. Thinking their homes would soon be condemned, people stopped fixing them. Because of lack of care, the homes became more vulnerable to destructive forces, like wind, water, and fire. As one or two homes were destroyed, the others became more vulnerable. Gradually, the neighborhood was eaten away, losing almost all of the enormous value it once had. This process of decline can start at any weak point in a city's armor. The urbanist's job is to find and repair the weak link so that the city can flourish again.

Cantal has identified a long list of processes that are analogous to broken windows, and he has an even longer list of interventions to counter the effects of each. When rowdies took over the one bench in a roadside park, other people stopped coming. Cantal installed twelve benches, on the theory that twelve benches would give each group of park users—rowdies, mothers, old people—a bench to call their own. This simple strategy revitalized the park and the surrounding area. When a small village was losing trade on its main street, Cantal proposed that they add a set of back streets, adding backbone, one might say. In that case, the intervention was not made, and the decline continued.

Principle Four: Ensure Freedom of Movement

The fourth thesis is that the urbanist must ensure the freedom of movement. Movement, as was demonstrated in the story of the Hill District prior to urban renewal, is the sine qua non of urban community. Without movement there can be no interrelationship. But movement is itself dependent on having an object: people move toward something. We see this most spectacularly in watching toddlers who work very hard to get to the next flower, and then stop and study it with an intensity we adults have all but forgotten. While trying to get my granddaughter to the zoo to see amazing things, I realized that the ants she was stopping to examine were just as astounding. Whether zoo or anthill, we are drawn forward, into the world, by the next great thing that we see.[6]

In the French tradition, the understanding of the role of perspective in the creation of landscape dates back to the work of André Le Nôtre. One Sunday in July 2000, while Bob and I were spending the

summer in Paris, Cantal called to say he was going to take us somewhere. On the way, he told us the story of Fouquet, treasurer for King
Louis XIV, who decided to build himself the most wonderful house
in France. He hired all the best people to help with this, including the
best landscape architect, André Le Nôtre. When the house and its gardens were ready, Fouquet gave a fabulous party to which he invited
the king.

The king looked around at the party and was furious that his treasurer had a better house than he did. He sent D'Artagnan and the
musketeers to arrest Fouquet. Then he confiscated Fouquet's money
and land, and hired all his people to design Versailles. Though much
grander, Versailles is rated by many—Cantal said—as inferior to what
Fouquet had created at Vaux-le-Vicomte. It was that original work of
André Le Nôtre that we were on our way to see.

Cantal emphasized that André Le Nôtre had mastered perspective. He had been trained in and had an incredible enthusiasm for geography, and used angles and lines to set everything in relation to
everything else. At Vaux-le-Vicomte, stables flank the entrance on
both sides, and a central path leads up to the château, which is surrounded by a moat. Circling to the back of the house, the garden
stretches before the visitor to a far point on the horizon.

This is not a garden concerned with flowers, and there are not
even very many plants. It is, rather, a garden that makes pleasure from
forms. It may help to give a few examples. As I pointed out, the stables for the château were placed at some distance from the house, on
either side. Yet as one proceeded down the major axis away from the
house, the stables seemed to become the wings of the house, completely changing its shape. Another marvel: each edge of every path
lined up with an architectural feature on the house—a door or window or another kind of edge. As one traveled through the park, the
exact nature of what one saw shifted dramatically. At different points,
we were in quite secluded spaces, at others in spaces with a clear view
of the windows of the château.

Walking down the central path, one seems to be able to walk directly to the statue of Hercules, placed at the edge of the horizon.
Suddenly, one encounters a theretofore invisible drop of thirty feet to

Fig. 8.3. Perspective in the classic French landscape tradition of André Le Nôtre, as exemplified in the garden at Vaux-le-Vicomte. Upper photograph: Mindy Fullilove. In the garden, looking toward the château. Lower photograph: Mindy Fullilove. In the garden, looking toward the statue of Hercules, on the horizon.

a different level, where a canal crosses at right angles to create the secondary axis of the design. This and other delights abound. Perhaps most marvelous of the pleasures of the garden was the experience of standing in one spot and turning slowly to see how the vista changed at different points in the compass. "One is always in the perspective," Cantal chortled, as we made circles all around the garden.

On the drive back, Cantal demonstrated everyday applications of perspective. Driving down Rue de l'Observatoire, he pointed out the long vista toward the center of Paris. As we drove away from the Odéon Theater, he had us look back to observe the manner in which the buildings on either side of the street appeared to meld with the roof of the theater. And he left us back at our Paris apartment with a book to read: *Portrait d'un homme heureux: André Le Nôtre, 1613–1700.*[7]

Perspective is a fundamental tool of French urbanists, and Cantal believes that its importance cannot be overestimated. Perspective creates both the intimacy of "here" and the wonder of "there." It allows rest and dwelling, but it also encourages exploration and travel. As such, it is the quintessential tool for creating a city that not only houses people but also encourages them to get to know one another. Perspective is, at heart, a democratic tool, because it is a linking tool. Cantal views it as essential to open perspective in many directions: to deepen connections with the past, to raise awareness of the bioregion, to create connections among producers and consumers, to create linkages with peoples near and far. Part of the work of creating perspective is *removing* barriers from the environment. Cantal's comments in Pittsburgh—"You must find the paths to the rivers"—was in this spirit of removing the roadblocks that were locking people into a segregated, and therefore starving, environment. To free movement as much as possible, every place must be connected to every other place. There can be no isolated places.

In sum, I have identified four major propositions for an aesthetics of equity. The first is the appreciation of the resource that is created when people live together in a place. The second is an appreciation of the habitat that has been created over time. The third is that breaking the cycle of disinvestment is essential to preserving and then revitalizing a place. The fourth is that all places must be connected to one another to ensure movement.

On the basis of these principles, Cantal is able to create lasting improvements in cities in France and abroad. His work is fully in line with the principles that animated the work of Haussmann in the 1800s: 1) to bring water and air into the city; 2) to unify all the parts of the city; and 3) to make the city more beautiful. What is striking is that this kind of urban transformation differs so dramatically from the clear-cutting strategies used by American planners during the era of urban renewal.[8]

Putting the Aesthetics of Equity into Practice

Embodying Freedom

Freedom is not simply an idea. As a lived experience, it is one of the emotions most deeply embedded in our bodies. I learned this not from anything Cantal told me, but from years of following him around. He would boldly move across thresholds that caused my feet to stop, allowing the moments or minutes in which I would decide: Might a black woman enter here? In following Cantal, I moved with the freedom of a white man, and this was a very different kind of movement than any I had ever experienced.

Cantal understands the hesitation I have, and his effort in designing environments is to erase the visual signals for the pause. This has at least two components: the signals to keep out and the signals for inferiority. Cantal sketched out for me the basic issue he had faced in designing the grounds for a school for prison guards. The first drawing showed the original proposal for a school enclosed by a wall. Cantal argued that such a design replicated the prison. By forcing the guards to move as prisoners, they would come to embody the hesitations and the fears that containment was meant to convey. They would experience themselves as confined away from the rest of society. In order to undo this reading of their own humiliation, Cantal reasoned, it would be necessary for them to degrade the prisoners in their charge.

Instead, he proposed an open park, organized around a canal that created a major axis between the school building and a distant church on the horizon, paralleling André Le Nôtre's alignment of the château at Vaux-le-Vicomte with the statue of Hercules on the horizon. In Cantal's design, the students were free to move in every direction. The landscape could thus train their bodies to be proud and confident. That stance of liberty would offer them a proud platform for reforming those who had offended society.

On a visit to the school in 2001, Cantal, Bob, and I had a meeting with the director of the school, who told us that the landscape was working as Cantal had predicted. The students were proudly at home, and moved from the school to the city with pleasure and confidence. The canal, home to hundreds of frogs, was a source of endless entertainment.

Equity in the Landscape

At Tarnos, a rapidly growing port town across from Bayonne, I had the opportunity to visit a center for handicapped people that Cantal had designed. I was deeply touched by that place, because I have spent so much of my life in the inferior places we Americans give to the physically and mentally most vulnerable among us. Cantal had designed the center around three villages, each with some unique facilities. The pavement of the center had slight inclines, enough to make travel interesting, but not too much for the residents' wheelchairs.

Most important, the interior of the center connected smoothly

Fig. 8.4. Mindy Fullilove. Perspective, as used by Michel Cantal-Dupart, to organize an open park at the school for prison guards. From the canal, looking toward the main classroom building.

with the sidewalks of the town. Cantal hates visual barriers, and in his design always seeks to extend the line of the place outward toward the horizon. Hence, the paving of the center doesn't stop at its door, but flows across the street and down the sidewalks, opening the horizon to those with limited ability to travel. It becomes one of his extraordinary tools for equity, visually stating, "You are *here*—and that's great—but you may also go *there*, and who knows what wonders you will find?"

While in Tarnos, we also visited a housing project. Although Cantal is fairly viscerally opposed to demolishing functional buildings, he thought that this case was an exception. The project consisted of a series of buildings set at an angle to the street, forming a visual wall. In exploring the site, he had discovered that there was a remarkable forest on the other side, but there was no clue about that pleasant vista from the roadway. Rather, the slabs, placed one after another, had the repulsive air of a poverty project. He had proposed selectively altering the site by eliminating one building, replacing the apartments by adding extra floors on the other buildings, and using the space to create a park that would set the whole in a worthy landscape.

On a return visit to Tarnos in 2001, Cantal took us to see the expensive condominiums closer to the beach. "There is no reason the housing projects couldn't look as good," he insisted. This insistence on beauty, which is an axiom of Cantal's urbanism, derives from his conviction that beauty is an essential element of places that work. Beauty is not simply skin deep, but represents that which is most pleasing, hence most satisfying, to the senses. Who would not choose to linger in the presence of pleasure? As an element of his fight for human rights, Cantal insists that beauty cannot be confined to the places of the rich. Beauty is an essential element, like air or water, and it must—and can—be shared by all. It is not, he contends, more expensive to have good design. He says we make places ugly because we lack technique, or because we hate. In his view, it is as simple as that.

Urbanism Against Terrorism

Urbanism, for Cantal, is the ecology of cities. The study of urbanism enables one to act within the laws of ecosystem and Cantal uses this science in many ways. In 1985, journalist Jean-Paul Kauffmann and several other people were taken hostage in Lebanon. Hostage-taking, in Cantal's view, poses a direct threat to the freedom of movement that is fundamental to urban life. Hence, fighting for the liberation of the hostages was an appropriate task for the urbanist to undertake. Jean-Paul was also his dear, dear friend and Cantal wanted him back.

Immediately on learning of the hostage-taking, Jöelle, wife of Jean-Paul, and Cantal went to see various ministers in the French government. The ministers blandly promised to do what they could. Cantal reasoned he and Jöelle had better act on their own: "We have the science of cities: that will provide our framework."

On that basis, they decided to travel abroad to meet with people in positions of power who might guarantee Jean-Paul's safety and eventual release. As part of this plan, Jöelle and Cantal traveled to Lebanon, where they were able to arrange one important meeting. Though it did not lead to Jean-Paul's immediate liberation, they felt that he would remain alive while they tried other channels.

They also sought to mobilize the French people to keep public pressure on the government. That meant mobilizing the cities. In Paris, every day a celebrity read a statement about freedom on the radio. One Paris broadcast started with the words, "Behind what wall? Behind what wall, hidden from liberty, are our four countrymen, Marcel Carton, Marcel Fontaine, Michel Seurat, my friend Jean-Paul, as well as Alfred Yagodsabeh?

"Is it a damp retaining wall of a narrow cave, poorly lit with little air?

"Is it a garden wall that holds the burning hot sun all day?

"Are they together in a single room or isolated and alone?"

Cantal's urbanism, so full of details, could easily be used to drive home the reality of captivity, mobilizing the listeners with the mundane horrors of possible rooms. In the same vein, Cantal used deep symbols derived from French life to emphasize that the hostages were far from home. On September 22, shortly after the hostages were captured, the wine growers of Bordeaux each brought a bottle of wine to make a *cave* for Jean-Paul, a great lover of that wine. The French public understood that Jean-Paul, held captive in a Muslim country, was not being offered wine with his meals, a concept that is so profoundly horrifying to the French soul, it is painful to even articulate it. Jean-Paul must come home, the creation of the *cave* said to people, so that he can have a drink.

The work of the "Free Jean-Paul Kauffmann" committee was housed on a *peniche,* a river barge that was moored on the Seine by the Pont Neuf. As it happened, Christo, the artist who wraps very large things like the Reichstag in Berlin, had come to Paris to wrap the Pont Neuf in gold cloth. In order to create the perfect spectacle, he asked Cantal to move the *peniche.*

Cantal said no. Cantal understood the symbolic meaning of the barge on the Seine, just as he had understood the symbolic meaning of the *cave* of fine Bordeaux.

Christo got threatening.

Cantal responded in kind, saying, "If you try to make us move the boat, I'll put posters all over Paris saying, 'Free Jean-Paul, Free the Pont Neuf.'"

Christo, who realized Cantal could play the symbols game better than he could, backed off.

The campaign continued without pause, until, on the fourth of May, 1988, the hostages were freed. "I'd love to know how many bottles of champagne were opened between 8 PM and midnight that day!" Cantal wrote.

Viewing this campaign through the lens of the science of cities, it is important to emphasize that, during the campaign, people came to reflect on the fundamental importance of freedom of movement, which is a right associated historically with, and essential for, cities. African Americans in Montgomery mobilized a thirteen-month bus boycott because they understood that if the segregationists could jail Rosa Parks, they could jail anyone. In fighting for her cause, they fought for their own. In fighting for the liberation of Jean-Paul, French citizens fought for their own freedom to travel the globe. They fought in continuity with hundreds of years of work to make cities safe for free people. In the ecology of cities, this is a fundamental protection: the protection of movement.[9]

Finally, every action of the campaign was conceived and carried out with panache. The headquarters was a *peniche* on the Seine. Famous people read texts on the radio. Wine growers created a *cave.* These elegant expressions of the best of the city added to the justness of the effort that certain something, the *je ne sais quoi,* the allure, the etiquette—that is to say, the packaging—that is integral to every aspect of life in France. In his understanding of the nuances of beauty as they are linked to French culture, Cantal has no peer.

Appropriation

The test of Cantal's aesthetics, he asserts, lies not in abstract assessments of attractiveness, but in appropriation: Do people take to heart the places that have been created? His most dramatic story of appropriation is from his work in Tunisia to preserve the ruins of the ancient Roman city of Carthage. On a hot day, sitting in Cantal's garden in the south of France, my husband, Bob, asked him, "What's your favorite project?"

"I think the project I prefer above all is the project to save Carthage, which is a suburb of Tunis, in Tunisia. Imagine that the site of Carthage is quadrilateral. On one side lies the Mediterranean and the oceanfront property, including the palace of the president of Tunisia and the villas of the major ministers—very chic. On the other side, to the north, you find Sidi Bou Saïd, which is a very typical village, very characteristic of the area, and almost mythical in its appearance. It's a village that, by its ambience, its color, and its geography is very dominant and very respected. There are villas there as well, with the sea and the cape in view. Then there are two other sides. To the south, there is La Villette, or, more precisely, the Kram, a rapidly growing industrial suburb, a little city, one might say. On the fourth side, which is the west side, there is a squatter village.

"When I arrived, which was in the 1970s, the rich people to the east wanted to continue to build villas. The people of Sidi Bou Saïd to the north, wanted to grow toward the south. The squatter settlement was horrible and uncontrolled. And, finally, the Kram, too, wanted to grow. So people turned to UNESCO, who turned to me,

to say, 'Come quick and dig out the treasures so we can build.' The
state of archaeology, at the time, just didn't permit one to imagine ex-
cavating the site and then turning it over to the builders. In fact, it's
very moving to be at the site of a city that has disappeared and to see
how it was organized. In the case of Carthage, it was astonishing to see
how—this ruined city—to see its *cardo* and its *decummanus*—its
Roman streets, which were continued into the modern streets where
the ministers lived, in the industrial areas of the Kram, and even into
the squatter settlement.

"For my part, I liked to say that it represented continuity with the
past. This continuity—this reading of the land—was something important. So I decided we wouldn't follow orders to clear the land for
building. Instead, we would make an archaeological park. This was an
idea that had been put forward by archaeologists for a long time, before anybody lived in the area. I wanted to make the park to limit the
encroachment of the surrounding cities.

"I left Tunisia in 1974, that is to say, more than twenty-five years
ago, and therefore the park idea had been put forward about thirty
years ago. Never, never would it have been possible to enact a law that
could protect the site. But something happened there. The people
know that it's a precious ancient site, an archaeological treasure. Little
by little, small shops sprang up around the park that were related to
the site. People learned to make copies of the mosaics, and the oil
lamps, and other kinds of things, and it became a whole enterprise,
selling goods to visitors who drove out to see the site. Additionally, the
archaeologists talked a lot about urbanism, that is, the way that ancient
Carthage had functioned as a city. It's the only site I know of where
urbanism is such an important part of what is talked about at the site.
Among the ancient Roman cities, it might be the only one that is
viewed through this lens of urbanism.

"I was back there this year and I went to see the site. The park was
the same. The villas of the ministers had stopped at the edge of the
park, the city of Sidi Bou Saïd had stopped at the edge of the park,
and even the squatter settlement had stopped at the edge. The people
of all walks of life had appropriated the site. Because of their appro-

priation, it could survive, something that no law could have done. The park survives because it is the will of the people. And that is the greatest test of any intervention an urbanist can make."

Bringing It All Back Home

September 11, 2001, started in the usual way, and then it changed. I was on a bus, going across the George Washington Bridge, when the bus stopped. The bus driver said, "If you're going to the World Trade Center, you can get off now. They've closed it."

Obviously, they didn't close the World Trade Center, so that was ridiculous. I clung to the sense of the ridiculous for several more minutes. Even when the driver announced the bridge was closed, I took it as an unexpected holiday under marvelously blue skies. As that illusion faded, I entered the world of towers falling, towers falling, towers falling, towers falling, endlessly and incomprehensibly.

Everyone watching in New York, and maybe in the world, thought, "What can I do?" In less time than it takes to tell, blood banks were overwhelmed, hospitals were filled with volunteers, and checks were in the mail to the Red Cross and other charities. As I sat thinking what to do, what to do, my thoughts kept circling back to Cantal's story of freeing Jean-Paul. "We have the science of cities," I thought. A weird incantation developed in my head that went like this:

> Science of cities,
> Therefore something urban;
> Something in city space;
> Something everybody can do to help;
> Something that will help people through the first year of mourning.

I mumbled this list to myself, over and over. Meanwhile, I was thinking about what I knew about the obliteration of neighborhoods. The World Trade Center occupied a small site in terms of acres. The urban renewal sites I have described in this book covered many times the sixteen acres of buildings obliterated in downtown New York.

Fig. 8.5. Root shock in New York. Compare this set of photographs to those of root shock in Paris (fig. 3.2) and root shock in Pittsburgh (fig. 7.3). Upper photograph: Rojelio R. Rodriguez. Fireman pausing as dust settles on 9/11.

Lower photograph: Rojelio R. Rodriguez. Fireman looking at the remains of the World Trade Center on 9/11.
COURTESY OF THE ARTIST.

One friend told me that she had flown over the site and been comforted by the small size of the affected area. What she missed, of course, was that the enormous acreage went up into the air. In all, 13,000,000 square feet of office space were lost, the equivalent of all the Class A office space in Miami or Atlanta. A number that helps to get a handle on the magnitude of what was lost: the eight basements of the World Trade Center held as much space as the entire Empire State Building.

That massive vertical neighborhood served as a crossroads for the region and a Main Street for the world. It was a shopping center and gathering place. The buildings could be seen from Bear Mountain in the North to Sandy Hook in the South. They were the first buildings children drew, a major tourist attraction, and the icon for New York. Those big utilitarian blocks were part of the ordinary in the lives of millions of people in the metropolitan region. Whether going there, seeing them, or being affected by work that was done there, all of us in the area were caught in a web of interconnections that had the World Trade Center at its core.

I had learned from Roanoke, Pittsburgh, Philadelphia, and Newark that the obliteration of a neighborhood destroys the matrix that holds people together on particular paths and in specific relationships. Absent the matrix, they cannot find each other in just that way, and in some cases, they cannot find each other at all. I had first heard of this in 1995 when Charles Meadows told me of the aftermath of urban renewal in Roanoke, but the message had been repeated many times in many cities.

Sala Udin, councilman for Pittsburgh's Hill District, captured the enormity of the problem when he told me, "The sense of fragmentation is a new experience that we can now sense, that we didn't sense then. We were all in the same location before. Now we are scattered literally to the four corners of the city, and we are not only politically weak, we are not a political entity. We are also culturally weak. And I think that has something to do with the easiness of hurting each other. How easy it is to hurt each other, because we are not that close anymore. We are not family anymore. You are a stranger. You are from another part of town. And, all of that, I think, contributes to a broken culture, broken values, and a broken psyche, and weakness in this city. And it all resulted from the blowup of the community into different pieces, scattered around the city."

There was no reason to think that the explosion of the World Trade Center would be any less shattering for the web of relationships that its existence had made possible. Furthermore, were a boom of destruction—such as the ones that had radiated out from the sites of urban renewal in Roanoke, Newark, and elsewhere—to echo out from the World Trade Center, it would make a very wide swath through the whole of the metropolitan area. No doubt existed in my mind but that the region was deeply implicated: businesses would leave Lower Manhattan for other parts of the region; grief would take its toll in communities large and small; and competition to avoid costs and reap benefits would sweep the neighborhoods of the region.

The public discourse, however, was not of the regional impact, but of the loss of heroes and innocent victims. Even that very understandable concern was soon perverted to justify a war against terrorism. Absent a workable understanding of the breadth and depth of what had happened, it seemed to me that we were headed for an out-and-out competition to see who would be left with the check when all was said and done.

The breadth of the emotional impact of the disaster was brought home at church, on that first Sunday after the tragedy. I went to church still in a hopeless daze of horror. Like everyone else in America, I was hoping for words of comfort. Our service involved answering the questions, what have you lost? how are you feeling? A microphone made its way around the packed room. Though the minister had announced, "Not everyone need answer," everyone *did* need to answer. The brief testimonials of sixty people were a revelation. I began to see how to measure the impact of 9/11 on the populace. I made rough calculations, based on comparing the congregation with others residing in the area. I took as my assumption that it was a metropolitan problem, because we, ourselves, were situated in Englewood, New Jersey, a comfortable distance from the World Trade Center site. By my estimates, a half million people had direct losses, another million had witnessed the collapse of the buildings, and everyone in the metropolitan area—millions of us—was in a state of shock.

My incantation continued through a restless night.

> Science of cities,
> Therefore something urban;
> Something in city space;
> Something everybody can do to help;
> Something that will help people through the first year of mourning.

I woke up with the idea of a walk for recovery. A walkathon like the March of Dimes or Race for the Cure, but, unlike those walks, not dedicated to a single organization. Rather, this walk would be sponsored by all the organizations in the metropolitan area, each with its own agenda for the recovery that lay ahead. Only Broadway, I concluded, was large enough to heal us all, all at once, and quickly. It was very odd, nearly two years later during the massive August 2003 blackout, to finally see people walking en masse, healing just as I had thought they would.[10] That's a backhanded way of saying I called it right, but it didn't happen exactly the way I wanted.

But other things did happen that demonstrated the power of the aesthetics of equity applied to an urban disaster. Under the umbrella of NYC RECOVERS, a group I helped organize, I worked on projects of all sizes. My favorite was a small project that we nicknamed the Luncheon of Champions. Staff of an American Express unit, Open the Small Business Network, were displaced from their office building by the destruction of the Towers, and wanted to do something to help. They convinced their group to use a portion of its community affairs budget for an event to help a restaurant in Lower Manhattan get back on its feet.

All the downtown businesses that had survived the blast were teetering on the brink of financial disaster because people were afraid to go downtown. So, killing many birds with one stone, the American Express team invited senior citizens from Washington Heights, a neighborhood at the other end of Manhattan, to have lunch with them in a downtown restaurant that was just reopening after a monumental cleanup. This seemed simple enough. The trick, it turned out,

was that the American Express team was English-speaking and the se-
niors were Spanish-speaking. Would it work?

I've never seen anything quite like that day for graciousness. There
wasn't a person on either side who wasn't courteous and hospitable.
In an atmosphere of people wanting to make connection, language
slowly faded and communication started. Then, the cakes were
brought out. The American Express team had baked chocolate cakes
to be decorated with New York City themes. As Stacy Lalin, the lead
organizer of the event, put it, "When those cakes came out, they could
all have been speaking a third language." It was profoundly therapeu-
tic, I found, to work with the people at my table to turn icing into the
South Street Seaport. For a few minutes, we were the makers of New
York, and we knew it was in good hands. Cities are bigger than language, but not bigger than art, I learned that day. Working with the
deep symbols of the city—as Cantal had worked with the deep symbols of France while fighting to free Jean-Paul—was a direct pathway
to hope and inspiration.

As the months went by, I found that the healing potential that lay
in such events was largely untapped, as the city focused on the heroes
and the victims. There is a powerful paper, "The Tragedy of the Commons," published some years ago in the prestigious journal *Science*.
Imagine, the authors ask the reader, that you have access to a commons for grazing cows, and imagine, further, that you would like to
get rich. It would make sense for you to graze many cows on the
commons, would it not?

"Yes," you answer, because of course it would.

But, the authors go on to point out, what makes sense for you also
makes sense for everyone else in the community. So imagine that
everyone has bought as many cows as they could and all grazing them
on the commons. Pretty soon there is no more grass left, the cows die,
and all the villagers are left impoverished.

This, they continue, is not an imaginary scenario, but the way we
live our lives. It explains why the fisheries are collapsing, the soil is depleted, and the grasslands are becoming deserts. This is the tragedy of
the commons. But it is a tragedy that has the markings of fate: we cannot stop ourselves from seeking to be rich, and thus we can't stop the

coming disaster. And the saddest part of tragic fate is that people blind themselves with dreams of immediate wealth, and refuse to see the future pain their greed will cause.

How do you get people to see the "commons" as belonging to all of us? Put into the context of 9/11, what would get people to see that the crisis of downtown was a crisis for all of us? As the dust settled over Manhattan, most people, themselves hoping to be helpful, were saluting the generosity of heroes, ironically acting out the very narrowness that leads to the tragedy of the commons. That heroes are concerned for *others* was somehow lost in that moment when the world turned upside down.

September 11 was not viewed as a tragedy of the region, but rather as an event upending the lives of special people, and taking out a building along the way. The science of cities teaches us that the World Trade Center was not simply a building: it was a central business district of the region and the world. Its obliteration knocked out a marketplace that organized a massive metropolitan area. The reknitting of what had been destroyed required both funds to educate the orphans, and money to make the system of the city make sense again.

In that regard, the largest tragedy, as the reaction to 9/11 unfolded, was that the selection of a beautiful plan for downtown buildings was the focus of attention. Beauty was confined to the narrowest vision of what a replacement skyscraper should look like. Every time the aesthetics of equity were brought up, they were shunted aside. "Not on the agenda" was the routine explanation.

I learned, watching New York cope, that the potential power of the city was beyond my imagination. But I also learned that, without an ecological consciousness founded on an aesthetics of equity, we would not use that power. Instead, we would go on with business as usual, more of the same, "Yes, the poor are always with us, but do we have to see them?"

Chapter 9

OUR PLACE, OUR HOME

One thousand six hundred segments of the African American archipelago nation suffered blows from the federal Housing Act of 1949. Imagine the pain of the Hill District, Gainsboro, and the Central Ward multiplied hundreds of times over. Imagine the loss of all the great streets of Black America: Henry Street in Roanoke, Springfield Avenue in Newark, Wiley Avenue in Pittsburgh, Fillmore Street in San Francisco, Beale Street in Memphis, Oak Street in New Haven, Walnut Street in Louisville, John R. Street in Detroit, Seventh Street in Oakland, the Block on Second Street in Charlotte, and on and on.

Imagine the significance of dispersing the communities that had created the *Pittsburgh Courier* and the *Chicago Defender;* of leveling the neighborhoods that housed jazz clubs too numerous to count; of breaking up coteries of people who had scrimped and saved to build a church where they could worship together, not to mention the costs they incurred when they had to build again.

Such upheaval, with its bizarre resemblance to wide-area bombing, might not have hurt so much had substantial rebuilding—on the order of the Marshall Plan, which rebuilt the cities of Europe after

World War II—followed the bulldozers and created housing, job opportunities, and education for the displaced African Americans.

Absent the appropriate postdisaster remedy, it was in a state of overwhelming injury that black people faced a series of crises: the loss of unskilled jobs, the influx of heroin and other addictive drugs, the slow collapse of the family, and the incursion of AIDS, violence, asthma, and obesity. Each disaster increased the impact of the next, and the spiral of community disintegration began to spin faster and faster, just as the last domino seems to fall much more quickly than the first. The present state of Black America is in no small measure the result of "Negro removal."

The howl of pain that went up with the first bulldozers has grown and deepened, as people began to understand, as Sala Udin did, what it meant to lose the lower half of our body. And this new pain, so different from the pain of slavery and so opposite the exuberance of the jazz era, required its own music and thus gave birth to rap, not simply the politically correct rap intellectuals can endorse, but the most brutal, most foul rap that expresses trauma as no other music ever has.[1] It is so agonized and agonizing that some black leaders wanted to crush it under the treads of bulldozers, not realizing that bulldozers are what called it into being.

What must be heard in these stories of urban renewal—their emotional core—is the howl of amputation, the anguish at calamity unassuaged, the fear of spiraling downward without cessation, and the rage at poverty imposed through repeated dispossession. The archipelago nation writhes in its dismemberment and longs to be whole again.

But, as John Donne told us so many years ago, "No man is an island, entire unto himself." Every person is a part of every other person, the way a peninsula is a part of the mainland. Each loss is a loss to all of us. And therefore, he admonished, "Send not to know for whom the bell tolls: it tolls for thee."

In the peculiar calculus of American racism—witness the Montgomery system of bus segregation—white people must occupy whole parts, like a whole row of bus seats or a whole neighborhood. As soon as any black people enter, the whole is spoiled, and the white people must either eject the black people—arrest Rosa Parks—or move away themselves. After the shame of arresting Rosa Parks became too much to bear, moving away became by far the better option. But what a bitter set of choices is presented in this fight-or-flight scenario, and the suffering imposed by the forced choice is enduring. White people, too, loved their neighborhoods and to this day mourn their lost homes. When they exchanged wonderful urban neighborhoods for cars, malls, and lawns, they abandoned not just the city but also the togetherness and sociability of their heritage. The pubs of the Irish, the street festivals of the Italians, the minyan of the Jews, the monumental buildings of the English: these were artifacts of the city that flourished amid tenements and, let me dare say it, diversity.

This dismemberment of our cities was sponsored by an elite that reorganized the metropolitan regions to maximize their wealth and power. Frank Moore, painter and AIDS activist, pointed out, "You cannot have healthy people in an unhealthy environment, and you can't have a healthy environment where unhealthy—greedy, exploitive—people predominate."[2] How we are diminished as a nation because we permitted the rich to remake the city by sending the poor and the colored away from downtown. Ask not for whom the bell tolls: it tolls for all of us.

But bells call our attention to other facets of life, and not just grief. My friend Sonia Rivera preached a sermon one Sunday about the church bells in her hometown in the Dominican Republic. There, the bells sounded each day to tell the children it was time to stop playing and go home for prayers. They marked the routine of everyday life; they were the spirit of dwelling in that place. The bell carries many messages: it is time for us to listen to it. In particular, I think we need to hear the messages that can stop the downward spiral of community collapse.

Time to Mourn

All that has happened and all that has been lost have yet to be mourned. I was struck, in the months post-9/11, at the hurry our leaders were in to get things "back to normal." With the first of January 2002, *The New York Times* ceased publishing its special section, "A Nation Challenged," and the city was officially off the injured list. It came as a shock to many when, three months later, Easter and Passover brought nearly intolerable pain triggered by being asked to remember just as we were trying so hard to forget.

Psychotherapist Miriam Greenspan says that our culture has "emotion-phobia." One of the ways we act out this phobia is that we want to limit the amount of time people are free to express their emotions, especially the painful emotions, like fear, despair, and grief. "Grief, perhaps the most inevitable of all human emotions, given the unalterable fact of mortality, is seen as an illness if it goes on too long. But how long is too long? My mother, a Holocaust survivor, grieved actively for the first decade of my life. Was this too long a grief for genocide? Time frames for our emotions are nothing if not arbitrary . . ."[3]

Rather than shy away from these emotions, Miriam Greenspan suggests instead that we learn from them. "If you are grieving, do so mindfully. Pay attention to your grief. Stop and listen to it. Befriend it and let it be. The dark emotions are profound spiritual teachers, like the Zen master who whacks you until you develop patience and spiritual discipline."[4]

This mourning is not simply a matter of the mind, but also of the body. The experience of place is encoded in our muscles and our bones: the sunshine on the longest day of summer, the distance to the corner store, the location of the tree with the best horse chestnuts. We moved across these distances in the joy of community, in the net of kindness. These distances exist no longer. In summer, in winter, our bodies remind us of those places no longer there to satisfy our wants and pleasures. It is an odd feeling to come up to the edge of the civic arena in Pittsburgh and watch a friend point to the vast parking lot and say, "My house was right there." It is an even odder feeling to get to the edge of a building from one's own life and find that one's past has been replaced by a hospital or a highway or a high-rise apartment tower.

Grieving mindfully has the power to open us up to new possibilities. Miriam Greenspan writes, "When grief shattered my heart after [my son]'s death, that brought with it an expansion, the beginning of a Self larger than my broken ego. Grieving mindfully—without recourse to suppression, intellectualization or religious dogmatism—made me a happier person than I'd ever been."

Mr. J. A. Reynolds, whom I met in the aftermath of 9/11, was from Pittsburgh and had watched the decline of the Hill District. He and his wife were the first blacks to move into an all-white enclave in northern Manhattan, but they made friends there and raised their son Bruce to be a part of that community. Bruce and a number of his friends died in the collapse of the World Trade Center. When I met Mr. Reynolds, his grief was still quite fresh, but I knew immediately that I was in the presence of a very wise man. And, indeed, as he talked of what he had been through and how he was managing, he made the comment, "You can make something beautiful of your grief."

In that process of making something of our grief, we stop that part of the downward spiral which is propelled by the weight of unshed tears. Former residents of the Hill District grappled with their grief in a number of ways, among them the establishment of a civil rights memorial at Freedom Corner, at the intersection of Centre Avenue and Crawford Street, across from the Church of St. Benedict the Moor. In the 1960s, community activists had erected a billboard there to say to the city and the urban renewal authorities that no more land could be taken from the African American community for urban renewal. That intersection became the starting point for civil rights marches. Carlos Peterson, who had lived in that area and spent so much of his life trying to grasp its transformations, was selected to design the memorial. In his hands, the figure of St. Benedict, drawn from the statue atop the church but given new grace and hope, became the symbol of freedom. At the opening ceremony for memorial, people gathered to celebrate a joyous occasion. The smile of Mrs. Thelma Lovette, matriarch of the Hill, captures the spirit of the day.

Although it may seem an unexpected turn, as groups work with their grief, not only does grief turn into something beautiful, but also it turns into something festive. As people are mindful of what they lost, they remember their pride and happiness. In that mood, people want to express their joy in a convivial setting. In gathering to cele-

Fig. 9.1. Robin Rombach. "At Freedom Corner." Celebration of the opening of the Freedom Corner Civil Rights Memorial Plaza, designed by Carlos Peterson. St. Benedict the Moor, who towers over the Church of St. Benedict the Moor on the opposite corner, is etched in the wall of the memorial. Thelma Lovette, matriarch of the Hill, smiles joyously in the center of the photo. COURTESY OF THE *PITTSBURGH POST-GAZETTE*.

brate the past, the people of the Hill continued a tradition of defiance of the city and organizations that had belittled their community. Thus, grief is assuaged by resistance, expressed through joy. The festival is the ultimate reworking of the grief of root shock.[5]

Time to Heal: Tasks for Black America

Education for the Digital World

In twelve-step fellowship, people who have faced the harms they did during the period of their addiction are encouraged to acknowledge those wrongs and to make amends where possible. There is not, as yet, a twelve-step fellowship for victims, but I do not doubt that when it emerges it will ask victims, after they have articulated what they have suffered, to pick up tasks they dropped as a result of their injuries. In my view, the central unfinished task facing Black America is education for the new world of work.

Prior to urban renewal and other kinds of upheaval that beset African Americans in the 1950s and '60s, the sense and reality of togetherness drove the accomplishment of many tasks, from child care to unionization. The decline in connection meant a disabling of the major mechanism for succeeding at collective goals. At the time of urban renewal African Americans had acknowledged some key goals, prominent among them the fight for civil rights. Any text on African American history examining the period 1950 to 1970 will focus on the civil rights struggles of the era and their accomplishments.

Sadly, the spatial and economic restructuring of American cities left many black people deeper in poverty and further marginalized from the dominant social structure. This structural disconnection has led to many problems, among them: an increase in joblessness, a decline in marriage, an acceleration of out-of-wedlock births, a widening disparity in rates of disease, rising rates of incarceration, and a greater proportion of African Americans living in poverty.

At the heart of the problem was the failure to transform the African American workforce from unskilled to skilled labor. The essential ingredient in this transformation was a higher level of education. Though grade school or high school education had sufficed in the past, the new information economy demanded college, and possibly graduate school, as the prerequisite for stable, remunerative employment.

Earlier in African American history—post-emancipation—education had been identified as one of the group's priorities. At that time, it was crystal clear that the ex-slaves would never be free if they did not know how to read and write. The establishment of schools throughout the South, many with the help of volunteers from the North, made possible a great leap in the levels of literacy of a group that had been actively denied all access to education. Brainard Institute was one such school, established in 1866 in Chester, South Carolina, for the children of newly freed slaves. It was the only school for black children in the country until the 1920s. In 1939, as public education became available and effective, Brainard closed its doors. Vivian Ayers, a resident of New Rochelle, New York, who was a student at the school in her youth, established a fund to create a museum telling the story of the school, and to commemorate the long struggle of black Americans to provide their children with a solid education.[6]

Mother to actress Phylicia Rashad and singer-choreographer Debbie Allen and friend of many rich and powerful people, Vivian Ayers had resources to back her in her preservation campaign. When developers threatened to take over the property in 1998, Phylicia Rashad bought it for her mother. "When you think of things you could give a person, most of those would not mean much to her," she said. "But this meant everything."[7] And, indeed, both as personal memory and collective symbol, the school has enormous importance for a circle of people that extends far beyond Vivian Ayers and her family.

In the epoch of urban renewal, sadly enough, there were no parallels to the achievements of the Brainard Institute. Quite the opposite: the newly dispersed communities were not able to identify the seriousness of the crisis nor to mount an appropriate response. Not only did the communities fail to instill the drive for more education, but also many fell victim to the thinking that "white=education/black=street," which has undermined school achievement among African American youth of all economic classes.

The transition would have been difficult in any event, because the move from country life to city life was still in progress. Writers who observed the early part of the Great Migration in the 1920s commented on the difficulty men and women faced in learning new rhythms of life. In agricultural life, work was seasonal, and time was fluid and forgiving. In the city, work was a daily event, and the time clock reigned. The people arriving from the South in the 1950s and '60s had little chance to be indoctrinated in the world of the factory before that world disappeared and was replaced by white-collar work, which was even more alien and less immediately accessible. As opposed to the transition from Africa to the New World, which was a transition from one set of farms to another, African Americans migrating to the cities post–World War II were faced with an enormous task of self-transformation. Without the upheaval of urban renewal, they might well have stumbled in making the transition, but in the chaos of upheaval and resettlement, the task was left undone.

At the beginning of the twenty-first century, education is more pivotal than ever in deciding children's fate. Those with an education have a chance; those without face prison and/or early death. That said, let us acknowledge that it is difficult to educate children living in unstable conditions. This poses a catch-22: we cannot educate children if we do not get them out of unstable conditions, and we cannot get them out of unstable conditions if we do not educate them. But the uncertainty facing children has its own stability. If the poor are forced to move, they will move to other sections of the city or the nearest suburbs offering affordable housing. They can't move to the rich neighborhoods, because they can't afford it, and they won't move far from friends and family, because they depend on what social networks they have. Thus, the child leaving one school is sure to show up in a predictable and small number of other schools. Therefore, the solution to instability is to create a system of schools that are in the rotation of the poor, such that each has substantial additional resources to support learning, and each resembles the other sufficiently for new children to blend in easily.

What are the resources these schools need? They need to be small, but housed in large buildings that offer plenty of room for activities, family meetings, community learning, and other kinds of gatherings that make the school a center for the neighborhood. They need to have long days, starting at seven and ending at five or six, and long school years, maybe forty weeks a year. Not only does this give parents time to work, it gives the children time to master all that is in the modern curriculum. We must abandon the unworkable assumption that schools will do half the teaching and parents will do the other half via homework and family enrichment activities. Instead, we must give schools the time they need to do the whole job.

Such schools also need to incorporate enormous amounts of emotional work into the curriculum. Children who are living unstable lives have much to process, and if we wish to avoid soul death, we must create the opportunities for them to be with their pain until it eases. These schools need to teach children to welcome newcomers, so that inclusion, and not exclusion, is the norm of group behavior.

These plans are not a state secret: they have been tried in one form or another in schools around the country, and they have been proven to work. Children are born ready to learn: we must put them in schools designed to compensate for the unstable nature of their lives.

Overcoming Fragmentation

I think it is abundantly clear that urban renewal fractured the African American ghetto communities. The dispersed people reconnected by class and by religion and by other tribal markers. But the groups did not reconnect across those lines. At this point, African Americans remain divided into haves and have-nots, religious and criminal, suburban and inner city. We are not one community anymore. To the extent that we all participate in one culture, many of the haves lament the fact that the most popular aspects of the culture are driven by the gangstas in the ghettos, rather than the milder middle-income group. They can't exactly grasp how this happened. Of course, the gangstas still live packed together in a culture-creating tension of poverty and overcrowding, while the more affluent blacks have settled in suburban sprawl that is not nearly so generative of new sounds and new moves. What Henry Belcher described of boys inventing dance moves on the streets of the Hill District does not exist in the genteel surroundings of Montclair, New Jersey, or Stone Mountain, Georgia. The wealth is located in one type of place, but the cultural hot spots are in another. That the former is law-abiding and the latter hedonistic complicates the matter enormously, and raises a profound question: Are African Americans still one people? Does racism still maintain the archipelago, albeit in different form? Or are the walls of Jim Crow falling and fading, permitting a new penetration into the American tossed salad? Would people live together if they could? Would the rich blacks want fancy homes cheek-by-jowl with prostitutes' shacks as in days of yore? Or does it feel more comfortable to park one's Cadillac SUV far from the madding crowd?

In thinking of solutions to these deep divisions, I am deeply influenced by the life and work of Jane Addams, who established the settlement house, Hull House, in Chicago in 1889.[8] What is most profound about her work is that Hull House was not her job but her home. Hull House grew rapidly from one modest house into the premier settlement house in the country, a place well equipped to help immigrants figure out how to make it in America. She and her coworkers adroitly combined a respect for the traditional cultures and crafts that immigrants brought to this country with plenty of access to the new: language classes, dancing classes, cooking classes, whatever seemed like it would help people get a handle on life in the New World.

A part of the Hull House story is that of distinctly different people gathering to help one another. It is that process—getting to know one another—that is the foundation of the community life. It is the essential transaction. If there is no exchange, there is no community. If there is no place for exchange, the community is thwarted in its development. Therefore, neighborhoods need to offer places for exchange. Furthermore—and this is the real genius of Hull House—people from different parts of the city must have the opportunity to meet one another. The women of Hull House learned a great deal by living among the poor immigrants of Chicago. They took these lessons to help make America a better country, serving in the administration of President Franklin Delano Roosevelt, and in many other posts of influence.

Every community—no matter how rich or how poor—needs a Hull House, an institution designed for gathering, where people can learn whatever it is they need to learn in order to go forward into the ever-changing future. We are all immigrants into the future, and we need the help that Hull House has to offer. (Need I say that the remarkable Hull House complex was destroyed by urban renewal?)

Time to Heal: Tasks for Everyone

Creating Neighborhoods in Which to Dwell

In addition to the unfinished work that victims themselves must do, there are tasks that require the participation of each and every American. In David Seamon's model, dwelling is not simply a family in a fine house, but rather a community in a fine place. We can deduce from his logic that we will never experience dwelling—the cycles of seasons and lives—unless we live together for generations in carefully tended places.

Instead, the United States has orchestrated for each of us a lifetime of moves in a country of movers. No one is allowed to dwell. Bulldozers happily eat fifty-year-old buildings—costs amortized thanks to the tax code—and now ready to be replaced for "higher uses." We are sacrificing a major portion of our mental health to chase the carrot of a "better life" at the end of the stick of impermanence, and it is important to understand our neurotic behavior.

The psychology of place is strange and wonderful. Historians who ask people about the near past often comment on what they consider the "utopian" visions people have of places that were poor and draining. "Nostalgia," a term coined in 1688 to describe loss of home as a life-threatening condition, has come to signify a false sense of the goodness of the past. How are we to understand people's insistence on the goodness of the past?

Indeed, the vision of past places is quite different from that of present places, our "here" in terms of both time and space. In the "here and now," we have to wash dishes, clean windows, calm angry children, deal with telemarketers, drive to stores, check email, and on and on. A day is always filled with tasks to do and problems to solve. In the "there and then," the daily recedes and a more holistic picture comes to the mind. If we think of the "there and then" of the past, we speak with the knowledge of the meanings that past had for us. If we think of the "there and then" of the future, we speak from our present longing to be free of burdens we are hard-pressed to manage. Thus, past, present, and future are concerned with different kinds of knowing, and each of these is true and useful and incomplete. When people are able to shift from one part of the picture to another, they typically do so by focusing on different parts. Some parts come into the foreground, while others recede into the background. Figuring out what is important and what is noise is a "figure/ground" problem. At any given moment, we must focus on one of the possible pictures, leaving the others in the background.

Put another way, in getting to work this morning, I need to focus on traffic. I am annoyed by the places where cars can't flow, because I must negotiate safely through those spaces. But in those places where the road is clear, I can drive without paying attention—focusing on other problems that I need to solve. Problem-solving is the essential task of the present, it is what keeps us alive. Those elements of the present that are working are typically relegated to parts of the mind that lie outside of consciousness. In this division of awareness into "need to know"/"don't need to know," we split the present into parts. We remain aware of the dysfunctional, but lose sight of the functional. This is a good strategy for staying alive, but has costs in terms of the holistic awareness of the present. Hence, the grass is greener on the other side, because I am not mowing that grass; public transportation is a better option for getting to work because I am driving; and "if you lived here, you'd be home now" is a fabulous highway advertisement because I am stuck in traffic far from my house.

In thinking of the past, problems fade from the foreground and slip out of consciousness, and the parts that were working take center stage. One is able to learn from the past because one is able to see parts that were not apparent at the time. Sala Udin captured this distinction in his comments about urban renewal, which contrasted the excitement of "then" with the frightening awareness of "now." It is essential to realize the foreground/background problems that we encounter in thinking about place.

Just as Miriam Greenspan argued that we must face grief mindfully, so too we must try to understand place mindfully. It takes an effort to visualize the parts of the present that *are* working, to still the din of problems enough to hear the quiet, fine parts that run smoothly and unconsciously. It is in mindful awareness of place that we will find the reasons to dwell despite the all-American pull of the green grass out there on the frontier.

But true mindfulness does not eliminate the problems of the present. Few of us emerged from the twentieth century with a strong, sustaining neighborhood to call home. We are sprawled away from one another, or packed into poverty. These two ends must be brought closer toward a middle of vital, dense, playful neighborhoods that nourish our souls and our communities.

During the Year of Recovery post-9/11, I participated in a workshop, Imagine New York, designed to elicit the public's ideas for rebuilding the World Trade Center site.[9] Perhaps the most important moment in that session was when the workshop leader said to us, "What do you want for the future?" Though I knew the question was coming, as I was an organizer of the event, I found it was not an easy question to answer. I, like others in my group, needed time to write a list. Then the leader asked for one item from that list. Each of our responses was then written down on master pages at the front of the room. My list contained items like world peace, affordable housing, emotional recovery. How was I to decide what I wanted *most*? One friend, after participating in an Imagine New York session, told me, "Now that I know what I want for the site, I'm going to be really upset if it doesn't go my way!"

Only partially a joke: we each cared about our ideas once they had been formulated and prioritized. It was a profound way to deepen and extend one's commitment to New York by thinking, "What is it I want to see?"

An outcome of the teach-ins that I worked with in Pittsburgh was that Bedford Dwellings tenants went back to the drawing board on the HOPE VI plans. They asked Terri Baltimore and others to help them think through technical issues. And they thought about what they, themselves, wanted. This led to a massive reorganization of the project, both in the process and the content. The tenants, having had a real opportunity to speak their minds, were in a much better position to face the future. Among other changes they made was that new houses would be built first, off site, and people would have the opportunity to move nearby. Then the housing projects would be leveled and replacement housing built there. It was rational, humane, and eminently doable, once everyone had clarified what they needed from the process.

Envisioning the future is essential, if the future is to be what we want.

Greed vs. Sustainability

This book is largely the story of African American dispossession by urban renewal. But African Americans were not the only people af-

fected by urban renewal, nor was urban renewal the only process tearing our cities apart. Highways, planned shrinkage, gentrification, densification, economic restructuring—all are profoundly important
processes that reshape cities. A city is not so much a solid, however
solid it looks, as a fluid, constantly taking new shapes as we clear and
build, clear and build. While many forces change the shape of the city,
the force most likely to lead to disaster is unmitigated greed, while the
concept most likely to save us is that of sustainability. But greedy people, chasing present profit, hate sustainability, which limits present re-
ward in favor of future survival.

As the world concentrates itself in cities, these issues of managing
urban reformation are going to be important for all of us. In 1942, so-
ciologist Pitirim Sorokin pointed out that calamities, such as war, revolution, famine, and pestilence, reshape society all the time. Add urban
renewal in its broadest sense to his list, and consider the following
statement. "The extraordinary migration and mobility attending
major disasters result, as we have seen, in a drastic disruption of social
relationships and social institutions. When the members of a family
are suddenly separated from one another by war or revolution, by
pestilence or famine, the family unit is seriously undermined . . . It is
weakened even more fundamentally and organically by the attitude of
'everyone for himself,' which results in the abandonment of children
by their parents, of wives by their husbands and vice versa . . .

"The same applies to other institutions, such as schools, clubs and
church organizations, business firms, labor unions, and political par-
ties. Like an explosive bomb, a calamity descends upon them and im-
pairs or destroys their unity by scattering their members and
disrupting their functions. Those that survive are profoundly transformed in their membership, constitution, and functions . . .

"For good or ill, calamities are unquestionably the supreme dis-
ruptors and transformers of social organization and institutions."[10]

Pitirim Sorokin did not contend that all the changes wrought by
calamity were bad. In fact, the disruption might lead to great advances
in invention, creativity, and social organization. What he did contend
was that the calamity would lead to change. In a wise society, much
could be done to minimize harm and increase good. In a blundering,

greedy society, actions might aggravate problems and, at their worst, could lead to hundreds of years of distress and the collapse of great civilizations.

It is this point that bears consideration. All calamities will end in time. But the mismanaged calamity will cost thousands, if not millions of lives, and will greatly alter the society that suffered through it. There is quite a difference between letting a calamity run its course, and intervening with what Sorokin called ". . . the best, most efficient and least costly techniques of countering the disaster."[11] To achieve the latter goal, he proposed, "The society must be capable of making new adaptations and inventions to alleviate the [calamity]. In brief, these measures can be and have been carried through only by well integrated societies with a strong system of values and social discipline. These permit the society to remove the necessary cause of [calamity] and to shorten or terminate the ordeal."[12]

In short, we must get to know one another, as Jane Addams got to know her Chicago neighbors, and we must ask one another, "What do you want for the future?" It is only on the platform of this clarity of community that we will be able to manage problems expeditiously, before the problems manage us.

White America has often taken the stance that it is not involved in the crisis of the inner city or the problems of minority citizens. In fact, by ordering the landscape so that the poorest and most vulnerable are hidden out of sight, white America has "invisibilized" (to invent a word) the problems of poverty and racial discrimination. This would seem to work, but, paradoxically, the creation of an apartheid system actually accelerates the spread of calamity, rather than reining it in. If illness simmers in the inner city, invisible to white America, the number of cases will reach levels and will extend over territory unimaginable had the illness been "seen" and managed.

Another example: destroying 400,000 low-income homes but rebuilding only 10,000 created a massive housing deficit at the low end of the scale. Some poor people doubled up and tripled up in order to be able to afford middle-income housing. This meant that middle-income people were left short of housing they needed. Hence, they overspent to move into higher-cost housing, and so on and so on.

Thus, all of us are spending excessive amounts of money for housing as a result of the ripple effects of urban renewal.

Thus, we learn again, at the beginning of the twenty-first century, what our ancestors figured out during the American Revolution: "We can hang together, or we can hang separately."

Time to Act

Pitirim Sorokin reminds us that calamity is both disaster and opportunity. In the aftermath of a calamity, people will be generous in unexpected ways, and they will focus on the problem at hand to a remarkable extent. When the crisis passes, it is true, they will go back about their business, but for the moment, all eyes are focused on the matter at hand. After a year of recovery post-9/11, people in my network could imagine the city of their dreams: it had colors, forms, and styles. That is a remarkable achievement, one that was repeated in many networks around the city. Though we pass through times of calamity, if we hang together, we can use the opportunity to imagine a better future. This is a great lesson to learn.

Ponder this possibility: given a past calamity—unjustly visited on the vulnerable and grossly mismanaged as it went forward—can we find a moment to borrow some focus from the past? Can we use that moment to think about better futures? Can we use the inspiration of that vision to move toward it?

What would happen if our society grappled with the calamity of urban renewal? How might past injustice be remedied? How might the injuries to the city be rectified? How might we create the dwelling places we all long for?

We are somewhere on the dwelling/journey spiral. We have all been forced from home but none of us has yet reached safety. We might choose to continue to proceed in blindness. But we might also recognize that we can use the journey to create the arrival of our dreams, in the community of all of us.

Let us listen to the bell: it tolls for us. It's time to go home.

NOTES

1. The Butterfly in Beijing

1. Prince, *Brooklyn's Dodgers: The Bums, the Borough, and the Best of Baseball.* Prince states, "When Bobby Thompson's home run cleared the high left field wall in the Polo Grounds in 1951, my mother, a normally voluble woman, got up from the sofa, turned the tiny television off, and went into the bedroom . . . She appeared the next day to take up her usual domestic responsibilities. She never said a word about that loss, that season, that home run. Not ever. We took our baseball seriously" (p. xi). Later in the Introduction, he apologizes that the book, published by a distinguished university press, ". . . is serious history, but I'm not sure it's very objective. I just couldn't do it this time" (p. xiii).

2. Grady, "Surgeons Prepare to Separate Conjoined Twins."

3. Bowlby, *Separation.* Bowlby, the theorist who developed the concept of attachment, proposed that there was attachment to place as well as to person, and described the natural environment as a second system of homeostasis. In elaborating on the development of an individual's particular manner of using the environment, he wrote, "Those trained in physiology may find it illuminating to view the behaviour under consideration as homeostatic. Whereas the systems studied by physiologists maintain certain physico-chemical measures, internal of the organism, within certain limits, the systems mediating attachment behaviour and fear behaviour maintain the individual within a defined part of the environment. In the one case the states held steady are interior to the organism, in the other the states held steady concern the relationship of the organism to the environment" (pp. 148–49).

4. A.F.C. Wallace, "Mazeway Disintegration." He notes, "[i]t is proposed that we regard physical objects external to the individual's perceptive apparatus, including natural objects, elements of material culture, and human beings, as constituting a 'maze,' which presents the individual with cues. . . . The individual's behavior in running the maze in order to obtain satisfactions is the learning of a *way* (systems of action-sequences). . . . The perception of the maze itself, or parts of it, and of the way as a reified abstraction, constantly maintains in the individual, to a greater or lesser degree, a sort of conditioned satisfaction, which derives both from developmental associations and from current reinforcements" (p. 25).

5. A.F.C. Wallace, *Mazeway,* In describing people's reactions to disaster, Wallace argued, ". . . many persons will suffer 'shock' and the subsequent characteristics of the disaster syndrome, partly or wholly as a result of the perception that *a part of their culture is ineffective or has been rendered inoperative, and the person reacts (unrealistically it may be) to this perception as if a beloved object were dead . . .* the emotional impact of the perception of cultural damage is as 'shocking' as, and for some is more shocking than, private loss; and conversely, many persons will suffer any degree of private loss, even death of self and family, before permitting loss of identification with their culture" (p. 24; emphasis in original).

6. M. Fullilove, "Psychiatric Implications of Displacement."

7. Erikson, *Everything in Its Path: The Buffalo Creek Flood.*

8. Davey, "Iowa Town Survived Flood."

9. Pohl, "What: Mob Scene. Who: Strangers. Point: None."

10. R. Fullilove, "Chaos, Criticality, and Public Health."

11. Gans, *Urban Villagers.*

12. Jacobs, *Death and Life of Great American Cities,* pp. 50–51.

13. Fogelson, *Downtown: Its Rise and Fall.*

14. I have not seen an exact number or a list from which I might infer the information. This estimate is based on the following pieces of information. According to the final report on urban renewal, there were 2,532 urban renewal projects in 992 cities (Garvin, *The American City,* 1996). A number of authors have reported that 75 percent of the people displaced were people of color and about 63 percent were African American. As most African Americans lived in ghettos, I have made the assumption that the proportion of displaced African Americans is similar to the proportion of bulldozed African American ghettos. Calculating 63 percent of 2,553 yields 1,608, which I have rounded off to 1,600.

2. Imagining Neon

1. I learned from Walter Prichard Eaton, author of *In Berkshire Fields,* that "A pet crow's name is always Jim, regardless of sex. Just why that is those wiser in folk-lore than I will have to answer" (p. 28).

2. During the Middle Ages, the plague killed about half the population of Europe, and weakened the hold of the feudal system. Many people went to the cities to be rid of feudal ties to the land.

3. Nesbitt, *Over the Line,* p. 309.

4. Ibid., p. 311.

5. Seamon, "Reconciling old and new worlds," p. 227.

6. Hansberry, *Raisin in the Sun.* Lorraine Hansberry was growing up in Chicago at around the time the terror attacks depicted in figure 2.1 were being made.

7. The first ghetto was established in Venice in 1516, by order of the Republic of Venice (http://www.doge.it/ghetto/storai.htm). In 1555, Pope Paul IV issued the Cum Nimis Absurdum Bull, which established the ghetto of Rome, confining three thousand Jews to an eight-acre site (http://www.geocities.com/Paris/Arc/5319/roma-c9.htm). See also Louis Seig, "Concepts of 'Ghetto,' " pp. 122–25.

8. Rose, *The Black Ghetto,* p. 4. Let me note that that day has not yet come.

9. Hart, "Changing Distribution of the American Negro," p. 50.

10. Robeson, *Here I Stand,* pp. 15–16. Peterson, in "As Princeton Changes, a Black Community Fears for Its Future," notes that this historic community is under enormous pressure from gentrification and may disappear.

11. Ellison, *Living with Music,* pp. 7–9.

12. Liner notes accompanying the compact disc set called *Billy Eckstine: The Legendary Big Band* point out, "The orchestra that Billy Eckstine led between 1944 and 1947 has a justifiably hallowed place in jazz history. It pointed the way for big band orchestration in the modern era, and cumulatively contained more soloists of lasting impact than even the star-studded ranks of the Duke Ellington and Count Basie ensembles. Despite the paucity of recorded evidence that it left for posterity, it remains one of the music's truly legendary units" (p. 1). Annotation by Bob Blumenthal, Savoy Jazz.

13. Davis, *Autobiography,* pp. 7–8. The gratuitous misogyny in the quote is not an accident, and led Pearl Cleage to write a book called *Mad at Miles: A Black Woman's Guide to Truth.* Cleage asks that we consider the following proposition: "[Miles Davis] is guilty of self-confessed crimes against women such that we should break his albums, burn his tapes and scratch up his CD's until he acknowledges and apologizes and rethinks his position on The Woman Question" (p. 13).

14. Where interview was taking place.

15. *Hillscapes,* pp. 1–2.

16. Hansberry, *To Be Young, Gifted and Black,* p. 17.

17. Herndon, *Let Me Live: The Autobiography of Angelo Herndon,* pp. 70–71.

18. Davis, *Communist Councilman from Harlem,* pp. 150–153.

19. Burns, *Daybreak of Freedom,* p. 70.

20. Garrow, *The Montgomery Bus Boycott and the Women Who Started It*, pp. 75–76.

21. Kenneth L. Smith and Ira G. Zepp, Jr., *Martin Luther King's Vision of the Beloved Community*, http://www.religion-online.org/egi-bin/relsearchd.dll/showarticle?item_id=1603.

22. Garrow, op. cit. 164–165.

23. Thompson, *Homeboy Came to Orange*.

24. Jacobs, *Death and Life*.

25. Jacobs, op. cit. She wrote, "The key link in a perpetual slum is that too many people move out of it too fast—and in the meantime dream of getting out" (p. 138). She continued, "The constant departures leave, of course, more than housing vacancies to be filled. They leave a community in a perpetually embryonic stage, or perpetually regressing to helpless infancy. The age of buildings is no index to the age of a community, which is formed by continuity of people" (p. 143).

26. Shapiro, *Jewish Ghetto in Rome*, http://www.audiowalks.com/read-a-walk/rome_ghetto.htm.

27. http://www.letsgo.com/ROMA/04-Sights-664.

3. URBAN RENEWAL . . .

1. Gould, *Insurgent Identities*; Carmona, *Haussmann*; de Moncan, *Villes Haussmanniennes*. One of the most useful books on the Paris Commune is Albert Boime's *Art and the French Commune: Imagining Paris After War and Revolution*. His principal thesis is that the Impressionists' paintings prettified Paris to cover up both the democracy of the Commune and the gore of its defeat. Boime wrote, "Once the military and political work [of defeating the Commune] was accomplished, the urban and intraurban sites transgressed by the Communards needed to be reinvested and reappropriated once again for bourgeois culture. The Communards constructed a new identity for themselves and in the process gave that urban space a new identity. . . . The worker-Communards, victims of Haussmann's architectural and social reorganization, descended into the center to reclaim the public space from which they had been evicted, to reoccupy streets they had formerly inhabited. . . . The impressonists . . . recovered the Parisian territory from the *canaille* who had rejected the privileged organization of that space, and reinvested it with bourgeois sensibility and symbolic value" (pp. 25–26).

2. Cantal-Dupart, *Merci la Ville!*, p. 104.

3. Gould, *Insurgent Identities*.

4. There is a large literature on urban renewal that falls into two eras. The first era, including books and articles written in the 1950s and 1960s, was concerned with describing and critiquing a program that was then in nationwide operation. Some of the most important writings of the era were

anthologized by Wilson, and by Bellush and Hausknecht. Key monographs include: Rossi and Dentler, *The Politics of Urban Renewal: The Chicago Findings;* Gans, *Urban Villagers;* Kaplan, *Urban Renewal Politics: Slum Clearance in Newark;* Greer, *Urban Renewal and American Cities;* Goodman, *After the Planners.* After the annulment of the program in 1973, a lull ensued. Retrospective analysis began about a decade later. Among the key books that have been published in this later period are: Teaford, *Rough Road to Renaissance;* Davis, *The World of Patience Gromes;* Saunders and Shackelford, *Urban Renewal and the End of Black Culture in Charlottesville;* Thomas, *Race and Redevelopment: Planning a Finer City in Postwar Detroit.* Two key articles that provide excellent summaries of this complex process are: Weiss, "The Origins and Legacy of Urban Renewal"; and Teaford, "Urban Renewal and Its Aftermath."

5. Sanders, *The Community,* p. 161.

6. For books on Native American dispossession see: Neihardt, *Black Elk Speaks;* Jahoda, *Trail of Tears;* Jacobs, *Dispossessing the American Indian.* For a later dispossession story, see Modell, *The Kikuchi Diary.*

7. See Fogelson, *Downtown,* for an extensive discussion of the invention of the concept of blight.

8. During a hearing on an urban renewal project in Newark, in June 1967, the legal definition of blight, as enacted in New Jersey Statute 49:55-21.1, was read into the meeting transcript (Housing Authority, "Public Hearing Transcript," pp. 6–7). It is highly informative because it describes the many ways in which an area might be designated as blighted. "The term 'blighted area' shall mean an area in any municipality wherein there exists any of the conditions hereinafter enumerated: the generality of buildings used as dwelling or the dwelling accommodations therein are substandard, unsafe, unsanitary, dilapidated or obsolescent, or possess any of such characteristics, or are so lacking light, air or space, as to be conducive to unwholesome living; the discontinuance of the use of buildings previously used for manufacturing or industrial purposes, the abandonment of such buildings or the same being allowed to fall into so great a state of disrepair as by untenable; unimproved vacant land, which has remained so for a period of ten years prior to the determination hereinafter referred to, and which land by reason of its location, or remoteness from developed sections or portions of such municipality or lack of means of access to such other parts thereof, or topography, or nature of the soil, is not likely to be developed through the instrumentality of private capital; areas (including slum areas), with buildings or improvements which by reason of dilapidated, obsolescence, overcrowding, faulty arrangement or design, lack of ventilation, light and sanitary facilities, excessive land coverage, deleterious land use or obsolete layout, or any combination of

these factors, are detrimental to the safety, health, morals or welfare of the community; a growing lack of proper utilization of areas caused by the condition of the title, diverse ownership of the real property therein and other conditions, resulting in a stagnant and unproductive condition of land potentially useful and valuable for contributing to and serving the public health, safety and welfare."

9. Greer, *Urban Renewal,* is the source for this description of the process by which urban renewal worked, pp. 7–12.

10. Weiss, op. cit., p. 253.

11. Ibid., pp. 253–54.

12. Ibid., p. 254; see also Lorant, *Pittsburgh;* Mohl, "Making the Second Ghetto in Metropolitan Miami"; Goodman, *After the Planners;* Hirsch, *Making the Second Ghetto.*

13. Lorant, *Pittsburgh,* pp. 432–33. At a June 29, 1943, luncheon meeting the Allegheny Conference on Post-War Community Planning came into being. In 1945, the group was renamed the "Allegheny Conference on Community Development" (pp. 383, 385).

14. Here are the degrees of separation linking me to that committee: The Maurice and Laura Falk Foundation was established by Leon Falk, Jr. That foundation terminated in 1965, and its monies were used to establish the Maurice Falk Medical Fund. Philip Hallen, director of the fund beginning shortly after its establishment in 1965, was the person who proposed that Bob and I become visiting professors at the University of Pittsburgh, a story told in Chapter 7.

15. Evans, "Here Is a Job for Postwar Pittsburgh"; Garvin, 1996, noted, "What Riis, Palmer, and other advocates of slum clearance ignored is that clearing slums also destroyed cheap housing and forced out residents who probably lived there because they could not afford anything better. They thought that replacing a slum and creating a desirable environment for future generations was sufficient justification for the slum dwellers to lose their homes" (p. 248).

16. I have not discovered the origins of this expression. It appears in print as early as 1950, and was derived from an earlier expression, "Slum Clearance Is Negro Clearance." The famous Pittsburgh journalist Frank Bolden told me that he came out of his office one day around 1956 and saw a mother and her children sitting on the street with nowhere to go. He went back to his office to write about the cruelty of the situation. He called his article "Urban Renewal Means Negro Removal." In Newark, New Jersey, for example, black people organized a group to fight urban renewal and called themselves The Committee Against Negro Removal. The phrase, whatever its origins, served as a shorthand for the black experience of urban renewal, which, in turn, was shorthand for the black experience of life in the United States.

17. Greer, op. cit., p. 147.

18. Rose, *The Black Ghetto,* p. 110.

19. Fogelson, op. cit., p. 319.

20. Garvin, op. cit., p. 122. Vincent Scully, Sterling Professor of Art History, Emeritus, at Yale University, gave the 24th Jefferson Lecture in the Humanities for the National Endowment for the Humanities, May 15, 1995. He observed: "The image of the free passage of the automobile coincided in the 1960s with the theories of modern urbanism as they had been propounded by Le Corbusier. . . . In 1925, he told us how awful the street as we knew it was. He told us that it cut off the sky and forced us to look into the faces of other human beings. . . . So we came to want to clean out all the mess of life and have instead the purest kind of death as in Le Corbusier's Voisin plan of 1925. . . . It was on that model that American redevelopment took shape. The two things coincided in the 1960s—a marriage made in hell right there—so that Le Corbusier's image of 1922 and 1925 about what an ideal city should look like was finally created in towns like New Haven. Eventually, all over the United States, the city centers were ripped out and the old density, the whole pedestrian scale, was gone. Not Le Corbusier's dreamy parks, but parking lots, took over" (p. 5).

21. Batelier, *Ni consignes, ni retour.*

22. Though ghettos did expand, there was enormous white resistance. Key literature on ghetto formation and white resistance: Rose, op. cit; Spear, *Black Chicago;* Hirsch, *Making the Second Ghetto;* Chicago Commission on Race Relations, "White Violence Versus Black Expansion"; Meyer, *As Long as They Don't Move Next Door.* See Goodman, *After the Planners,* for a discussion of tools used by planners to shape the city. My analysis of spatial changes in Pittsburgh and elsewhere draws heavily on his ideas.

23. Clark, *Ghetto Game.*

24. Hirsch, *Making of the Second Ghetto.*

25. Garvin, op. cit., p. 168.

26. Adams, "The Geography of Riots," p. 291.

27. National Commisssion on Civil Disorders, 1968.

28. Ibid., p. 142.

29. Reddy, "The Key Issue."

30. Knell, *To Destroy a City.* Compare the map on p. 30 of *To Destroy a City* with the maps of U.S. urban renewal plans; see especially figure 6.7 in this volume, and contrast those with Haussmann's plans, figure 3.1.

4. . . . Means Negro Removal

1. Rouse, *The Great Wagon Road.*

2. Woods, Rogers and Hagelgrove, "Hand that rocks the cradle . . . pulled the strings."

3. Bishop, "Natives visit lost neighborhood," E2, E6.

4. Bishop, "Street by Street."

5. Nine hundred ninety-two American cities carried out one or more urban renewal projects. More and more affected communities are posting materials on the Internet about what happened to them. These materials include photographs, oral histories, maps, and documents. "Urban renewal is Negro removal" is an excellent search term.

6. Robert Lunsford, artist for the *Roanoke Times,* spent time driving around the area to ensure that the map was a correct representation of what existed and what had been lost, as of 1995. He also drew the Henry Street map, which appears in this chapter.

7. Bishop, "Street by Street," p. 2.

8. Ibid.

9. Ibid., p. 4.

10. Pardue, "A neighborhood gone and a lesson learned," B1, B4. The article states, "More than 20 years ago James Robertson helped destroy Kimball. It was a predominantly black Roanoke neighborhood of more than 300 homes leveled so the main post office and other businesses could be built. Robertson did it in the name of urban renewal, with hope that Roanoke would use the cleared land to prosper and grow. It was a mistake, he says now. He wants to add his name to those of residents of Gainsboro, another black neighborhood, now fighting to stop the city from tearing down more of its homes to make way for roads, a convention center and a rejuvenated Hotel Roanoke" (B1).

11. Bishop, op. cit., p. 4.

12. Ibid., pp. 5–6.

13. Elders and Chanoff, *Jocelyn Elders.*

14. Bishop, op. cit., p. 10. Redlining, she notes, is the systematic refusal by banks to give loans to neighborhoods they think are deteriorating.

15. Ibid., p. 7.

16. Claytor, "Reflections." He wrote about helping to build the family's clinic, "I . . . unloaded bricks from a railway freight car and brought them to the site. This is how I spent the break between classes in dental school—helping to have the office ready when and if I graduated . . . My aching and sore back muscles also impressed upon me what my Mother used to preach '. . . you learn to use your head or this type of labor will become your life's work.' My studies became a lot easier after the experience of helping to build the Clinic" (p. 1).

17. Bishop, op. cit., p. 7.

18. Ibid., p. 12.

19. Bishop and Harrington, "The Invisible Inner City."

20. Reed, "Roanoke Segregated." Three maps (fig. 4.8n) demonstrate how the city was changing. The outline of the "Invisible Inner City" neighbor-

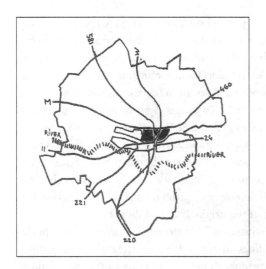

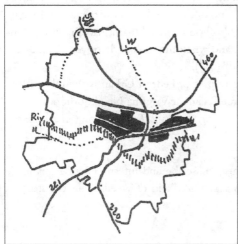

Fig. 4.8n. Land use in Roanoke. On the upper map, the darkened area represents the urban renewal tracts, depicted in greater detail in fig. 4.1. On the middle map, the darkened areas represent the "invisible inner city," the poverty tracts extending out on either side of the urban renewal zone. (Note that the outline of the invisible inner-city areas is included in all three maps.) On the lower map, the darkened area represents the majority black area of Roanoke, which is home to 65 percent of the city's African American population. Adapted by Michel Cantal-Dupart from: Mary Bishop, 1995; Mary Bishop and Shannon Harrington, 1997; Ray Reed, 2002. COURTESY OF THE *ROANOKE TIMES*.

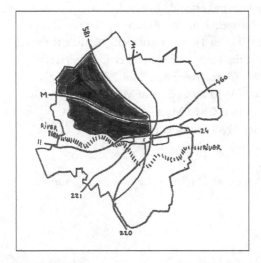

hoods—the center map—is replicated on all three maps, to provide an area for comparison. The top map overlays the urban renewal area, detailed in figure 4.1, and demonstrates both the former area of black settlement and the area that has been largely cleared of its former residents in order to provide land for new uses. The bottom map demonstrates the area of concentrated black settlement, according to the 2000 census. Approximately 65 percent of Roanoke's black population lives in that area. In studying the overlaps among these three maps, we realize that the processes of urban renewal and contagious housing destruction moved the black population away from downtown to the northwest section of the city. The contagious housing destruction that started in Gainsboro has spread dramatically, and now affects an area many times the size of the original zone of disinvestment.

21. Scully, "Architecture of Community." He noted, ". . . while we were destroying irreplaceable buildings in the 1960s, we were also doing much worse. We were destroying neighborhoods, we were destroying populations, we were destroying cultures . . . no one seemed to know that a low-income neighborhood could be a neighborhood, indeed that it had a cultural identity. It had social structures . . . and when those were destroyed . . . individuals were uprooted, disoriented" (p. 4).

22. Shareef, "An Evaluation of the Impact of Federal Urban Renewal and Redevelopment Programs on Three Roanoke Virginia Neighborhoods."

23. Hobfoll, *Stress, Culture, and Community;* Watkins, *Fantasy, Decay, Abandonment.*

5. When the Center Fails . . .

1. The QRM class of 2001 helped transcribe and interpret transcripts made with David. Harold Franklin's video "A Field of Weeds" tells the story of urban renewal in Eastwick.

6. . . . What Will Hold?

1. David Fullilove, a brother of Bob and Harold, deceased 1991.

2. This map is based on the Newark Housing Authority, "Urban Renewal Progress Map, February 22, 1971," in Housing Authority, "Urban Renewal Progress," pp. 20–22. The site of the start of the Newark civil disorders is taken from Tom Hayden, "City of Newark and Rebellion Zone," *Rebellion in Newark,* p. 25. The original area for the New Jersey College of Medicine and Dentistry was shown in Shabazian, "Newark Is Given March 1 Deadline," p. 21.

3. Johnson, *The Books of American Negro Spirituals,* p. 48.

7. Unceasing Struggle

1. Dickens, "Lawsuit Revives Anger," and "Claytor Lawsuit Sees Victory."

2. Cunningham, *Newark,* p. 316.

3. The Pittsburgh Photographic Project was a remarkable undertaking, designed to document the complexity and beauty of the city. It was headed by Roy Stryker, famous for his work with the WPA photographic projects. It brought famous photographers to Pittsburgh. Thousands of photographs were taken. For the most part, the photographs are in the collection of the Carnegie Library of Pittsburgh and are available at a nominal charge to the public. For an outstanding sample of photographs from the collection, see Schultz and Plattner, *Witness to the Fifties.*

4. Fried, "Grieving For a Lost Home," p. 242.

5. M. Fullilove, "Psychiatric Implications of Displacement."

6. HOPE VI legislation was enacted in 1992 and was designed to clear large stretches of land. At the 1991 reunion picnic of neighbors from Northeast in Roanoke, we note the following: ". . . Roanoke Vice Mayor Howard Musser told a reporter he doubts that whole neighborhoods like Northeast will ever be destroyed again. 'Mass clearing of houses, mass destruction of a neighborhood is a thing of the past . . .'" Bishop, "Northeast Reunion."

7. Barclay, *People Need Roots.*

8. Perlmutter, "Psychiatrist Tries to Dispel Fear."

9. M. Fullilove, "Is My Community Dead?"

10. M. Fullilove, "Mapping the Neighborhood," pp. 25–27.

11. Rodgers-Melnick, "A look at how to save a place," B1–2.

12. Editorial, "Building a Balance."

13. Addams, *Twenty Years at Hull House.*

14. Charles Elliott, *The Transplanted Gardener,* p. 187.

8. HUMAN RIGHTS IN THE CITY

1. Goodman, *After the Planners.*

2. Wallace and Wallace, "Coming Epidemic of AIDS in the Suburbs."

3. Michel Cantal-Dupart's major publications are *Merci la Ville!* and *La Ville à Livre Ouvert: Regarde sur Cinquante Ans d'Habitat* (with Roland Castro and Antoine Stinco). The report *Atelier Cantal-Dupart* is a portfolio of recent projects, published by Michel Cantal-Dupart in 2003. "Le Grand-Paris: Pour une Capitale à l'Echelle Européene" gives an excellent description of "Banlieue 89," a major project led by Roland Castro and Michel Cantal-Dupart. It was published in *MURS, MURS,* supplement to number 14, April 1986. "Banlieue 89" has received renewed attention as it approaches its twentieth anniversary; for example, the magazine *Urbanisme* devoted forty pages in its September–October 2003 issue to an examination of the concepts and impact of "Banlieue 89."

4. Dripps, *The First House.*

5. Wilson and Kelling, "Broken Windows."

6. Traveling in the direction of something we can see is reminiscent of the old camp song "The Bear Went over the Mountain" (to see what he could see).

7. Orsenna, *Portrait d'un homme heureux.*

8. Knell, *To Destroy a City.*

9. Derrida, *Cosmopolitanism.*

10. Hernandez, *Fostering Collective Recovery.*

9. OUR PLACE, OUR HOME

1. T. Rose, *Black Noise.*

2. Smith, "Frank Moore," A27.

3. Greenspan, "The Wisdom in the Dark Emotions," p. 58.

4. Ibid.

5. There are two independent sources of the idea of the festival. One is Michel Cantal-Dupart who writes of this in *Merci La Ville!* The second is Hirofumi Minami, an environmental psychologist from Hiroshima who worked with us in NYC RECOVERS post-9/11. Hirofumi Minami has studied urban renewal in Hiroshima (see Minami, "Urban renewal and the elderly"). His ethnographic work included close observations of neighborhood ritual life before and after urban renewal. As he observed the activities of NYC RE-COVERS, he emphasized that it was the festival that was helping people to recover.

6. Hershenson, "Faraway School," B8.

7. Ibid.

8. For an overview of Jane Addams's work, see the following: Addams, *Twenty Years at Hull House;* Bryan and Davis, *100 Years at Hull House;* Johnson, *The Many Faces of Hull House.*

9. Imagine New York was a massive project sponsored by the Municipal Art Society in 2002. It included 350 workshops with four thousand participants who discussed their vision for the future of New York.

10. Sorokin, *Man and Society in Calamity.*

11. Ibid., p. 296.

12. Ibid., p. 297.

BIBLIOGRAPHY

Adams, John S. "The Geography of Riots and Civil Disorders in the 1960s." *Black America: Geographic Perspectives*, edited by R. T. Ernst and L. Hugg. Garden City, NY: Anchor Books, 1976.

Addams, Jane. *Twenty Years at Hull House*. Chautauqua, NY: Chautauqua Press, 1911.

Adler, Patricia A., and Peter Adler. "The Promise and Pitfalls of Going Into the Field." *Contexts* 2 (2):41–47, 2003.

Afolayan, A. A. "The Sasa Resettlement Project: A Study in Problems of Relocation." *Habitat International* 11 (2):43–57, 1987.

Alexander, Christopher. "The Goodness of Fit and Its Source." In *Environmental Psychology: Man and His Physical Setting*, edited by H. M. Proshansky, W. H. Ittelson, and L. G. Rivlin. New York: Holt, Rinehart and Winston, Inc., 1971.

Anderson, Marian. *My Lord, What a Morning*. Urbana: University of Illinois Press, 2002.

Ansary, Tamim. *West of Kabul, East of New York: An Afghan American Story*. New York: Farrar, Straus, and Giroux, 2002.

Artis, Jeff. "At Last, Roanoke Will Have a King Memorial Worthy of Him." *Roanoke Times*, March 9, 2003, Horizon 3.

Aubespin, Mervin. *With Urban Renewal, a Community Vanishes* (Internet). Courier Journal-Online, December 18, 2002, 1999 (cited October 12, 2002). Available from http://www.courier-journal.com/2000/times_waln.html.

Bacon, Edmund. *Design of Cities*. New York: Penguin Books, 1974.

Barclay, Irene. *People Needs Roots: The Story of the St. Pancras Housing Association*. London: Bedford Council of Social Service, 1976.

Barton, Craig E., ed. *Sites of Memory: Perspectives on Architecture and Race*. New York: Princeton Architectural Press, 2001.

Batelier, JF. *Ni consignes, ni retours*, Édite par L'auteur, Paris, 1993.

Bauman, John F., Roger Biles, and Kristin M. Szylvian, eds. *From Tenements to the Taylor Homes: In Search of an Urban Housing Policy in Twentieth-Century America*. University Park, PA: Pennsylvania State University Press, 2000.

Baxandall, Rosalyn, and Elizabeth Ewen. *Picture Windows: How the Suburbs Happened*. New York: Basic Books, 2000.

Beagle, Ben. "Loss of Homes Major Concern: Kimball Worried as Renewal Project Nears." *Roanoke Times*, March 3, 1966.

———. "Kimball Families Wait in Fear." *Roanoke Times*, April 26, 1964.

Beardsley, John, William Arnett, Paul Arnett, and Jane Livingston. *Gee's Bend: The Women and Their Quilts*. Atlanta: Tinwood Books, 2002.

Beatley, Timothy. *Green Urbanism: Learning from European Cities*. Washington, DC: Island Press, 2000.

Beck, Henry Charlton. *The Roads of Home: Lanes and Legends of New Jersey*. New Brunswick, NJ: Rutgers University Press, 1984.

Beck, Henry Charlton, and William F. Augustine. *Tales and Towns of Northern New Jersey*. New Brunswick, NJ: Rutgers University Press, 1983.

Behura, N. K. "Socio-Economic Problems and Social Change Among the Relocatees of Rengali Dam—a Case Study." *The Uprooted: Displacement Resettlement Development*, edited by V. Sudarsen and M. A. Kalam. New Delhi: Gian Publishing House, 1990.

Bellush, Jewel, and Murray Hausknecht. "Urban Renewal: An Historical Overview." *Urban Renewal: People, Politics, and Planning*, edited by J. Bellush and M. Hausknecht. Garden City, NY: Anchor Books, 1967.

The Beloved Community of Martin Luther King, Jr. (Internet). The King Center (cited October 13, 2002). Available from http://www.thekingcenter.org/bc.html.

Benmayor, Rina, and Andor Skotnes, eds. *Migration and Identity*. Oxford: Oxford University Press, 1994.

Bernard, Gilles. *L'Aventure des Bastides: Villes Nouvelles du Moyen Age*. Toulouse: Edition Privat, 1998.

Bihu, Barbara Vitale. *You Might Be From Newark, New Jersey if You . . .* (Internet). Old Newark Memories (cited November 8, 2002). Available from http://oldnewark.com/memories/newark/bihus.htm.

Bishop, Mary. "Natives Visit Lost Neighborhood." *Roanoke Times*, September 1, 1991, E1, E6.

———. "On Henry St., Renewed Interest." *Roanoke Times*, April 9, 1995.

———. "Street by Street, Block by Block: How Urban Renewal Uprooted Black Roanoke." *Roanoke Times*, 1995.

Bishop, Mary, and S. D. Harrington. "The Invisible Inner City: Poverty, Crime and Decay in Roanoke's Oldest Neighborhoods." *Roanoke Times*, 1997.

Blassingame, John W. *Black New Orleans, 1860–1880*. Chicago: University of Chicago Press, 1973.

Blumenthal, Bob. *Liner Notes: The Legendary Big Band of Billy Eckstine.* Santa Monica, CA: Savoy Jazz, 2002.

Boesel, David, and Peter H. Rossi, eds. *Cities Under Siege: An Anatomy of the Ghetto Riots, 1964–1968.* New York: Basic Books, 1971.

Boime, Albert. *Art and the French Commune: Imagining Paris After War and Revolution.* Princeton: Princeton University Press, 1995.

Bolin, Doub, and Christopher Moore. *Wylie Avenue Days* (Internet). WQED Multimedia 1991 (cited October 13, 2002). Available from http://www. wqed/.org/erc/pghist/logs/wylie.html.

Bontemps, Arna, and Jack Conroy. *Any Place But Here,* third ed. New York: Hill and Wang, 1967.

Booth, Tim, Ken Simons, and Wendy Booth. "Moving Out: Insiders' View of Relocation." *British Journal of Social Work* 19:369–85, 1989.

Borden, Iain, Joe Kerr, Rendell, and Alicia Pivaro, eds. *The Unknown City: Contesting Architecture and Social Space.* Cambridge: MIT Press, 2001.

Bosselmann, Peter. *Representation of Places: Reality and Realism in City Design.* Berkeley: University of California Press, 1998.

Bowlby, John. *Separation: Anxiety and Anger.* New York: Basic Books, 1973.

Bowser, Benjamin P. "Community and Economic Context of Black Families: A Critical Review of the Literature, 1909–1985." *The American Journal of Social Psychiatry* 6 (1):17–26, 1986.

Bowser, Benjamin P., and Louis Kushnick, eds. *Against the Odds: Scholars Who Challenged Racism in the Twentieth Century.* Amherst: University of Massachusetts Press, 2002.

Bracey, John H., Jr., August Meier, and Elliott Rudwick, eds. *The Rise of the Ghetto.* Belmont, CA: Wadsworth Publishing Company, 1971.

Bradford, Alexandre, Julie Burkley, Mark Feild, Manuel Maysonet, John Van Decker, and Jia Wei. *Property Tax Analysis* (Internet). Center for Urban Policy Research, Department of Urban Planning and Policy Development, Edward J. Bloustein School of Planning and Public Policy, Rutgers, the State University of New Jersey, 1998 (cited November 11, 2002). Available from http://policy.rutgers.edu/cupr/community/organizations/projcomm/wsp/west8.html.

Brand, Dionne. *No Burden to Carry: Narratives of Black Working Women in Ontario 1920s to 1950s.* Toronto: Women's Press, 1991.

Brand, Elizabeth. *Community Action at Work: TAP's Thirty-Year War on Poverty.* Blacksburg, VA: Total Action Against Poverty, 2000.

Bronfenbrenner, Urie. *The Ecology of Human Development: Experiments by Nature and Design.* Cambridge: Harvard University Press, 1979.

Brossault, Pierre-Alain, Francois Breteau, Jean-Luc Dumesnil, Laure Schnieter, and Isabelle Lopez, eds. *L'écologie à Paris.* Paris: Abacus Edition, 1995.

Brown, Patricia Leigh. "From the Bottomlands, Soulful Stitches." *The New York Times,* November 21, 2002, F1.

Bruce, Carolyn Hale. *Roanoke: A Pictorial History.* Norfolk, VA: Donning, 1976.

Bryan, Mary Lynn McCree, and Allen F. Davis, eds. *One Hundred Years at Hull House.* Bloomington and Indianapolis: Indiana University Press, 1990.

Buchanan, A. Russell. *Black Americans in World War II.* Santa Barbara: Clio Books, 1977.

"Building a Balance." *Pittsburgh Post-Gazette,* April 22, 1998, E1.

Bullard, Robert D., III, J. Eugene Grigsby, and Charles Lee, eds. *Residential Apartheid: The American Legacy.* Los Angeles: CAAS Publications, 1994.

Burns, Elizabeth K. "Nested Hexagons: Central Place Theory." In *10 Geographic Ideas That Changed the World,* edited by S. Hanson. New Brunswick, NJ: Rutgers University Press, 1997.

Burns, Stewart, ed. *Daybreak of Freedom: The Montgomery Bus Boycott.* Chapel Hill: University of North Carolina Press, 1997.

Busch, Akiko. *Geography of Home: Writings on Where We Live.* New York: Princeton Architectural Press, 1999.

Bush, Esther L. *Daybreakers: The Story of the Urban League of Pittsburgh: The First Eighty Years,* second ed. Pittsburgh: Urban League of Pittsburgh, 1999.

Buttimer, Anne. *Geography and the Human Spirit.* Baltimore: Johns Hopkins University Press, 1993.

Cantal-Dupart, Michel. *Merci la Ville!* Bordeaux: Investigations Le Castor Astral, 1994.

Carmon, Naomi. "Three Generations of Urban Renewal Policies: Analysis and Policy Implications." *Geoforum* 30:145–58, 1999.

Carmon, Naomi, and Moshe Hill. "Neighborhood Rehabilitation Without Relocation or Gentrification." *Journal of the American Planning Association* 54 (4):470–81, 1988.

Carmona, Michael. *Haussmann: His Life and Times, and the Making of Modern Paris.* Chicago: Ivan R. Dee, 2002.

Castro, Roland, Michel Cantal-Dupart, and Antoine Stinco. *La Ville à Livre Ouvœrt: Regarde sur Cinquante Ans d'Habitat.* Paris: La Documentation Française, 1980.

Cha-Jua, Sundiata Keita. *America's First Black Town: Brooklyn, Illinois, 1830–1915.* Urbana: University of Illinois Press, 2000.

The Changing Face of Anacostia: Public Housing and Urban Renewal (Internet). American Studies at the University of Virginia, August 20, 2002 (cited October 12, 2002). Available from http://xroads.virginia.edu/~CAP/ANACOSTIA/public.html.

Chanin, Abe, and Mildred Chanin. *This Land, These Voices: A Different View of Arizona History in the Words of Those Who Lived it.* Tucson: Midbar Press, 1977.

Chicago Commission on Race Relations. "White Violence Versus Black Expansion." *The Rise of the Ghetto,* edited by J. John H. Bracey, A. Meier, and E. Rudwick. Belmont, CA: Wadsorth Publishing Company, 1971.

Childs, Mark C. "Civic Ecosystems." *Journal of Urban Design* 6 (1):55–72, 2001.

Choay, Francoise. *L'urbanisme, Utopies et Realités: Une Anthologie.* New York: Le Corbusier, 1965.

Civil Rights in Pittsburgh: Timeline 1800's–1960 (Internet). Freedom Corner (cited October 11, 2002). Available from http://www.freedomcorner.org/civil_rights_in_pittsburgh.html.

Clark, Dennis. *The Ghetto Game: Racial Conflicts in the City.* New York: Sheed and Ward, 1962.

Clark, John L. " 'Ike' Makes Plea for Full Equality." *Courier: America's Best Weekly,* January 31, 1953.

Clark, Kenneth B. *Dark Ghetto: Dilemmas of Social Power.* New York: Harper & Row, 1965.

Clark-Lewis, Elizabeth. *Living In, Living Out: African American Domestics and the Great Migration.* New York: Kodansha International, 1996.

Clay, Grady. *Close-Up: How to Read the American City.* Chicago: University of Chicago Press, 1973.

Claytor, Walter S. "Reflections about the Claytor Memorial Clinic." Roanoke: undated typescript.

Claytor, Walter S., Evelyn D. Bethel, Virginia J. Board, Helen E. Davis, and George H. R. Heller. "Black Community Observations Over the Past Forty (40) Years in the City of Roanoke." Roanoke, VA.

Cleage, Pearl. *Mad at Miles: A Blackwoman's Guide to Truth.* Southfield, MI: Cleage Group, Inc., 1990.

Cline, Ann. *A Hut of One's Own: Life Outside the Circle of Architecture.* Cambridge: MIT Press, 1997.

Clubs and the Social Scene . . . (Internet). Groundbreaking Cities in America (cited November 8, 2002). Available from http://www.northbysouth.org/2000/Beauty/Crawford.htm.

Cohen, Lizabeth. "Trying to Buy Our Way Out of Trouble." *The New York Times,* December 11, 2002, A35.

Comeaux, Malcolm. "Creating Indian Lands: The Boundary of the Salt River Indian Community." *Journal of Historical Geography* 17 (3):241–56, 1991.

Cooke, Mervyn. *Jazz.* Slovenia: Thames and Hudson, Inc., 1998.

Cunningham, James, ed. *Neighborhood Shock: Case Study of Pittsburgh's East Street Expressway and Citizen Participation, 1952–1976.* Pittsburgh: University of Pittsburgh Press, School of Social Work, 1976.

Cunningham, John T. *Newark.* Newark: New Jersey Historical Society, 1988.

———. *This Is New Jersey,* fourth ed. New Brunswick, NJ: Rutgers University Press, 1994.

Curry, Leonard P. *The Free Black in Urban America, 1800–1850: The Shadow of the Dream*. Chicago: University of Chicago Press, 1981.

Dailey, Jane. *Before Jim Crow: The Politics of Race in Postemancipation Virginia*. Chapel Hill: University of North Carolina Press, 2000.

Daily, Kathleen Krieger, and Gaylord T. Guenin. *Aspen: The Quiet Years*. Aspen, CO: Red Ink, Inc., 1994.

Damon J. Keith Biography (Internet). Wayne State University, 2001, 1993 (cited May 5, 2002). Available from http://www.reuther.wayne.edu/keith_bio.html.

Daniels, Douglas Henry. *Pioneer Urbanites: A Social and Cultural History of Black San Francisco*. Philadelphia: Temple University Press, 1980.

Darden, Joe T. *Afro-Americans in Pittsburgh: The Residential Segregation of a People*. Lexington, MA: D.C. Heath and Company, 1973.

Davey, Monica. "Iowa Town Survived Flood, but Teetered in the Aftermath." *The New York Times,* July 14, 2003, A5, A10.

Davis, Benjamin J. *Communist Councilman from Harlem: Autobiographical Notes Written in a Federal Penitentiary*. New York: International Publishers, 1969.

Davis, Miles, and Quincy Troupe. *Miles: The Autobiography of Miles Davis*. New York: Simon & Schuster, 1989.

Davis, Scott C. *The World of Patience Gromes: Making and Unmaking a Black Community*. Lexington: University of Kentucky Press, 1988.

Derrida, Jacques. *On Cosmopolitanism and Forgiveness*. Translated by M. Dooley and M. Hughes. London: Routledge, 1997.

Des Cars, Jean, and Pierre Pinon. *Paris: Haussmann*. Paris: Éditions du Pavillon de l'Arsenal, 1998.

Dickens, Tad. "Claytor Lawsuit Sees Small Victory in Court." *Roanoke Times,* June 19, 2003, A1.

———. "Lawsuit Revives Anger About Treatment of Blacks During Urban Renewal." *Roanoke Times,* April 13, 2003, A1, A2.

Dohrenwend, Bruce P. "Psychological Implications of Nuclear Accidents: The Case of Three Mile Island." *Bulletin of the New York Academy of Science* 59 (10):1060–76, 1983.

———. "The Role of Adversity and Stress in Psychopathology: Some Evidence and Its Implications for Theory and Research." *Journal of Health and Social Behavior* 41:1–19, 2000.

Drake, St. Claire, and Horace A. Cayton. *Black Metropolis: A Study of Negro Life in a Northern City*. Chicago: University of Chicago Press, 1993.

Dripps, R. D. *The First House: Myth, Paradigm, and the Task of Architecture*. Cambridge: MIT Press, 1997.

Du Bois, W.E.B. *The Philadelphia Negro*. Millwood: Kraus-Thomson Organization Limited, 1973.

———. *The Souls of Black Folk*. New York: Random House, 2003.

Eaton, Walter Prichard. *In Berkshire Fields.* New York: Harper and Brothers Publishers, 1920.

Eckholm, Erik. "Sadly, There Goes the Neighborhood. There's No Stopping 'Urban Renewal.' " *The New York Times,* May 26, 2003, A4.

Elders, Joycelyn, and David Chanoff. *Joycelyn Elders: From Sharecropper's Daughter to Surgeon General of the United States of America.* New York: William Morrow and Co., 1996.

Elliott, Charles. *The Transplanted Gardener: An American in England Looks at Hedges, Ha-ha's, History, and More.* New York: Lyons & Burford, 1995.

Ellison, Ralph. *Living with Music: Ralph Ellison's Jazz Writings.* New York: Modern Library, 2001.

Erikson, Kai T. *Everything in Its Path: Destruction of Community in the Buffalo Creek Flood.* New York: Simon & Schuster, 1976.

Ernst, Robert T., and Lawrence Hugg, eds. *Black America: Geographical Perspectives.* Garden City, NY: Anchor Press, 1976.

Evans, George. "Here Is a Job for Postwar Pittsburgh: Transforming the Hill District." *Greater Pittsburgh,* July–August 1943.

Ewing, Reid, Tom Schmid, Richard Killingsworth, Amy Zlot, and Stephen Raudenbush. "Relationship Between Urban Sprawl and Physical Activity, Obesity, and Morbidity." *American Journal of Health Promotion* 18 (1):47–57, 2003.

Fainstein, Norman. "Race, Class, and Segregation: Discourses about African Americans." *Readings in Urban Theory,* edited by S. S. Fainstein and S. Campbell. Malden, MA: Blackwell Publishers, Inc., 2002.

Fainstein, Susan S., and Scott Campbell, eds. *Readings in Urban Theory,* second ed. Oxford: Blackwell, 2002.

Fainstein, Susan S., N. I. Fainstein, R. C. Hill, D. Judd, and M. P. Smith. *Reconstructing the City: The Political Economy of Urban Redevelopment.* New York: Longman, 1983.

Fanzo, Michelle. "The Hill District." *The Observer,* June 1995, 15–19.

Feimer, Nickolaus R., and E. Scott Getter, eds. *Environmental Psychology:* Praeger, 1983.

Feld, Kate. "The Future of Jarvis Street." *Valley News,* December 9, 2001, A1, A6.

Finkelstein, Sidney. *Jazz: A People's Music.* New York: International Publishers, 1988.

Fitch, James Marston. *American Building: The Forces That Shape It.* Boston: Houghton Mifflin Company, 1948.

Fitch, James Marston, and William Bobenhausen. *American Building: The Environmental Forces That Shape It.* New York: Oxford University Press, 1999.

Fitzpatrick, Don. *The Story of Urban Renewal* (Internet). Post-Gazette.com 2000 (cited October 12, 2002). Available from http://www.post-gazette.com/businessnews/20000521eastliberty1.asp.

———. "What Happened to the Hill District." *Minority Business Times,* July 1, 1996, 8–11.

Fitzpatrick, Kevin, and Mark LaGlory. *Unhealthy Places: The Ecology of Risk in the Urban Landscape.* New York: Routledge, 2000.

Fogelson, Robert M. *Downtown: Its Rise and Fall, 1880–1950.* New Haven: Yale University Press, 2001.

Ford, Larry R. *America's New Downtown: Revitalization or Reinvention.* Baltimore: Johns Hopkins University Press, 2003.

Franklin, Harold L. "A Field of Weeds," Produced, directed, written, and edited by H. L. Franklin. Philadelphia: EKO Productions, 1989.

Fridlington, Robert, and Lawrence Fuhro. *Cranford, NJ Volume Ii.* Arcadia: Arcadia Tempus Publishing Group, Inc., 1996.

Fried, Marc. "Grieving for a Lost Home: Psychological Costs of Relocation." *Urban Renewal: The Record and the Controversy,* edited by J. Q. Wilson. Cambridge: MIT Press, 1966.

Fried, Marc, and Peggy Gleicher. "Some Sources of Residential Satisfaction in an Urban Slum." *The Journal of the American Institute of Planners* 27 (4):305–315, 1961.

Fried, Marc, and Joan Levin. "Some Social Functions of the Urban Slum." In *Urban Planning and Social Policy,* edited by B. J. Frieden and R. Morris. New York: Basic Books, 1968.

Fullilove, Mindy Thompson. "Psychiatric Implications of Displacement: Contributions from the Psychology of Place." *American Journal of Psychiatry* 153 (12):1516–23, 1996.

———. *The House of Joshua: Meditations on Family and Place.* Lincoln: University of Nebraska Press, 1999.

———. "Is My Community Dead?" In *Hillscapes: A Scrapbook,* edited by A. Robins. Pittsburgh: University of Pittsburgh Press, 1999.

———. "Links Between the Social and Physical Environments." *Children's Environmental Health* 48 (5):1253–66, 2001.

———. "Mapping the Neighborhood." In *Hillscapes: A Scrapbook,* edited by A. Robins. Pittsburgh: University of Pittsburgh Press, 1999.

Fullilove, Robert E., Jennifer Choe Edgoose, and Mindy Thompson Fullilove. "Chaos, Criticality, and Public Health." *Journal of the National Medical Association* 89 (5):311–16, 1997.

Fuoco, Michael. "Future Investment: Crawford Square Is One of Many Vibrant New Hill Projects." *Pittsburgh Post-Gazette,* April 12, 1999, A1, A6–7.

———. "Grand Old Theater in Spotlight Again." *Pittsburgh Post-Gazette,* April 12, 1999, A7.

———. "Heroin Holds Him in Its Vicious Thrall." *Pittsburgh Post-Gazette,* April 13, 1999, A9, A14–15.

——. "Heroin on the Hill." *Pittsburgh Post-Gazette,* April 13, 1999, A1, A8–9.

——. "Keeping the Faith." *Pittsburgh Post-Gazette,* April 14, 1999, A1.

——. "Return to Glory: Hill District Determined to Regain Lost Greatness." *Pittsburgh Post-Gazette,* April 11, 1999, A1, A10–11.

Gangadhar, V., and D. Padmavathi. "The Tiger Triumph and the Timid Tribal: the Chenchu Case." *The Uprooted: Displacement Resettlement Development,* edited by V. Sudarsen and M. A. Kalam. New Delhi: Gian Publishing House, 1990.

Gans, Herbert. *People, Plans, and Policies: Essays on Poverty, Racism, and Other National Urban Problems.* New York: Columbia University Press, 1993.

——. *The Urban Villagers.* New York: Free Press, 1962.

——. "The Failure of Urban Renewal." In *Urban Renewal: The Record and the Controversy,* edited by J. Q. Wilson. Cambridge: MIT Press, 1966.

Garrow, David J., ed. *The Montgomery Bus Boycott and the Women Who Started It.* Knoxville: University of Tennessee Press, 1987.

Garvin, Alexander. *The American City: What Works, What Doesn't.* New York: McGraw-Hill, 1996.

——. *The American City: What Works, What Doesn't,* second ed. New York: McGraw-Hill, 2002.

Gebhardt, Nicholas. *Going for Jazz: Musical Practices and American Ideology.* Chicago: University of Chicago Press, 2001.

Glasco, Laurence. "Double Burden: The Black Experience in Pittsburgh." In *City at the Point,* edited by S. P. Hays. Pittsburgh: University of Pittsburgh Press, 1989.

Glassie, Henry. *Vernacular Architecture.* Bloomington: Indiana University Press, 2000.

Goings, Kenneth W., and Raymond A. Mohl, eds. *The New African American Urban History.* Thousand Oaks, CA: Sage Publications, 1996.

Goodman, Robert. *After the Planners.* New York: Simon & Schuster, 1971.

Gottlieb, Peter. *Making Their Own Way: Southern Blacks' Migration to Pittsburgh, 1916–30.* Urbana and Chicago: University of Illinois Press, 1987.

Gottlieb, Robert, ed. *Reading Jazz: A Gathering of Autobiography, Reportage, and Criticism from 1919 to Now.* New York: Vintage Books, 1996.

Gould, Roger V. *Insurgent Identities: Class, Community, and Protest in Paris from 1848 to the Commune.* Chicago: Chicago University Press, 1995.

Grady, Denise. "Surgeons Prepare to Separate Conjoined Twins." *The New York Times,* September 9, 2003, B4.

Gratz, Roberta Brandes. *The Living City: How America's Cities Are Being Revitalized by Thinking Small in a Big Way.* Washington, DC: Preservation Press, 1994.

Gratz, Roberta Brandes, and Norman Mintz. *Cities Back from the Edge: New Life for Downtown.* New York: John Wiley & Sons, Inc., 1998.

Greenberg, Michael, and Dona Schneider. "Violence in American Cities: Young Black Males Is the Answer, but What Was the Question?" *Social Science and Medicine* 39 (2):179–87, 1994.

Greenspan, Miriam. "The Wisdom in the Dark Emotions." *Shambala Sun,* January 2003, 57–61.

Greer, Scott. *Urban Renewal and American Cities.* Indianapolis: Bobbs-Merrill Company, 1965.

Grier, William H., and Price M. Cobbs. *Black Rage.* New York: Basic Books, 1968.

Grinberg, Leon, and Rebecca Grinberg. *Psychoanalytic Perspectives on Migration and Exile.* New Haven: Yale University Press, 1989.

Grossman, James R. *Land of Hope: Chicago, Black Southerners, and the Great Migration.* Chicago: University of Chicago Press, 1989.

Groth, Paul, and Todd W. Bressi, eds. *Understanding Ordinary Landscapes.* New Haven: Yale University Press, 1997.

Gutman, Robert, ed. *People and Buildings.* New York: Basic Books, 1972.

Halpern, Robert. *Rebuilding the Inner City: A History of Neighborhood Initiatives to Address Poverty in the United States.* New York: Columbia University Press, 1995.

Hamburg, Perry. *Downtown Stores* (Internet). Old Newark Memories, October 14 (cited November 8, 2002). Available from http://oldnewark.com/memories/downtown/hamburgstores.htm.

Jennings, Carol A. *The Hand That Rocks the Cradle, Pulled the Strings.* Produced and directed by Carol Jennings. Blue Ridge Public Television, 1997.

Hansberry, Lorraine. *Raisin in the Sun.* New York: New American Library, 1966.

———. *To Be Young, Gifted and Black.* Englewood Cliffs, NJ: Prentice Hall, Inc., 1969.

Hare, Clyde. *Pittsburgh: Four Decades of Pittsburgh, Frozen in Light,* first ed. Pittsburgh: Pittsburgh History and Landmarks Foundation, 1994.

Hart, John Fraser. "The Changing Distribution of the American Negro." In *Black America: Geographic Perspectives,* edited by R.T. Ernst and L. Hugg. Garden City, NY: Anchor Books, 1976.

Hartman, Chester W. "The Housing of Relocated Families." In *Urban Renewal: People, Politics, and Planning,* edited by J. Bellush and M. Hausknecht. Garden City, NY: Anchor Books, 1967.

Hartshorn, Truman A. *Interpreting the City: An Urban Geography,* second ed. New York: John Wiley & Sons, Inc., 1992.

Hayden, Tom. *Rebellion in Newark: Official Violence and Ghetto Response.* New York: Vintage Books, 1967.

Hayes, Samuel P., ed. *City at the Point: Essays on the Social History of Pittsburgh.* Pittsburgh: University of Pittsburgh Press, 1989.

Heard, Nathan C. *Howard Street*. New York: Dial Press, Inc., 1968.

Heinz Architectural Center. *Manchester: A Neighborhood Sketchbook*. Pittsburgh: Carnegie Museum of Art, 1998.

Herbert, David. *Urban Geography: A Social Perspective*. New York: Praeger Publishers, 1972.

Hernandez, Daisy. "With Plumbers' Candles and Guest Traffic Cops, Region Perseveres." *The New York Times,* August 15, 2003, A21.

Hernández-Cordero, Lourdes. *Fostering Collective Recovery: Exploring the Role of Organizations in Post-disaster Trauma Recovery.* New York: Mailman School of Public Health, Columbia University, 2004.

Herndon, Angelo. *Let Me Live: The Autobiography of Angelo Herndon.* New York: Random House, 1937.

Hershenson, Roberta. "Faraway School Close to Mount Vernon Woman." *The New York Times,* 2002, B8.

Hinton, Milt, and David G. Berger. *Bass Line: The Stories and Photographs of Milt Hinton.* Philadelphia: Temple University Press, 1988.

Hirsch, Arnold R. "Choosing Segregation: Federal Housing Policy Between Shelley and Brown." *From Tenements to the Taylor Homes: In Search of an Urban Housing Policy in Twentieth-Century America,* edited by J. F. Bauman, R. Biles, and K. M. Szylvian. University Park: Pennsylvania State University Press, 2002.

Hirsch, Arnold. *Making the Second Ghetto: Race & Housing in Chicago.* Chicago: University of Chicago Press, 1998.

Hiss, Tony. *The Experience of Place: A Completely New Way of Looking at and Dealing with Our Radically Changing Cities and Countryside.* New York: Alfred A. Knopf, Inc., 1990.

History of the Ghetto and the Jewish Community (Internet). Business Project 2002 (cited October 20, 2002). Available from http://www.doge.it/ghetto/storiai.htm.

Hobfoll, Stevan E. *Stress, Culture, and Community: The Psychology and Philosophy of Stress.* New York: Plenum Press, 1998.

Homer. *The Odyssey.* Translated by R. Fagles. New York: Penguin Books, 1996.

Honey, Michael Keith. *Black Workers Remember: An Oral History of Segregation, Unionism, and the Freedom Struggle.* Berkeley: University of California Press, 1999.

Housing Authority, Newark, N.J. *Public Hearing Transcript: Medical Center Urban Renewal Project Area.* Newark City Hall, June 1967. Winard and Winard Printing.

———. *Urban Renewal Progress, 1972–73,* 1973.

Hughes, Charles C., Marc-Adelard Tremblay, Robert N. Rapoport, and Alexander H. Leighton. *People of Cove and Woodlot: Communities from the Viewpoint of Social Psychiatry.* Vol. II, *The Sterling County Study of Psychiatric Disorder & Sociocultural Environment.* New York: Basic Books, 1960.

Hurley, Andrew. *Diners, Bowling Alleys, and Trailer Parks: Chasing the American Dream in Postwar Consumer Culture.* New York: Basic Books, 2001.

Images in Time (Internet). Old Newark Images in Time (cited November 8, 2002). Available from http://oldnewark.com/imagepages/images/streets/springfield/build/73springfield.jpg.

Isay, Dave, David Miller, and Harvey Wang. *Milton Rogovin: The Forgotten Ones.* New York: Quantuck Lane Press, 2003.

Jacobs, Jane. *The Death and Life of Great American Cities.* New York: Random House, 1993.

Jacobs, Wilbur R. *Dispossessing the American Indian.* New York: Charles Scribner's Sons, 1972.

Jahoda, Gloria. *The Trail of Tears: The Story of the American Indian Removals, 1813–1855.* New York: Wings Books, 1975.

Jargowsky, Paul A. *Poverty and Place: Ghettos, Barrios, and the American City.* New York: Russell Sage Foundation, 1997.

Johnson, James Weldon. *The Book of American Negro Spirituals.* New York: Da Capo Press, 1969.

Johnson, Mary Ann, ed. *The Many Faces of Hull House: The Photographs of Wallace Kirkland.* Urbana and Chicago: University of Illinois Press, 1989.

Johnson, Whittington B. *Black Savannah, 1788–1864.* Fayetteville: University of Arkansas Press, 1996.

Jones, Emrys, and Eleanor Van Zandt. *The City: Yesterday, Today, and Tomorrow.* Garden City, NY: Doubleday & Co., 1974.

Jones, E. Michael. *The Slaughter of Cities: Urban Renewal as Ethnic Cleansing.* South Bend: St. Augustines's Press, 2004.

Kalter, Robert P. "Medical Center Site: Are the Cards Stacked?" *Sunday Newark Star Ledger,* October 30, 1966, 1, 33.

Kaplan, Edward H., and Oded Berman. "OR Hits the Heights: Relocation Planning at the Orient Heights Housing Project." *Interfaces* 18 (6):14–22, 1988.

Kaplan, Harold. *Urban Renewal Politics: Slum Clearance in Newark.* New York: Columbia University Press, 1963.

Kardiner, Abram. *The Individual and His Society: The Psychodynamics of Primitive Social Organization.* New York: Columbia University Press, 1939.

Kardiner, Abram, and Herbert Speigel. *War Stress and Neurotic Illness.* New York: Paul B. Hoeber, Inc., 1947.

Kawachi, Ichiro, and Lisa F. Berkman, eds. *Neighborhoods and Health.* Oxford: Oxford University Press, 2003.

Kennedy, Liam. *Race and Urban Space in Contemporary American Culture.* Edinburgh: Edinburgh University Press, 2000.

King, Coretta Scott. *My Life with Martin Luther King, Jr.* New York: Holt, Rinehart, and Winston, 1969.

King, Martin Luther. *Stride Toward Freedom*. New York: Harper & Row, 1958.

Kirby, Jack Temple. *Rural Worlds Lost: The American South 1920–1960*. Baton Rouge: Louisiana State University Press, 1987.

Kleppner, Paul. *Chicago Divided: The Making of a Black Mayor*. DeKalb: Northern Illinois University Press, 1985.

Klineberg, Eric. *Heat Wave: A Social Autopsy of Disaster in Chicago*. Chicago: University of Chicago Press, 2002.

Knell, Hermann. *To Destroy a City: Strategic Bombing and Its Human Consequences in World War II*. Cambridge: Da Capo Press, 2003.

Knox, Paul. *Urban Social Geography: An Introduction,* second ed. New York: John Wiley & Sons, Inc., 1989.

Kostof, Spiro. *The City Shaped: Urban Patterns and Meanings Through History.* Little, Brown, and Company, Inc., 1991.

Kusmer, Kenneth L. *A Ghetto Takes Shape: Black Cleveland, 1870–1930*. Urbana: University of Illinois Press, 1976.

Kytle, Elizabeth. *Willie Mae: A Poignant First-Person Account of a Black Woman's Life in the Segregated South*. Athens: University of Georgia Press, 1993.

Landau, Bernard, Claire Monod, and Evelyne Lohr. *Les Grand Boulevards*. Paris: Action Artistique de la Ville de Paris, 2000.

Lane, Roger. *Roots of Violence in Black Philadelphia, 1860–1900*. Cambridge, MA: Harvard University Press, 1986.

Lang, John. *Urban Design: The American Experience*. New York: John Wiley & Sons, Inc., 1994.

Lang, Robert E., and Rebecca R. Sohmer. "Legacy of the Housing Act of 1949: The Past, Present, and Future of Federal Housing and Urban Policy." *Housing and Policy Debate* 11 (2):291–98, 2000.

Lasch, Christopher, ed. *The Social Thought of Jane Addams*. New York: Irvington Publishers, Inc., 1982.

LeDuff, Charlie. "A Self-Taught Artist's Blue-Collar City and What's Left of It." *The New York Times,* March 24, 2002, CY 5.

Lee, Alfred McClung, and Norman Daymond Humphrey. *Race Riot*. New York: Dryden Press, 1943.

Leighton, Alexander H. *My Name Is Legion: Foundations for a Theory of Man in Relation to Culture*. Vol. I, *The Stirling County Study of Psychiatric Disorder & Sociocultural Environment*. New York: Basic Books, 1959.

Leighton, Dorthea C., John S. Harding, David B. Macklin, Allister M. MacMillan, and Alexander H. Leighton. *The Character of Danger: Psychiatric Symptoms in Selected Communities*. Vol. III, *The Stirling County Study of Psychiatric Disorder & Sociocultural Environment*. New York: Basic Books, Inc., 1963.

Leonard, Herman. *Jazz Memories*. Levallois-Perret Cedex: Filipacchi, 1995.

Lesko, Kathleen M., Valerie Babb, and Carroll R. Gibbs. *Black Georgetown Re-*

membered: A History of Its Black Community from the Founding of the "Town of George" in 1751 to the Present Day. Washington, DC: Georgetown University Press, 1999.

Lesy, Michael. *Long Time Coming: A Photographic Portrait of America, 1935–1943.* New York: W.W. Norton & Company, Inc., 2002.

Logan, John. "Life and Death in the City: Neighborhoods in Context." *Contexts* 2 (2):33–40, 2003.

Lorant, Stefan. *Pittsburgh: The Story of an American City.* Garden City, NY: Doubleday, 1964.

Lowe, Jeanne R. 1967. *Cities in a Race with Time: Progress and Poverty in America's Renewing Cities.* New York: Random House, 1967.

Lubove, Roy. *Twentieth Century Pittsburgh: Government, Business and Environmental Change.* New York: John Wiley and Sons, Inc., 1969.

———. *Twentieth Century Pittsburgh: The Post Steel Era, Volume 2.* Pittsburgh: University of Pittsburgh Press, 1996.

Lucey, Donna M. *I Dwell in Possibility: Women Build a Nation, 1600–1920.* Washington, DC: National Geographic Press, 2001.

Luebke, Paul. "Activists and Asphalt: A Successful Anti-expressway Movement in a 'New South City.' " *Human Organization* 40 (3):256–63, 1981.

Manoni, Mary. *Bedford-Stuyvesant: The Anatomy of a Central City Community.* New York: New York Times Book Co., 1973.

Mariage, Thierry. *The World of André Le Nôtre.* Translated by G. Larkin. Philadelphia: University of Pennsylvania Press, 1999.

Marshall, Alex. *How Cities Work: Suburbs, Sprawl, and the Roads Not Taken.* Austin: University of Texas Press, 2000.

Massey, Douglas S., and Nancy A. Denton. *American Apartheid: Segregation and the Making of the Underclass.* Cambridge: Harvard University Press, 1993.

McKelvey, Blake. *The Urbanization of America, 1860–1915.* New Brunswick, NJ: Rutgers University Press, 1963.

Meeropol, Robert. *An Execution in the Family: One Son's Journey.* New York: St. Martin's Press, 2003.

Meier, August, and Elliott Rudwick. *Black Detroit and the Rise of the UAW.* New York: Oxford University Press, 1979.

Meyer, Stephen Grant. *As Long as They Don't Move Next Door: Segregation and Racial Conflict in American Neighborhoods.* Lanham, MD: Rowman & Littlefield Publishers, Inc., 2000.

Miller, Otha. *The Central Ward* (Internet). Old Newark Memories, October 14 (cited November 8, 2002). Available from http://oldnewark.com/memories/central/miller.htm.

Minami, Hirofumi. "Urban Renewal and the Elderly: An Ethnographic Approach." In *Handbook of Japan–United States Environment-Behavior Research,* edited by S. Wapner, J. Demick, T. Yamamoto, and T. Takahashi. New York: Plenum Press, 1977.

Mitchell, J. Paul, ed. *Federal Housing Policy & Programs: Past and Present.* New Brunswick, NJ: Center for Urban Policy and Research, 1985.

Modell, John, ed. *The Kikuchi Diary: Chronicle from an American Concentration Camp.* Urbana: University of Illinois Press, 1993.

Moffatt, George. "Blight Carries Seeds for New Urban Growth." *The Newark Star-Ledger,* December 24, 1979.

———. "Urban Renewal: A Bold Experiment for Cities 30 Years Later." *The Newark Sunday Star-Ledger,* December 23, 1979.

Mogey, J. M. *Family and Neighbourhood: Two Studies in Oxford.* Oxford: Oxford University Press, 1956.

Mohl, Raymond A. "Making the Second Ghetto in Metropolitan Miami, 1940–1960." *The New African American Urban History,* edited by K. W. Goings and R. A. Mohl. Thousand Oaks, CA: Sage Publications, 1996.

Moncan, Patrice de, and Claude Heurtex. *Le Paris D'Haussmann.* Rennes: Les Éditions du Mécène, 2002.

Moncan, Patrice de, Marc Saboya, Marie-Josèphe Lussien-Maisonneuve, Jean-Paul Duffieux, Denise Jasmin, and Claude Jasmin. *Villes Haussmanniennes: Bordeaux, Lille, Lyon, Marseille.* Rennes: Les Édition du Mécène, 2002.

Mumford, Esther Hall. *Seattle's Black Victorians: 1852–1901.* Seattle: Ananse Press, 1980.

Mutatkar, R. K. "Public Health Problems of Urbanization." *Social Science and Medicine* 41 (7):977–81, 1995.

National Advisory Commission on Civil Disorders. *Report of the National Advisory Commision on Civil Disorders.* New York: Bantam Books, 1968.

"Neighborhoods of Roanoke." Roanoke, VA: City Planning Commission, n.d.

Neihardt, John G. *Black Elk Speaks: Being the Life Story of a Holy Man of the Oglala Sioux.* Lincoln: University of Nebraska Press, 1979.

Nesbitt, George A. "Break Up the Black Ghetto?" *The Crisis,* 48–52, 1949.

———. "Relocating Negroes from Urban Slum Clearance Sites." In *Land Economics,* edited by R. T. Ely and G. S. Wehrwein. Madison: University of Wisconsin Press, 1964.

Nesbitt, Peter T., and Michelle DuBois. *Over the Line: The Art and Life of Jacob Lawrence.* Seattle: University of Washington Press, 2001.

Neveil, Ray. *Off Broad Street* (Internet). Old Newark Memories, October 14, 2002 (cited November 8, 2002). Available from http://oldnewark.com/memories/downtown/neveiloff.htm.

Niehaus, Isak A. "Relocation Into Phuthaditjhaba and Tseki: A Comparative Ethnography of Planned and Unplanned Removals." *African Studies* 48 (2):157–81, 1998.

Niles, Dawn, Jeff Veenema, Heidi Domine, Luis Rico-Gutierrez, and David Lewis. *The Hill Rebuilds Itself.* Pittsburgh: Carnegie Mellon University, 1999.

Nolen, John, ed. *City Planning: A Series of Papers Presenting the Essential Elements of a City Plan.* New York: D. Appleton and Company, 1929.

O'Brien, Tim. "Urban Illness Plagues Newark Despite 'Renewed' Prescription." *The Newark Star-Ledger,* December 1973.

Oliver, Paul. *Blues Fell This Morning: Meaning in the Blues,* second ed. Cambridge: Cambridge University Press, 1990.

O'Meally, Robert G., ed. *Ralph Ellison's Jazz Writings: Living with Music.* New York: Random House, Inc., 2001.

Orsenna, Erik. *Portrait d'un homme heureux: André Le Nôtre, 1613–1700.* Paris: Fayard, 2000.

Osofsky, Gilbert. *Harlem: The Making of a Ghetto.* New York: Harper & Row, 1966.

O'Sullivan, Michael, and Paul J. Handal. "Medical and Psychological Effects of the Threat of Compulsory Relocation for an American Indian Tribe." *American Indian and Alaskan Native Mental Health Research* 1 (1):3–19, 1988.

Ouf, Ahmed M.S. "Authenticity and the Sense of Place in Urban Design." *Journal of Urban Design* 6 (1):73–87, 2001.

Palm, Risa. *The Geography of American Cities.* Oxford: Oxford University Press, 1981.

Parizot, Isabelle, Pierre Chauvin, Jean-Marie Firdion, and Serge Paugam, eds. *Les Megapoles Face aux Defi des Nouvelles Inegalités.* Paris: Médecine-Science Flammarion, 2000.

Parke, Rouse, Jr. *The Great Wagon Road: From Philadelphia to the South: How Scotch-Irish and Germanics Settled the Uplands.* Richmond, VA: Dietz Press, 2000.

Parris, Guichard, and Lester Brooks. *Blacks in the City: A History of the National Urban League.* Boston: Little, Brown and Company, 1971.

Passic, Frank. *Historic Albion Michigan* (Internet). Morning Star, 1994 (cited October 12, 2002). Available from http://www.albionmich.com/history/histor_hotebook/940213.shtml.

Patterson, T. William, and Charles Worley. "Virginia Tech Plan for Commonwealth Urban Renewal." Roanoke, VA: Virginia Tech, 1959.

Perlmutter, Ellen. "Psychiatrist Tries to Dispel Fears of Future." *Pittsburgh Post-Gazette,* July 25, 1997.

Peterson, Iver. "As Princeton Changes, a Black Community Fears for Future." *The New York Times,* September 3, 2001, B1.

Pittsburgh Revealed: Photographs Since 1850. Pittsburgh: Carnegie Museum of Art, 1997.

Pohl, Otto. "What: Mob Scene. Who: Strangers. Point: None." *The New York Times,* August 4, 2003, A4.

Pollack, Craig Evan. "Burial at Srebrenica: Linking Place and Trauma." *Social Science and Medicine* 56:793–801, 2003.

———. "Intentions of Burial: Mourning, Politics, and Memorials Following the Massacres at Srebrenica." *Death Studies* 27:125–42, 2003.

Prince, Carl E. *Brooklyn's Dodgers: The Bums, the Borough, and the Best of Baseball.* Oxford: Oxford University Press, 1996.

"A Proposal for Public Housing and Urban Renewal in the South Gainsboro Area." Roanoke, VA: Department of City Planning, 1965.

Proshansky, Harold M. "Prospects and Dilemmas of Environmental Psychology." *Environmental Psychology: Directions and Perspectives,* edited by N. R. Feimer and E. S. Geller. New York: Praeger, 1983.

Proshansky, Harold M., William H. Ittelson, and Leanne G. Rivlin, eds. *Environmental Psychology: Man and His Physical Setting.* New York: Holt, Rinehart and Winston, Inc., 1971.

Rae, Douglas W. *City: Urbanization and Its End.* New Haven: Yale University Press, 2003.

Rainwater, Lee. *Behind Ghetto Walls: Black Family Life in a Federal Slum.* Chicago: Aldine Publishing Company, 1970.

Reddy, N. Subba. "The Key Issue: Development, Displacement and Resettlement." In *The Uprooted: Displacement Resettlement Development,* edited by V. Sudarsen and M. A. Kalam. New Delhi: Gian Publishing House, 1990.

Reed, Ray. "Census Data Made No Quality Judgements: Roanoke Listed Among Nation's Most Segregated Metro Areas." *The Roanoke Times & World News,* December 10, 2002, A1, A12.

Ridington, Robin. "When Poison Gas Came Down Like a Fog: A Native Community's Response to Cultural Disaster." *Human Organization* 41 (1):36–42, 1982.

"Roanoke Population Levels and Traits." Roanoke, VA: Department of City Planning, 1974.

Roanoke: Story of a County and City. Compiled by Workers of the Writers' Program of the Works Projects Administration in the State of Virginia. Roanoke, VA: Stone Printing and Manufacturing Company, 1942.

Roanoke Valley Regional Planning Commission. "Population Analysis and Projections for the Roanoke Valley Region." Roanoke: Roanoke Valley Regional Planning Commission, 1967.

Roanoke, Virginia, Department of City Planning. "Population Trends in the Roanoke Valley Region." Roanoke Valley Regional Planning Commision, 1962.

Robins, Anthony. "Progress Report on the Maurice Falk Medical Fund Minority Fellows Program: The Power of Health and Space Project." Pittsburgh: University of Pittsburgh, 1999.

Robins, Anthony, Terri Baltimore, Rich Brown, Mindy Thompson Fullilove, Robert Fullilove, and Tracy Myers. *Hillscapes: A Scrapbook, Envisioning a Healthy Urban Habitat.* Pittsburgh: University of Pittsburgh Press, 1999.

Robeson, Paul. *Here I Stand.* Boston: Beacon Press, 1958.

Rodgers-Melnick, Ann. "A Look at How to Save a Place." *Pittsburgh Post-Gazette,* 1998.

Roessner, Jane. *A Decent Place to Live from Columbia Point to Harbor Points: A Community History.* Boston: Northeastern University Press, 2000.

Roman, Harry T. *Branch Brook Park* (Internet). Old Newark Memories (cited November 8, 2002). Available from http://oldnewark.com/memories/bloomave/romanbbp.htm.

———. *Candy Stores* (Internet). Old Newark Memories, October 14, 2002 (cited November 8, 2002). Available from http://oldnewark.com/memories/bloomave/romancandy.htm.

Rome's Ghetto: The Old Jewish Quarter (Internet). Virtual Roma, March 2003 (cited October 20, 2002). Available from http://www.geocities.com/Paris/Arc/5319/romac9.htm.

Rose, Harold M. *The Black Ghetto: A Spatial Behavioral Perspective.* New York: McGraw Hill, 1972.

———. "The Development of an Urban Subsystem: The Case of the Negro Ghetto." *Black America: Geographic Perspectives,* edited by R. T. Ernst and L. Hugg. Garden City, NY: Anchor Books, 1976.

———. "The Origin and Pattern of Development of Urban Black Social Areas." In *Black America: Geographic Perspectives,* edited by R. T. Ernst and L. Hugg. Garden City, NY: Anchor Books, 1976.

Rose, Harold M., and Paula D. McClain. *Race, Place and Risk: Black Homicide in Urban America.* Albany: State University of New York Press, 1990.

Rose, Tricia. *Black Noise: Rap Music and Black Culture in Contemporary America.* Hanover: Wesleyan University Press, 1994.

———. *Longing to Tell: Black Women Talk About Sexuality and Intimacy.* New York: Farrar, Straus and Giroux, 2003.

Rosenwald, Mike. "The Bold(en) Story." *Pitt Magazine,* September 1999, 31–35.

Rossi, Peter H., and Robert A. Dentler. *The Politics of Urban Renewal: The Chicago Findings.* New York: Free Press of Glencoe, Inc., 1961.

Rubenstein, James M. "Relocation of Families for Public Improvement Projects: Lessons from Baltimore." *Journal of the American Planning Association,* 185–96, 1988.

Rymer, Russ. *American Beach: How "Progress" Robbed a Black Town—and Nation—of History, Wealth, and Power.* New York: HarperPerennial, 1998.

Sanders, Irwin T. *The Community: An Introduction to a Social System.* New York: Ronald Press Co., 1958.

Sandler, Stanley. *Segregated Skies: All-Black Combat Squadrons of World War II, Smithsonian History of Aviation Series.* Washington, DC: Smithsonian Institute Press, 1992.

Sandweiss, Eric. *St. Louis: The Evolution of an American Urban Landscape.* Philadelphia: Temple University Press, 2001.

Sassen, Saskia. *The Global City: New York, London, Tokyo.* Princeton, NJ: Princeton University Press, 1991.

Saunders, James Robert, and Renae Nadine Shackelford. *Urban Renewal and the End of Black Culture in Charlottesville, Virginia.* Jefferson, VA: McFarland & Company, Inc., 1998.

Schultz, Constance B., and Steven W. Plattner, eds. *Witness to the Fifties: The Pittsburgh Photographic Library, 1950–1953,* first ed. Pittsburgh: University of Pittsburgh Press, 1999.

Scully, Vincent. *The Achitecture of Community.* Washington, DC: National Endowment for the Humanities, 1995.

———. "The Architecture of Community." Paper read at Twenty-fourth Annual Jefferson Lecture in the Humanities; National Endowment for the Humanities, May 15, 1995, at Washington, DC.

Seamon, David. "Reconciling old and new worlds: the dwelling-journey relationship as portrayed in Vilhelm Moberg's 'Emigrant' novels." *Dwelling, Place, and Environment: Towards a Phenomenology of Person and World,* edited by D. Seamon and R. Mugerauer. New York: Columbia University Press, 1985.

Seamon, David, and Robert Mugerauer, eds. *Dwelling, Place, & Environment: Towards a Phenomenology of Person and World.* New York: Columbia University Press, 1985.

Seig, Louis. "Concepts of 'Ghetto': A Geography of Minority Groups." In *Black America: Geographic Perspectives,* edited by R. T. Ernst and L. Hugg. Garden City, NY: Anchor Books, 1976.

Shabazian, Bob. "Newark Is Given March 1 Deadline to Provide Medical Center Land," *Newark Sunday News,* December 11, 1966, 1, 19, 20.

Shaffer, Carolyn R., and Kristin Anundsen. *Creating Community Anywhere: Finding Support and Connection in a Fragmented World.* New York: G. P. Putnam's Sons, 1993.

Shapiro, Carol. *Jewish Ghetto in Rome* (Internet). Sound Travel, March 31, 2000 (cited October 20, 2002). Available from http://www.audiowalks.com/read-a-walk/rome_ghetto.htm.

Shareef, Reginald. *An Evaluation of the Impact of Federal Urban Renewal and Redevelopment Programs on Three Roanoke Virginia Neighborhoods.* Report to: Howard University, Institute for Urban Affairs and Research, Washington, DC, 1991.

———. *Healing the Wounds of Urban Renewal* (Internet). Roanoke.com 2001 (cited November 26, 2001). Available from http://www1.roanoke.com.

——. *Tapping Black Experience to Combat Terror* (Internet). Roanoke.com 2001 (cited December 3, 2001). Available from http://www1.roanoke.com.

Shay, Jonathan. *Odysseus in America: Combat Trauma and the Trials of Homecoming.* New York: Scribner, 2002.

Short, John R. *The Humane City.* Cambridge, MA: Basil Blackwell, Inc., 1989.

Shumaker, Sally Ann, and Ralph B. Taylor. "Toward a Clarification of People-Place Relationships: A Model of Attachment to Place." In *Environmental Psychology: Directions and Perspectives,* edited by N. R. Feimer and E. S. Geller. New York: Praeger, 1983.

Silberman, Eve. "We Almost Lost Kerrytown." *Ann Arbor Observer,* January 1998, 31–37.

Silver, Christopher. "The Ordeal of City Planning in Postwar Richmond, VA: A Quest for Greatness." *Journal of Urban History* 10 (1):33–60, 1983.

Simon, Arthur R. *Faces of Poverty.* New York: Macmillan, 1968.

——. *New Yorkers Without a Voice: A Tragedy of Urban Renewal* (Digital Edition). The Atlantic Online 1966 (cited May 3, 2002).

Singer, Christopher M. *New Hamtramck Homes Settle Civil Rights Lawsuit* (Internet). detnews.com, April 17, 2003, 2001 (cited May 3, 2002). Available from http://detnews.com/2001/metro/0107/04/a08-243322.htm.

Sitton, Ron. *Beale Street Culture Blues* (Internet). The Southerner, 2001, 1999 (cited May 3, 2002). Available from http://www.southerner.net/v1n4_99/soculture4.html.

Smith, Jock M., and Paul Hemphill. *Climbing Jacob's Ladder: A Trial Lawyer's Journey on Behalf of "The Least of These."* Montgomery, AL: NewSouth Books, 2002.

Smith, Kenneth L., and Ira G. Zepp, Jr. *Search for the Beloved Community: The Thinking of Martin Luther King, Jr.* Valley Forge, PA: Judson Press, 1974.

Smith, Neil. *The New Urban Frontier: Gentrification and the New Revanchist City.* London and New York: Routledge, 1996.

Smith, P. J. "The Rehousing/Relocation Issue in an Early Slum Clearance Scheme: Edinburgh 1865–1885." *Urban Studies* 26:100–114.

Smith, Roberta. "Frank Moore, 48, a Painter with Activism on His Palette." *The New York Times,* April 20, 2002, A27.

Soares, Joseph. *Urban Renewal on Oak Street* (Internet). Yale University Library and Sociology Department, February 7, 1997 (cited October 12, 2002). Available from http://www.yale.edu/socdpet/slc/urban/oak88.html.

Sorin, Gerald, ed. *The Nurturing Neighborhood: The Brownsville Boys Club and Jewish Community in Urban America, 1940–1990.* New York: New York University Press, 1990.

Sorokin, Pitirim A. *Man and Society in Calamity.* New York: E. P. Dutton and Co., 1942.

Spear, Allan H. *Black Chicago: The Making of a Negro Ghetto, 1890–1920.* Chicago: University of Chicago Press, 1967.

Spirit of a Community: The Photography of Charles "Teenie" Harris. Greensburg, PA: Westmoreland Museum of Art, 2001.

Stack, Carol B. *All Our Kin: Strategies for Survival in a Black Community.* New York: Harper & Row, 1974.

Stange, Maren. *Bronzeville: Black Chicago in Pictures, 1941–1943.* New York: New Press, 2003.

Stansfield, Charles A. *A Geography of New Jersey: The City in the Garden,* second ed. New Brunswick, NJ: Rutgers University Press, 1998.

Stephenson, Sam, ed. *Dream Street: W. Eugene Smith's Pittsburgh Project.* New York: W. W. Norton & Company, Inc., 2001.

Sterling, Dorothy, ed. *The Trouble They Seen: The Story of Reconstruction in the Words of African Americans.* New York: De Capo Press, 1994.

Stern, Gerald M. *The Buffalo Creek Disaster: How the Survivors of the Worst Disaster in Coal-Mining History Brought Suit Against the Coal Company—and Won.* New York: Vintage Books, 1976.

Stillwell, Paul, ed. *The Golden Thirteen: Recollections of the First Black Naval Officers.* Annapolis, MD: Naval Institute Press, 1993.

Stokes, W. Royal. *The Jazz Scene.* Oxford: Oxford University Press, 1991.

Stolz, Rich. *Race, Poverty, Transportation* (Internet). Poverty and Race Research Action Council 2000 (cited October 11, 2002). Available from http://www.prrac.org/topics/mar00/stolz.htm.

Suchantke, Andreas. *Eco-Geography: What We See When We Look at Landscapes.* Great Barrington, MA: Lindisfarne Books, 2001.

Sudarsen, V., and M. A. Kalam, eds. *The Uprooted: Displacement, Resettlement, Development.* New Delhi: Gian Publishing House, 1990.

Sugrue, Thomas J. *The Origins of the Urban Crisis: Race and Inequality in Postwar Detroit.* Princeton, NJ: Princeton University Press, 1996.

Tate, Thad W. *The Negro in Eighteenth-Century Williamsburg.* Williamsburg, VA: Colonial Williamsburg Foundation, 1965.

Taylor, Quintard. *The Forging of a Black Community: Seattle's Central District from 1870 Through the Civil Rights Era.* Seattle: University of Washington Press, 1994.

Tchen, John Kuo Wei, ed. *The Chinese Laundryman: A Study of Social Isolation.* New York: New York University Press, 1987.

Teaford, Jon C. *The Rough Road to Renaissance: Urban Revitalization in America, 1940–1985.* Baltimore: Johns Hopkins University Press, 1990.

——. "Urban Renewal and Its Aftermath." *Housing and Policy Debate* 11 (2):443–65, 2000.

Tervalon, Jervey, ed. *Geography of Rage: Remembering the Los Angeles Riots of 1992.* Los Angeles: Really Great Books, 2002.

Thomas, June Manning. *Redevelopment and Race: Planning a Finer City in Postwar Detroit.* Baltimore: Johns Hopkins University Press, 1997.

Thomas, June Manning, and Marsha Ritzdorf, eds. *Urban Planning and the African American Community: In the Shadows.* Thousand Oaks, CA: Sage Publications, 1997.

Thompson, Ernest, and Mindy Thompson. *Homeboy Came to Orange: A Story of People's Power.* New Jersey: Bridgebuilder Press, 1976.

Toker, Franklin. *Pittsburgh: An Urban Portrait.* Pittsburgh: University of Pittsburgh Press, 1986.

Townley, Joseph E. "NAACP Loses Plea for Addison High School." *The Roanoke Tribune,* August 23, 1973, A1.

Travis, Dempsey J. *An Autobiography of Black Jazz,* first ed. Chicago: Urban Research Institute, 1983.

Vale, Lawrence J. *From the Puritans to the Projects: Public Housing and Public Neighbors.* Cambridge: Harvard University Press, 2000.

Venkatesan, D., and V. Sudarsen. "Ecological Consequences of Rehabilitation Programmes in Andamans." *The Uprooted: Displacement, Resettlement, Development,* edited by V. Sudarsen and M. A. Kalam. New Delhi: Gian Publishing House, 1990.

Venkatesh, Sudhir Alladi. *American Project: The Rise and Fall of a Modern Ghetto.* Cambridge: Harvard University Press, 2000.

Von Eckardt, Wolf. "Bulldozers and Bureaucrats." *The New Republic,* September 14, 1963, 15–19.

———. "There Is No There There." *The New Republic,* September 21, 1963, 17–20.

———. "Conserving the Old." *The New Republic,* September 28, 1963, 16–18.

———. "Beauty and the Planners." *The New Republic,* October 5, 1963, 21–24.

———. "Black Neck in the White Noose." *The New Republic,* October 19, 1963, 14–17.

———. "New Towns in America." *The New Republic,* October 26, 1963, 16–18.

Von Hoffman, Alexander. "Why They Built Pruitt-Igoe." *From Tenements to the Taylor Homes: In Search of an Urban Housing Policy in Twentieth-Century America,* edited by J. F. Bauman, R. Biles, and K. M. Szylvian. University Park: Pennsylvania State University Press, 2000.

Waldram, James B. "Relocation, Consolidation, and Settlement Pattern in the Canadian Subarctic." *Human Ecology* 15 (2):117–31, 1987.

Wallace, Anthony. "Mazeway Disintegration: The Individual's Perception of Socio-Cultural Disorganization." *Human Organization* 16:23–27, 1957.

Wallace, Deborah, and Rodrick Wallace. *A Plague on Your Houses: How New York Was Burned Down and National Public Health Crumbled.* London: Verso, 1998.

Wallace, Rodrick. "A Synergism of Plagues: 'Planned Shrinkage,' Contagious Housing Destruction, and AIDS in the Bronx." *Environmental Research* 47:1–33, 1988.

Wallace, Rodrick, and Deborah Wallace. "The Coming Crisis of Public Health in the Suburbs." *The Milbank Quarterly* 71 (4):543–64, 1993.

Washington, Jack. *The Quest for Equality: Trenton's Black Community: 1890–1965.* Trenton, NJ: Africa World Press, Inc., 1993.

Watkins, Beverly Xaviera. "Fantasy, Decay, Abandonment, Defeat, and Disease: Community Disintegration in Central Harlem 1960–1990." New York: Graduate School of Arts and Sciences, Columbia University, 2000.

Weaver, Robert C. *Dilemmas of Urban America.* Cambridge: Harvard University Press, 1965.

———. *The Negro Ghetto: What Negro Residential Segregation Costs the Community and How Democratic Housing Can Be Achieved.* NY: Harcourt, Brace and Co., 1948.

———. *The Urban Complex: Human Values in Urban Life.* Garden City, NY: Doubleday & Company, Inc., 1964.

Weiss, Marc A. "The Origins and Legacy of Urban Renewal." In *Federal Housing Policy and Programs: Past and Present,* edited by J. P. Mitchell. New Brunswick: NJ: Rutgers University Press, 1985.

Whiteman, Dorit Bader. *The Uprooted: A Hitler Legacy.* New York: Plenum Press, 1994.

Whitmire, Tim. *Restoring Life After Urban Renewal* (Internet). *The Philadelphia Inquirer,* April 17, 2003, 2002 (cited October 12, 2002). Available from http://www.philly.com/mld/inquirer/2002/08/25/news/nation/ 3934242.htm?template=contentModules/printstory.jsp.

Whitwell, W. L., and Lee W. Winborne. *The Architectural Heritage of the Roanoke Valley.* Charlottesville: University Press of Virginia, 1982.

Whitworth, Clifton B., Jr. "The Yard" Part I. *The Roanoke Tribune,* August 23, 1973, A1.

———. "The Yard," Part II. *The Roanoke Tribune,* August 30, 1973, A1.

———. "The Yard," Part III. *The Roanoke Tribune,* September 6, 1973, A1.

Wilgoren, Jodi. "Many Face Street as Chicago Project Nears End." *The New York Times,* August 7, 2003, A14.

Wilson, James Q. "Planning and Politics: Citizen Participation in Urban Renewal." *Urban Renewal: The Record and the Controversy,* edited by J. Q. Wilson. Cambridge: MIT Press, 1966.

———, ed. *Urban Renewal: The Record and the Controversy.* Cambridge: M.I.T. Press, 1966.

Wilson, James Q., and George L. Kelling. "Broken Windows." *The City Reader,* edited by R. T. LeGates and F. Stout. London: Routledge, 2000.

Wilson, William Julius. *When Work Disappears: The World of the New Urban Poor.* New York: Alfred A. Knopf, Inc., 1996.

Winstead, Mary. *Back to Mississippi: A Personal Journey Through the Events That Changed America in 1964,* first ed. New York: Hyperion, 2002.

Wolff, Daniel. "There Always Was Pride." *Doubletake,* Winter 1999, 56–61.

Woodbury, Margaret Claytor, and Ruth Claytor Marsh. *Virginia Kaleidoscope.* Ann Arbor, MI: Woodbury/Marsh, 1994.

Young, Bonnie. *A Walk Through the Cloisters.* New York: The Metropolitan Museum of Art, 2000.

Zurawsky, Christopher. "Stories and Neighboring Key to Future of Hill District." *Tribune Review,* October 15, 1998, B3.

TECHNICAL NOTE

The data reported here were collected in the course of a variety of projects. The formal research project "Root Shock: The Longterm Consequences of African American Dispossession" was funded by a Health Policy Investigator Award from the Robert Wood Johnson Foundation, 2001–2. It supported travel to five cities, three of which are discussed in this book. The plans for protection of human subjects were approved by the Columbia University Institutional Review Board.

The design of the study was "situation analysis," a theoretically derived method developed by our research group. Situation analysis operates from the assumption that complex interpersonal interactions can be described using the following parameters: key actors, roles, rules, setting, timing, and context. Thus, we talked to people who were in key roles: planners, uprooted people, historians, and advocates. We collected photographs and maps to assist in analysis. We reviewed the secondary literature and newspaper articles on urban renewal. Using these methods, we developed a "definition of the situation."

In addition to formal research, this book draws on my experiences as a visiting professor in Pittsburgh, as a student of urbanism in France, and as the authorized biographer of David Jenkins.

ACKNOWLEDGMENTS

Many people helped me accomplish the research for the book and put the manuscript together. Some of the people who helped me I can't thank in person because they are deceased. My father, Ernest Thompson, inspired me to write books that would help people. My best professor, Herbert Aptheker, taught that being angry about injustice was part of the scientific process. Charles Meadows and Della Wimbs, whom I met as part of the work and to whom this book is dedicated, allowed me to witness unceasing struggle. What a legacy these beloved teachers left for me to build on!

I am grateful to all the people who helped the process get started in 1994. Deborah Tall got me started thinking about the psychology of place. Estelle Schecter gave me key texts to read. My landlord in Brittany, Yann Le Loupp, was generous with stories of his "Bretagnitude" and made the concept of displacement come to life. I met David Jenkins at about that time, and he and I have worked together ever since. I would never have come to understand these issues without his deep commitment to the project.

I met Mary Bishop in 1995, and she has been my role model and mentor over the years. She is a gifted reporter, working in the highest traditions of investigative journalism. Tirelessly and fearlessly, she chipped away at the story, until she had identified every house in the affected areas, and the fate of nearly every uprooted person. She is as kind as she is brave, opening her home and heart to me, and giving me the benefit of all her accumulated wisdom. She is an extraordinary person and I am proud to call her my friend.

Mary's work received remarkable support from the *Roanoke Times*. That paper devoted substantial resources to the publication of Mary's two special reports. The whole paper worked to support her efforts. She has described to me the contributions of many people, including the printers who laid the first copies of "Street by Street" tenderly in her arms. I am indebted to all of them. I would like to thank, in particular, editor Rich Martin, librarian Belinda Harris, and mapmaker Robert Lunsford. What they accomplished will surely help all of America grapple with the heretofore hidden story of black upheaval due to urban renewal.

As I got to know Roanoke, a number of other people offered to teach me about their city. Arleen Ollie, Evelyn Bethel, Helen Davis, Reginald Shareef, and Walter Claytor all devoted time to this project. In the Southern tradition, they offered warmth and friendship in addition to facts, which made it a great pleasure to pass time with them.

In 1997, Don Mattison, then dean of the Graduate School of Public Health, University of Pittsburgh, invited me to Pittsburgh. Della Wimbs, Tamanika Howze, Angela Howze, and Terri Baltimore invited me to the Hill. Phil Hallen, then president of the Maurice Falk Medical Fund, provided generous financial support for my husband, Bob, and me to travel to Pittsburgh monthly over a fifteen-month period. The staff of the Center for Minority Health, particularly Angela Ford and Anthony Robbins, gave us their utmost support. Many other people in Pittsburgh were generous with their time and insights: Clarke Thomas, Phil Pappas, George Moses—in fact, the list is too long to mention everyone. I must add that many a pleasant evening was spent at Foster's, the restaurant of the Holiday Inn next door to the University of Pittsburgh, and our home away from home on many an occasion. In all, those months visiting Pittsburgh provided an unparalleled opportunity to learn and to contribute.

Friends and family helped me understand the recent history of Newark. My thanks to Patty and Harold Fullilove and their wonderful sons for enthusiastically embracing this undertaking. I am especially grateful to DeCosta Dawson and the Essex Chorale for permitting me to be a part of their music-making. In creating a photographic essay on Newark, I had the help of Tamara Coley and Sara Booth, who searched the archives of the Newark Public Library and the New Jersey Historical Society. We are grateful to people at both organizations for their support, especially Charles Cummings whose tireless efforts to document the history of Newark have been invaluable for those interested in the city. I owe a special debt of thanks to Tamara Coley's family. They graciously shared their family albums and gave permission to reprint "Children at the Wedding."

Michel Cantal-Dupart gave me what amounts to a master's degree in urbanism so that I might write this book. He took Bob and me all over southwest France. We met the mayors of about forty French cities, and dined in even more French homes. This inside look at another country, and how it manages its cities, made a deep impression on me. The southwest of France, like our South, is famous for its hospitality. Cantal and his family took my family into their homes with a generosity that is hard to imagine and impossible to repay. I am also grateful to Cantal's coworkers at Marchands des Villes in Paris—Gilles Rousseau, Didier Richard, Sibyle Rerolle, and Christine Larousse—who welcomed us into their workspace and shared their vast knowledge of urbanism.

Turning to the issues of research, this project received generous support from the Robert Wood Johnson Foundation, through its Health Policy Investigator Award Program, which helps researchers write books that pull together a body of thinking and investigation. I am proud that *Root Shock* will join the distinguished list of publications produced by recipients of those awards. New York City RECOVERS became a part of the Root Shock project after 9/11. We received additional support from the Macy Foundation, the Unitarian Universalist Service Committee, the Citizens Committee for New York, and the Columbia Center for Youth Violence Prevention. The development of the ideas underlying this project received critical financial support from the National Center for Environmental Health of the U.S. Centers for Disease Control and Prevention (the psychology of place) and from the Open Society Institute (the meanings of race/ethnicity).

I am lucky to work with a remarkable team. Robert E. Fullilove, III, my husband, codirects our team, the Community Research Group. Lesley L. Green and Jennifer Stevens Madoff completed their doctoral work with us, and have helped us to develop our research. It was Jen who demonstrated the potential for "situation analysis," and Lesley who suggested that we use it for this project. Both conducted a substantial number of interviews for the project, and have helped with the analysis of data. Lourdes Hernandez-Cordero, another doctoral student with our team, has worked as the art director for the book. She developed a vision for the illustrations and worked with designers, photographers, and artists to bring the materials together.

Caroline Moore did a brilliant job of transcribing the taped interviews and tracking their key ideas. Ericka Phillips and Mark Boutros have managed the complex tasks of getting transcripts approved by interviewees and ready for deposit in Columbia's Oral History Archive. Evelyn Joseph deftly handled both project administration and staff morale. Paula Mitchell, Tamara Coley, and Sara Booth worked tirelessly to pin down details, from references to photographs. There is a point at which this project ceased to be my new idea and became a creation of our remarkable team.

In a big university system, one acquires debts to many people. Jack Gorman, who was chair of my department at the New York State Psychiatric Institute, has a broad vision of psychiatry and understood my undertaking from its inception. Such support is of immeasurable importance when one is trying to chart new ground. Allan Rosenfield, dean of the Mailman School of Public Health, was equally supportive and never hesitated to demonstrate his faith in Bob and me. The members of the institutional review boards, who oversee the proper conduct of research; the administrators who balance the budgets; the security guards who watch over us; the parking attendants who remind me to smile even when things look bleak: all have made it safe and easy for me to do my part. No one helps more than graduate students, and I am indebted to the public health students who took my Qualitative Methods in Research course over the years. The students helped me understand the concepts of "upheaval," "situation," and "occasion," as well as untangling the complex threads in David Jenkins's life story.

As the work ground to a close, and the illustrations were selected, the task of acquiring permissions started. Gil Pietrzak was unfazed by my many requests for pictures from the Pittsburgh Photographic Project. Heather Domencic, of the Carnegie Museum of Art, was equally flexible in helping me access the newly established Charles "Teenie" Harris Collection. Keith Helmatag kindly supplied the maps that he had made for the John Heinz Wildlife Refuge in Pennsylvania. Michel Cantal-Dupart, Rich Brown, Cynthia Golembeski, and Richard V. Miller helped to translate complex ideas into beautiful graphics. Helen M. Stummer, Carlos F. Peterson, Arlene Corsano, Rogelio R. Rodriguez, Rich Brown, and Jennifer Stevens Madoff kindly supplied photographs. Carlos F. Peterson and Jean-François Batelier generously gave permission to reprint their artworks. A really unexpected favor came from Jose Marrero, of the American Dock and Doors Company, who brought his truck and ladder to Springfield Avenue to help us re-create a several-stories-high picture taken in the 1950s.

A number of people helped me put together a photographic essay about Roanoke. Mary Bishop examined a number of archives and found "Parade on Gainsboro/Peach Road." Bobby Smith, owner of the photograph, gave permission for its use. Claudia Whitworth and Stan Hale, editors at *The Roanoke Tribune,* provided a digital copy. Mary Bishop also located the photograph of the Norfolk and Western Colored Veterans assembled in front of the Lincoln Theater. Kent Chrisman, of the Virginia Museum and Historical Society, supplied a digital version. Arleen Ollie gathered a number of photographs from friends and family, among them "Church Supper," reprinted with the permission of Judith Muse.

Quite a number of people read versions of the manuscript and gave helpful feedback, including Lise Funderburg, Francine Rainone, Rodrick Wallace, and Michel Cantal-Dupart. My agent, Angela Miller, was an enormous and continuous source of support. My editor, Elisabeth Dyssegaard, believed in the project from the beginning. Her quiet requests for little changes drove massive revisions, and I was always happily surprised at how much better the book became by following her instructions.

My whole family worked hard to get me through the process. Bob Fullilove traveled with me throughout this period. He has debated every idea, read every chapter thirty times, and provided support or sternness as needed to move the process along. Molly Kaufman, my daughter, provided writing axioms, books on writing, and comments on manuscripts. She has also taken me to yoga classes and spas to remind me to be holistic even under pressure. My mother, Maggie Thompson, believed in me first and still does, which is an enormous help in the middle of the night. My other children and grandchildren and the rest of the family forgave my grumpiness, forgetfulness, incessant traveling, and preoccupation, and they never forgot to ask, "So how's it going?" They'll be so glad to hear me say, "Hey, it's finally done!"

Having said all that, though many people helped me, I am solely responsible for the contents of this book.

INDEX

ABOUT THE AUTHOR

MINDY THOMPSON FULLILOVE, MD, Hon AIA, is Professor of Urban Policy and Health, Milano School for International Affairs, The New School for Public Engagement.

She is a former professor of clinical sociomedical sciences, Mailman School of Public Health, and former professor of clinical psychiatry, College of Physicians and Surgeons, at Columbia University. Trained at Bryn Mawr College and Columbia University, she has conducted research on AIDS and other pathologies that disproportionately affect communities of color. Her research examines the mental health effects of environmental toxins, violence, segregation, and displacement.

Dr. Fullilove has authored numerous articles and five books including *Urban Alchemy: Restoring Joy in America's Sorted-Out Cities*, published in 2013 by New Village Press. She lives in Orange, New Jersey, and is founding president of a popular education center, the University of Orange.

CPSIA information can be obtained
at www.ICGtesting.com
Printed in the USA
JSHW041934110822
29182JS00007B/135